# A LIFETIME
# BURNING IN
# EVERY MOMENT

## ALSO BY ALFRED KAZIN

*Writing Was Everything*
*Our New York* (with David Finn)
*A Writer's America: Landscape in Literature*
*Bright Book of Life: American Novelists and Storytellers from Hemingway to Mailer*
*An American Procession*
*On Native Grounds*
*Starting Out in the Thirties*
*The Inmost Leaf*
*New York Jew*
*Contemporaries*
*A Walker in the City*

Editor:
*The Viking Portable Blake*
*F. Scott Fitzgerald: The Man and His Work*
*The Stature of Theodore Dreiser* (with Charles Shapiro)
Herman Melville, *Moby-Dick*
*Emerson: A Modern Anthology* (with Daniel Aaron)
*The Works of Anne Frank* (with Ann Birstein)
*The Open Form: Essays for Our Time*
*Selected Short Stories of Nathaniel Hawthorne*
Henry James, *The Ambassadors*
Walt Whitman, *Specimen Days*

# A
# LIFETIME
# BURNING
# IN EVERY
# MOMENT

From the
Journals of

# Alfred
# Kazin

Selected and Edited
by the Author

HarperCollins*Publishers*

*The late Carol Saltus assisted me in making selections from the great mass of my journals. In grateful memory.*

Excerpt from *East Coker* in *Four Quartets* copyright © 1943 by T. S. Eliot and renewed 1971 by Esme Valerie Eliot, reprinted by permission of Harcourt Brace & Company.

Portions of this book have appeared, in slightly different form, in *The New Yorker*, the *Paris Review*, and the *New York Review of Books*.

HarperCollins books may be purchased for educational, business, or sales promotional use. For information please write: Special Markets Department, HarperCollins Publishers, Inc., 10 East 53rd Street, New York, NY 10022.

FIRST EDITION

*Designed by Rebecca Caitlin Daniels*

ISBN 0-06-019037-X

96 97 98 99 00 ❖/HC 10 9 8 7 6 5 4 3 2 1

For Judith

*Je suis né pour te connaître.*
Paul Eluard

Home is where one starts from. As we grow older
The world becomes stranger, the pattern more complicated
Of dead and living. Not the intense moment
Isolated, with no before and after,
But a lifetime burning in every moment
And not the lifetime of one man only
But of old stones that cannot be deciphered.

T. S. Eliot, *East Coker*

# CONTENTS

| ONE | 1938-1945 | 1 |
|---|---|---|
| TWO | 1946-1950 | 49 |
| THREE | 1950-1978 | 121 |
| FOUR | 1978-1993 | 181 |
| FIVE | 1993-1995 | 313 |

# PART ONE

## 1938-1945

*B*efore Asya and I were married, we decided to keep a daily record of our lives. Of course we won't keep it up. I do need a note-book-journal-record of some sort, and this may be it. Asya is like nothing I ever anticipated or even hoped for. She's priceless.

"They will more than arrive there, every one."

A Sunday afternoon walk to the East River with Asya. In this industrial kitchen of Long Island City, where the factories lie scrubbed and waiting in the sun like so many pots and pans hung up to dry, there is a weariness in the air. The river is not the sluice of New York Harbor it usually is, but a pallid, turgid stream breaking weakly against neglected docks, piers, and river dumps.

Sunday: The fog over the river and the long line of yellow lamps all along the subway line near the "project," where Italians live in modern-art slums, cut and parceled like cheap dresses in a factory. The Italians play an old game with a few balls and a hole in the ground. It just needs a little earth, a wall, a gutter for us to have a game.

I remember the sadness of Sunday because I was so terrified of school the next day—the waiting, the fear before the soul returns to its treadmill, the fear of stammering in class the next day as my mother stammered when she was afraid. And when was she not afraid, even as she passed the fear on to me? She could not speak my

English, and I hated falling into her Yiddish—it was so broken with her fear, her grief over everything she had left, full of dark Poland, Jew-hating Poland. Even when there was no school I wanted not to leave the sand at Coney Island as the beach emptied and I could still look to another world in the water.

Sunday: The walk to Highland Park out of Brownsville and East New York, out of everything I knew to the wonderful line of yellow lamps across the embankment before the park—the dumped earth we used to climb over to the playing grounds, where the boys had a last game of touch football in the twilight, and we would sit on the benches near the reservoir, petting so madly as the lights of the YMCA spread out before us, challenging us, that I came, astonished to ecstasy by the weights in my body steadily falling.

Sunday: Playing Bach duets with Anne, my partner in the violin section of the Franklin K. Lane High School orchestra. Then her mother's Polish cups of tea. The sharp, reproving taste of lemon in my mouth as we go over French irregular verbs for tomorrow. Sunday: Always Highland Park and the reservoir, around which my teacher Julian Aaronson and I walked, dissecting the first stories I wrote in high school. Sunday: Always Highland Park and the trees in shadow, the flower garden we could barely see in the growing dark. Darkness, the darkness! And then the walk through the Italian neighborhood to home—the butcher shops busy of a "Jewish" Sunday, the pushcarts lining Belmont Avenue, Cousin Sophie's old room with bed and a table for me to write on and the fragrance of Sophie still where she had kept her dresses, behind a curtain, forever bring her back. And sitting there, looking out on Sutter Avenue, and I thinking, Israel! Israel! Why have you forsaken me! Sunday: The long-remembered waiting and then Nancy's rhinestone-studded dress as we huddled together against the wall of the toilet, hoping her parents would not return too soon. Sunday: The waiting, the waiting for the next day, the benches in Highland Park, the cold, the kitchen sink, the water in the reservoir.

\* \* \*

Every once in a while some token—a sentence in a book, a voice heard, will recall for me the fresh instant delight in American landscape and culture that I felt when I really got into *On Native Grounds.* The sentence this morning, fresh as a spring wind, comes from Constance Rourke's book on Audubon, on the sudden realization that his ornithology showed a national sense of scale, that like Whitman he was a great voice of American nationality.

I recall the excitement under which I lived for weeks in 1939, when I knew that I had this passionate and even technical interest in images of the American past. Thomas Eakins, always a hero to my spirit. I would walk up and down the "American" rooms of the Metropolitan Museum, taking in the portraits of solemn colonial and Revolutionary figures—dull, glazed transcriptions of a Sunday morning in ye olde Flatbush, 1836. Images that brought back the delight I had taken even as a boy in old narratives of American discovery—the indomitable Henry Hudson always at the center—in life stories of Americans at all times and in all conditions. As a college student during the depression, one of my jobs for the National Youth Administration (fifteen dollars a month) was to comb the *Dictionary of American Biography* for Southerners who had graduated from college before the Civil War. I never got tired of reading their stories. I have never been able to express the excitement I get from "Americana," from Constance Rourke's saying, "the poet of American nationality"—from the very names Cope, James, Peirce, Dickinson, and Roebling in Lewis Mumford's *The Brown Decades*—from Thomas Beer's *Hanna* and *The Mauve Decade*—from the letters of William James. To think of Albert Pinkham Ryder and Henry James, of Emerson and Whitman and Dickinson in the same breath, as it were, gives me extraordinary satisfaction. Makers and movers and thinkers—observers in the profoundest sense. I loved to think of America as an idea, to remember the adventure and the purity, the heroism and the *salt.*

Of course I love all this from the outside, as the first native son after so many generations of mud-flat Russian Jews who never saw the United States. But my personal need is great, my inquiry is urgent.

\*　\*　\*

His name is Howard Nott Doughty, and he comes from a family that despite its long settlement in Ipswich, Massachusetts, is still in touch with its English cousins. They don't, it seems, quite approve of these relatives across the sea, who are so backward in our advanced American ways that in sending over some silver spoons as a wedding present, they neglected to add the bride's initials to the groom's.

At Harvard in the twenties (he was born in 1904), he was, with Lincoln Kirstein and Varian Fry, one of those advanced undergraduates who put out *The Hound and Horn*, that great founding journal of an American modernism. Tall, rangy, languidly humorous about his descent in the world, he is still the proud Yankee and is writing a biography of his distant kinsman Francis Parkman. He is so glad to meet up with another literary bloke in dreary Long Island City that he has taken to presenting me with rare editions inscribed to me in French—*Moby-Dick* illustrated by Rockwell Kent, and Madame de La Fayette's beautiful little seventeenth-century novel, *La Princesse de Clèves*, the story of the exquisite heroine's overcoming the temptation to illicit passion.

The question about this Yankee patrician and kindly friend is, What is he doing in Long Island City? He is teaching at the Police Academy! Why he is fallen this low is a question around which he genially circles without ever telling me anything. Until the other day, when he said, as if exasperated, "Of course you know I'm homosexual." Of course I hadn't known any such thing, and probably exasperated him even more by having nothing whatever to say on the subject.

He is married, with a daughter, and is regularly unwell. He suffers such spasms from colitis, which he offhandedly describes as "a stress disease," that he frequently doubles up as he is talking to me. What interests me is his stoical sense of failure, his clearly having a "failing," as his ancestors might have said.

He is interested in me because of my book, but my being a Jew seems to be a problem to him. His feisty little wife, Binx, laughs in a knowing way as she makes "jokes" about Jews. These pass over me like air since, despite her malice on the subject, I never quite know what she is talking about. In his turn Howard seems to feel that my being a Jew is a terrible loss to me. This bothers him a lot. The other day, assuming for no reason that I observe the dietary laws, he came by not only with his usual gift of a book but with a bag of oysters that he carefully shucked and cleaned, and then to my amazement demanded that I eat them right then and there.

Thinking of John Dewey this morning. Some weeks ago, as I was walking to the subway after my day at the Fifth Avenue Library, I saw Dewey on Lexington Avenue with a woman I took to be his daughter. I looked at him with affection and pleasure that I had recognized him. He stared back. After half a block I looked back. He was still staring, talking to his daughter as if to say, "Now, when did I have him in my classes?"

I was thinking of Dewey because my impression of his career and significance is different from that of students of his philosophy alone. For me Dewey represents more than the pragmatic adaptable twentieth-century intelligence that was going to fit philosophy to the scientific age. He really speaks with the security and serenity of a vanished world. I think not of his lack of elegance, the clumsy handiwork of his style, but of his nobility, his steadiness, the work of immense, quiet usefulness, the moral achievement that constitutes his life.

In *On Native Grounds* I described Dewey's influence on and embodiment of the "H. G. Wells period" in uplift in "progressive" Wilsonian America. All that has turned into ashes, but Dewey the man represents its vital force still. The tang of the Vermont woods. The philosopher of the frontier. The good American teacher and scholar with absolute integrity and quiet originality. If he is not the peer of William James, he is more than any other native philosopher the man whose whole career has been a continuing happiness for the rest of us. Dewey has proved that a man can give his whole life to purposive teaching and make of it a moral as well as an intellectual example. William James was of course a genius. His personality was his greatest contribution to philosophy. Dewey's reforming career—his whole example from the 1880s on—is as great a contribution as his social psychology and the galvanizing influence of his attack on the old education. He may not have given us a truly serviceable new idea of education, but he certainly shamed the old.

Passing under our kitchen window on my way home from the subway at Borough Hall, I loved to look up at Asya standing in the window in the last light, preparing our evening meal. And then all the ease and charm of our young marriage would unfold for me, right there on Clinton Street, before I got to our front door on Remsen.

Brooklyn Heights, 1938: The downtown streets dense with traffic bound for Brooklyn Bridge on a winter's day, and lined with churches, banks, courts, municipal offices, stationers', the old Brooklyn Central Library on Montague Street, the main offices of the Brooklyn Union Gas Company, the one big street clock in the neighborhood, lawyers on Court Street hungrily bunched together but looking to grab any passerby who could be turned into a client. The air was resonant with bailiffs, city marshals, and lined legal paper, foolscap size. But in the center of the center, one room and a kitchen, fifty dollars a month, we had our love.

The minute I left the house for the Forty-second Street Library and my excited all-day reading in American writers for my first book, I could feel in an instant flush of delight how that grid of dark, radiating lines, offices, marble bank fronts, subway openings, the Elevated on Fulton Street, and the trolleys for the bridge—how all that dark, busily official, and endless hum of topmost Brooklyn life—enclosed us, enclosed us tight. So that at night, as we lay on our just-made-up sofa bed listening to a Haydn cello concerto on WQXR, against the fits and starts of city traffic, we had a delicious sense of being alone and all to ourselves on one sluggishly turning flywheel of the city. In the sudden stillness of a Sunday night, one shining cross in the venerable church across the street (Brooklyn, the city of churches) burned at our windows.

None of that belonged to us—not the documents being turned over all day, not the proprietary New England airs Brooklyn Heights still gave itself as we walked down Remsen Street to the harbor against a solid line of classic brownstones. Beautiful wooden doors with exquisitely etched glass inserts. At night you could often see the hall light, and even the curve of the stairs as they mounted. Another world, another world! I could write about the mansion dominating Columbia Heights that figured in Ernest Poole's *The Harbor* (or so I guessed), but I could not imagine myself in it.

All this before the Esplanade. At the end of Remsen Street, however, you could wedge through the fence to face the great jeweled breast of Manhattan floating on the water. Now everything was ours—the cobblestones leading down to the piers under the old "Japanese" iron bridge at the end of Montague Street, the iron-doored warehouses, the freighters tied up below with one small light in the rigging, and, out there to the right, above all and mastering all, great Brooklyn Bridge itself. Everything on Columbia Heights was related for me to the bridge's hard, leaping and thrusting glory. The immigrant John Roebling had dreamed it; the immigrant's son, Washington—though near paralyzed by the bends—the caisson disease he had contracted working below the East River on the foundation for the Brooklyn tower—had built it after the dreamer was struck by the Fulton Street ferry the bridge was going to replace. And here, right on Columbia Heights, Hart Crane had written the only lines—

O harp and altar, of the fury fused
(How could mere toil align thy choiring strings!)

Terrific threshold of the prophet's pledge,
Prayer of pariah, and the lover's cry,

—that could match John Roebling's dream.

We were radicals; our friends Richard and Felice Hofstadter on one side of Montague Street, Richard and Eleanor Rovere, Bertram D. Wolfe and his wife, Ella, on the other. The depression lasted until the war; Hitler was on our minds day and night; Franco was killing his own people with the help of Nazi Germany and Fascist Italy. It was inconceivable that anyone intelligent and of goodwill was not on our side, along with Auden, Malraux, Silone, Orwell, Hemingway, Dos Passos, Steinbeck, Wilson, Farrell, and every young writer, scholar, painter, and medical student we knew. It was 1938. Thirteen men from City College—students, faculty, alumni— were to die in Spain.

At 68 Montague Street, Bert Wolfe (an early leader of the American Communist Party, long since expelled as a Lovestoneite, a right deviationist), and his jolly wife, Ella, covered a wall with photographs of their old comrades and friends from many countries in the "movement" (O holy word!). The central photograph was of Lenin, looking (it seemed to me) at all the others with his usual disapproval of anyone not up to his harsh standards. There was also a lot of Mexico on the wall. The Wolfes had been close to Diego Rivera (whose life Bert was writing when he was not writing *Three Who Made a Revolution: Lenin, Trotsky and Stalin*) and his stormy wife, the painter Frida Kahlo.

Bert and Ella of course ended up, like so many other exhausted radicals and neocons, at the Hoover Institution in Palo Alto, Californio. Bert died there. Forty years later, when I was at Stanford's Center for Advanced Studies, I was happy to see Ella, as delightful as ever, but was not prepared to see in Palo Alto the same lineup of photographs I had seen forty years before at 68 Montague

Street, Lenin still looking disapprovingly at everyone else. Living amid the Hoover Institution's remarkable collection of documents relating to the international Communist movement, Ella was more awash than ever in her old history. Just as she had joked in 1938 that a Comintern congress had no delegate from the jungle because "they couldn't find a Jew willing to wear a nose ring," so now she laughingly related Trotsky's affair with Frida Kahlo and that Kahlo had given him up as "that tiresome old man."

The thirties were an age of faith, and for a time, a great many people I knew and knew of were soldiers of faith. We alone were pure. The only evil in the world was fascism. That took care of all other things, like our personal lives.

I came home from the library one afternoon, radiantly happy, to find Asya face down on the floor, sobbing in anger, hitting the floor with her fists. The excessive smell of fresh paint in our newly occupied flat hit me as I bent to her. She had just had a visit from her mother, whose only way of dealing with a charmingly errant husband was to harangue Asya to the point of hysteria.

Her parents were Jews who proudly let me know that they considered themselves Russian "intelligentsia" and condescended to my easily subdued parents because they spoke Yiddish to each other. There was not a thing about the USSR that Asya's parents did not find holy, perfect, and adorable. The mother amused me—only her pretensions were amusing—by wearing severe suits and routinely choosing a straight kitchen chair to sit in with a fixed frown—I never saw her smile—rather than the wing chair that was our one luxury. This showed her contempt for "bourgeois" frippery. Otherwise she was an absolute terror, always on the attack. She just could not manage her husband. Often enough she could not even locate him.

Everything about Asya's parents was strange to me. The mother's cruelty to Asya and her younger brother, Leon, who was to succumb at an early age to the unbearable stress his mother forced on her children—went hand in hand with an idolatry of Stalin that made me laugh. Asya's father and I were fond of each other; he even confided that his terrible wife had a sexual hold on him that explained his inability to tear himself away from her. He loved his daughter madly and loved me even when, with my friend Richard Hofstadter, I jeered at his political orthodoxy.

The Hofstadters were another left-wing couple in marital disarray, but here the problem was startlingly, openly, one of rival careers. The unstoppable Felice (only cancer would stop her at twenty-nine, after she had borne a son she—typically—named Dan, for "the smallest and most belligerent tribe in Israel") had come downstate from a prominent medical family in Buffalo as if she expected New York City to fall at her feet—which it damned near did. At first the Hofstadters in their rough lodgings over a bakery on Montague Street were so poor that Felice seriously tried to get Dick work in a nightclub as a stand-up comic. We all howled when he did his imitation of FDR and of the Ozark farmer whose daughter had fallen into the well: "Must get her out of there one of these days."

Before long Felice—starting only as a researcher for the medical columnist on *Time*—was writing the column. Women had traditionally been restricted to research for writers exclusively male, but of course Felice broke through all that. She was irresistible in her ability not only to accept and affirm but to *display* her various loyalties. Only robustly left-wing Felice could have decided to live close to the harbor so that she could keep up with members of the Norwegian Seamen's Union. They would wander in of a Saturday afternoon for a taste of Felice's famous version of cholent, the Sabbath dish traditionally prepared by Orthodox Jews before the Sabbath, when no cooking is allowed.

Felice publicly loved being Jewish, as she publicly flourished feeding her "comrade" Norwegian seamen, shining to advantage as one of the first women writers on *Time*. When she left her office high up in the Chrysler Building of a Saturday night (working the weekend "for Luce" was routine), she never seemed surprised to be greeted by the many male friends waiting to take her out to dinner. She carried in every step the pride, the gusto, and for me the very romance that comes with sudden success for the young in New York, and that from that time forward remains embodied for me in the Chrysler Building itself, rising up there over Forty-second Street like the only true New York cathedral, its shining spire scraping the sky all right and challenging it to find another so confident in its potency and silver beauty. And this in the midst of a depression, weighing down millions, a whole quarter of the American working class unemployed, that aroused all Felice's scorn and indignation as a radical.

After uneasily trying this and that, Dick was in graduate school at Columbia and began writing *Social Darwinism in America* as I was lurching into *On Native Grounds*. We were soon doing our reading side by side in the great reading room, 315, of the Forty-second Street Library. He was never an outspoken public personality like his wife—not even when he was recognized as one of the most significant contemporary American historians. But, not uninfluenced by his early Marxism, he had attained an intellectual certainty that won me, along with the gift for mimicry he displayed in private. The mimicry—of all possible American characters but always returning to that central presence, the president of the United States, who in our eyes was just not doing enough—was the voice of his essential skepticism. His German-background Lutheran mother had died early; his Polish-Jewish father had given his gift for Yiddish an irresistible turn. Between two such worlds—who would have guessed that the middle name of this former Lutheran altar boy was *Irving?*—he had become the amused outsider who looked Gentile, was married to a Jew, and whose friends were regularly Jews.

I was linked to Richard Hofstadter by our passion for America as history. America was more than the radical alienation, the critical edge we brought to it. When Dick read aloud from Mencken's unforgettable portrait of William Jennings Bryan at the Scopes trial in Tennessee, when he laughingly quoted Mr. Dooley on Theodore Roosevelt's looking all teeth—"Teddy bit his way to the platform"—I would sit back in an ecstasy of enjoyment that someone else equally relished every little bit of the American scene. Dick would say of Columbia University that he loved observing it as "a society." In the same way I was fascinated by the depression crowds jostling us in Room 315 as we did our reading, the mass of impatient, often clearly troubled unemployed people in the Automat across the street on Forty-second where we often gobbled our lunch at the standup table before going off to a local pool parlor to play Ping-Pong. We had left our books and notes on one of the golden library tables under a note—BACK SOON. PLEASE DO NOT DISTURB.

All the while Dick was quietly preparing himself for the great career that was to end all too soon in 1970 of leukemia, Felice was growing more restive. I was not prepared to understand—not until my separation from Asya cut my life in half—the urgency of rebellion that erupted in the Hofstadters' public quarrels over the way she drove their new car. Their increasing prosperity and fashionableness made them as a couple less fun than they had been in their old Bohemian lodgings in Brooklyn Heights. Felice loved being important to *Time* more than she could ever love *Time* itself. Writing up a frightful industrial accident in which a worker had been pressed to death by a machine, she had thought it clever to write that the victim could now be slipped under a door. On her way home she felt horrified by her callousness, rushed back to the office to change the piece, and found the managing editor roundly congratulating her.

Felice was ambitious, morally sensitive to a degree, but she was not as serious as she thought, not a serious thinker like her husband. She wanted to be a novelist, she wanted to be acclaimed, she wanted, she wanted! When I could not respond as expected to her one published novel, of intense social content, the roof fell in. I pretty well never saw her again. As the war was ending, she became deathly ill. Dick, looking after her, sitting by her side in a darkened room, began *The*

*American Political Tradition* in the dark, on a yellow pad, not always able to see his words.

I began *On Native Grounds* in 1938 with the instinct that I should ground my book in the crucial last decades of the nineteenth century, which saw genuine religious belief derided by "scientific" determinism. The ever mounting tide of American power since the Civil War confronted a violently aroused social discontent among farmers and the immigrant working class.

The nineteenth century did not seem at all far away to me, sitting in the Forty-second Street Library, surrounded, as it were, by *The Education of Henry Adams*, Thorstein Veblen's *The Theory of the Leisure Class*, Gustavus Myers's *History of the Great American Fortunes*, Theodore Dreiser's *Sister Carrie*, Mark Twain's "The United States of Lyncherdom," Jane Addams's *Twenty Years at Hull House*, and Abraham Cahan's *The Rise of David Levinsky*. My Russian Polish immigrant parents, born in the 1880s, represented the period to me as did my Brooklyn neighborhood, its tenements, its clotheslines hanging out of windows, its synagogues in street after street given over to radical protest, its peddlers and their horses collapsing in the street before my eyes of a hot summer morning.

The harsh, combative end of the nineteenth century in America naturally drew me. It was still going on. I really did not believe that the "socialism" of my father and so many other Jewish workmen would change anything. The purge trials just then going on in Russia were a shock and a warning long before the Nazi-Soviet pact left me gasping. Stalin turned out to be as great a murderer as Hitler. But radicalism was a perspective. We were intellectually armed. We were the vanguard on the side of history. This added to the sense of purpose with which I was writing my book, though the subject was only America. The age was with me, the excitement of the thirties was in my book and getting me to write it—along with my being twenty-three and lusting for everything in sight.

So at first it did not matter when the book was published—in the midst of the war—and my wildest hopes were amazingly realized. After four years of trudging to the library, teaching evenings at City College ($2.50 an hour), I spent my days at Madison and Forty-ninth as literary editor of the *New Republic*.

Asya and I were now at Twenty-fourth and Lexington. I was exhilarated feeling myself at the center of things in midtown, meeting writers—Saul Bellow just in from Chicago, his old schoolmate Isaac Rosenfeld, the Italian Jewish exile from Rome Paolo Milano, William Barrett. I was excited by the whirl of New York and the high, lean towers of Radio City, excited even more by the women in the morning light, the proud, beautiful women of New York, the breasts and hot purple mouths of the Bergdorf women, the fantastic sexiness of New York at lunch in certain cool restaurants—all of it hot and cold at once, frightening to dream about. But I dreamed continually, was ashamed, but not so ashamed that I did not go on dreaming and wanting.

What is it men in women do require?
The lineaments of gratified desire.
What is it women in men do require?
The lineaments of gratified desire.

This morning on Second Avenue near the Queensboro Bridge I waited for the bus in front of a fruit stand. The fruits and vegetables out under the awning, still dripping with water from the can, suddenly aroused in me by their look of careless richness a whole world of memories about the summers in Brownsville when I was a kid. The early summers, when I was either too young or we were too poor for me to go anywhere. The hot afternoons and the tenement women sitting out front on kitchen chairs. And then that moment that made summer, the unbelievable moment of pause, when Mama would admit (after hours at the sewing machine), "Oh, it's so hot, too hot!" And I would walk down to P.S. 66, where the other kids gathered to play in the cool basketball sweat of the hall downstairs.

The fruits on the stand, the bowling on the cool brown floor in the dust, Mama in her eternal housedress. Why is this dim memory suddenly dear to me? Looking back is opening myself to everything out of childhood I've wanted desperately to lose.

Lord, come out of the wilderness!

In Durham, North Carolina, a week ago I saw a white boy throw a lighted cigarette right at a Negro soldier. Bob Wunsch of Black Mountain College told me that when he was a boy studying at the family table, an uncle came in and threw something across that left a red splotch. It was the finger of a Negro the uncle had just helped to lynch. The education of a Southerner. Wunsch now wants to admit Negroes to the college, and spends much of his time in Negro schools.

Woke too early again, as I have for so long—much too early, straining against the light, hoping it will dissolve, that the night will return and protect me. But it never does, and the long, awful day begins, and the fear. The sudden tide of nausea, and waiting for the letter from the invisible hostile stranger who has never actually met me but has condemned me in advance. These faults, these omissions. Yet the punishment remains mockingly indistinct. It is my whole life that is now condemned, not just my fault.

I am tired of these dreamlike mornings of guilt. I am tired of being always afraid, waiting for the letter. All the accusing letters anyone might write me have mischievously long been in my heart. I am tired of reproaches, for as yet I have done nothing to deserve them—nothing, that is, but allow myself forever to be judged by *them*—nothing but fail to be true to my innermost conception of myself. And that is why I have turned again here, to plot the curve, its rise and fall, that must end now. It must end now. It must, dear God, for I cannot go on like this. I had hoped to lose all this in the army, and when I was rejected and learned that I had to go to the hospital for an operation, it was too much. Whatever it costs me, I must, I *must* get into the war somehow.

*Fortune*'s managing editor took his new writer to lunch with Henry Luce this afternoon. I proposed "The American Prophetic Books" in our literature for the "philosophy" series with which Luce plans to manage the American mind. Luce different from what I had imagined. Eyebrows like growing plants. Getting bald, hair in back very long. The luncheon was on the sixty-fourth floor of the RCA Building in the private dining room of the Time Inc. executives. Much clatter, heavy gloss. I could not understand everything Luce said. He has what I would call the Yale mumble. I've heard it in Paine, John Chamberlain, Charlie Poore. The mumble shows off their colloquialism and friendliness, their divorce from the formality and remoteness of power life in their fathers' day. It shows their youth and happy carelessness.

Luce wanted to talk about AMERICA AND WHAT'S WRONG WITH IT. He confirmed what I had suspected about the "philosophy series" in *Fortune*—it's a naive attempt to bring mind, purpose, etc., into the lives of the business class by buying pronouncements on the good life by Hocking, Whitehead, Hutchins, et al. It's not misleading, just an attempt to create intellectual order and serenity for people who have everything else. The hitch is that, Mortimer Adler–like, they're trying to add this *to* Time Inc. culture.

All this nauseates me a little. *Time* is dead cold so far as a single real ideal is concerned. But the provincial *Saturday Evening Post* formula won't work anymore. This is a world-conscious generation, etc. So the news capsules in *Time* and the glossy pages of *Fortune* are all trumpeted as "educational."

I was talking of Henry Adams and the disillusionment after the Civil War. Said we had to know now that the emperor has no clothes on. Luce looked puzzled, then frowned—asked, "What emperor?" I said, with fingers crossed, "The materialist emperor." "But America is not materialist!" cried Luce. "*Fortune* was organized not to celebrate business but to explore it!"

*Fortune* is now what it had set out to "explore." Part of Luce really wants to know about the mental world today. But wants the Robert Hutchins Great Books Great Ideas formula. Wants to add "purpose" without dropping anything. I love John Dewey, especially at this moment. Henry Luce—Henry Luce!—said, "John Dewey sold philosophy out." The most pragmatic salesman of ideas in America complains that John Dewey—is not an Aristotelian.

The *New York Times* notes in an easy-to-miss corner of a back page that on May 12, in London, the Polish Jew Shmuel Ziegelboim, who represented the Jewish Workers Bund in the Polish cabinet-in-exile, was found dead by his own hand in a London flat. His wife and child had been murdered by the Nazis. His letter was addressed to the president of Poland and to Prime Minister Wladyslaw Sikorski:

> I take the liberty of addressing to you my last words, and through you to the Polish government and to the Polish people, the governments and peoples of the Allied states—to the conscience of the world. From the latest information received from Poland, it is evident that the Germans, with the most ruthless cruelty, are now murdering the few remaining Jews in Poland. Behind the ghetto's walls the last act of a tragedy unprecedented in history is being performed. The responsibility for this crime of murdering the entire Jewish popula-

tion of Poland falls in the first instance on the perpetrators, but indirectly it is also a burden on the whole of humanity, the people and the governments of the Allied states which thus far have made no effort toward concrete action for the purpose of curtailing this crime.

By the passive observation of the murder of defenseless millions, and of the maltreatment of children, women and old men, these countries have become the criminals' accomplices.

I must also state that although the Polish government has in a high degree contributed to the enlistment of world opinion, it has yet done so insufficiently. It has not done anything that would correspond to the magnitude of the drama being enacted now in Poland. From some 3,500,000 Polish Jews and about 700,000 other Jews deported to Poland from other countries—according to official statistics provided by the underground Bund organization—there remained in April of this year only about 300,000. And this remaining murder still goes on.

I cannot be silent—I cannot live—while remnants of the Jewish people of Poland, of whom I am a representative, are perishing. My comrades in the Warsaw ghetto took weapons in their hands on that last heroic impulse. It was not my destiny to die there together with them, but I belong to them, and in their mass graves. By my death I wish to express my strongest protest against the inactivity with which the world is looking on and permitting the extermination of my people. I know how little human life is worth today; but as I was unable to do anything during my life, perhaps by my death I shall contribute to breaking down the indifference of those who may now—at the last moment—rescue the few Polish Jews still alive from certain annihilation. My life belongs to the Jewish people of Poland and I therefore give it to them. I wish that this remaining handful of the original several millions of Polish Jews could live to see the liberation of a new world of freedom, and the justice of true socialism. I believe that such a Poland will arise and that such a world will come. I trust that the President and the Prime Minister will direct my words to all those for whom they are destined, and that the Polish government will immediately take appropriate action in the fields of diplomacy. I bid my farewell herewith to everybody and everything dear to me and loved by me. S. Ziegelboim.

The *Times* added: "That was the letter. It suggests that possibly Shmuel Ziegelboim will have accomplished as much in dying as he did in living."

At my strenuous urging the *New Republic* has reprinted Ziegelboim's last message. Under it *I* add:

Something has already been done—by us the bystanders as well as by the Nazi killers—that will never be undone. Hitler will leave hatred of the Jews as his last political trick, as it was his first. The people who have been most indifferent to the massacre of the Jews will be just those who wonder why all the pacts and all the formal justice will have done so little to give them their prewar "security" again.

You who want only to live and let live, to have the good life back—and think you can dump three million Jews into the furnace, and sigh in the genuine impotence of your undeniable regret, and then build Europe back again! Where so great a murder has been allowed, no one is safe.

This cry in a "liberal" weekly brings no handwringing and head-shaking. Exactly three people—Lewis Mumford, Daniel Bell, Eugene Lyons—have responded. They praise my "courage" in writing so directly about the "Jewish tragedy."

They are killing us off in Europe. They are killing us by the thousands from the Rhine to the Volga. The blood of the Jews is like the vapor in the air that Faustus saw when the Devil claimed his due. But no one claims us but death. Our due is the "sympathy" of a few men of goodwill. From this morning's *Times* I learn that a few French Catholic priests have been opposing Vichy's submission to Nazi Jewish policy. Saliège, the archbishop of Toulouse, has written this pastoral letter:

> There is a Christian morality, there is a human morality, that impose duties and confer rights. These duties and these rights derive from the very nature of man. They may be violated. No mortal may endeavor to suppress them. That children, women, men, fathers, mothers should be treated as a wretched herd, that members of the same family should be separated from one another and embarked for unknown destinations, was a spectacle reserved for our bad times to see.
>
> Why does the right of asylum no longer exist in our churches? Why are we a vanquished people? Lord, have mercy on us! Our Lady, pray for us! These Jews are men, these Jewesses are women; these aliens are men and women. All is not permissible against them, against these men and women, against these fathers and mothers. They belong to mankind. They are our brethren as are so many others. No Christian can forget that.
>
> France, beloved motherland; France, who preserves in the conscience of all children traditional respect for the individual; chivalrous and generous France, I do not doubt that thou are not responsible for these errors.

Croton: Sitting in this screened-in porch is like occupying a mound in the forest. The fixed, monotonous cries of the birds. When Asya and I rented this cottage nobody told us that in this area Stalin is still God. And that "gangster, that enemy of the people" Max Eastman, is still playing daily tennis at the other end! As I was working a woman came up to the porch and stared at me bitterly.

"Aren't you coming to the meeting?" "What meeting?" She looked as if she couldn't believe my response and stormed off in disgust.

The sidewalk preachers in New York on Sunday afternoons. There is nothing so empty as walking alone in New York on Sunday. The gutters seem to throw back all one's thoughts. The pavements are creased and dull. All that life which has been flung out here all week, only to reach a point in a schedule, has now been emptied into great boxes and thrown away. The storefronts are glass: the walkways are glass; the sky, which before might have gone unnoticed in its beauty, is now just too remote. Life has dissolved, been dusted away into the corners of endless carpets. Stray men are waiting for buses or breathing in the litter of chewing-gum wrappers and subway latrines down below, where the trains make such a roar when they come. Or they are gathered in hostile congregations in the Bowery, at the entrances to parks, near bridges, listening to the funny men who are crying to Jesus on a New York Sunday. Once I saw a man talking to himself in the shadows of the El's pillars and the newsstands at the entrance to Brooklyn Bridge, crying with genial desperation, "*Jesus saves.*" They write their lessons for the day in chalk on the sidewalk, mount a box, and shout, though there may be no one there. At most they draw a handful—boys and girls on an outing; people looking for the subway; the Bowery women in dirty fur collars and Queen Mary hats who live nowhere and everywhere. And the city's tramps, the fuzzy-wuzzies of New York's self-disgust. The preachers look like small-town insurance agents; some still wear the high collar of 1912. Their faces are content; their hearts are full of belief.

Who are they? The amateurs of the faith, slaves to the office all week and missionaries to Sin City on Sunday? If they are believers, why do they look so pleased with themselves? If they are fakes, why are they so serene? They are not fakes. They have enough religion to talk to anyone who will listen on a Sunday afternoon. It does not matter that I will not listen, that you will scoff, that little boys will laugh and run away. They have divested themselves of the obligation to be someone else. What I see most in them—refugees from the slave week. They are preaching not to convert but to express themselves, to be themselves, for once, on the empty glass-walk Sundays; in the shadows and in the Sunday latrine stench. To be free, where everyone is absent.

The *Times* reports "The story of a British Medical major named Shorlee—who refused to be repatriated from a German prison camp because he felt his duty lay in serving blind fellow-prisoners."

I joined *Fortune* so that I could get overseas. So now I am on my way to the Great Lakes Naval Training Station. First week Washington, second week Camps Lee in Virginia and Bainbridge in Maryland, A white plume of smoke over the brown crusted earth in Ohio. Red barns. Earth looks cold and scrubbed between the bales of straw wheat, villages that make me think of Senator Bricker, they are so stately, proper looking. All night long, bouncing in the upper berth of Car 73. Where am I going? Where? Yet it is a happy day for all my terror—a good Sunday morning. I am full of love for Mary Lou, expectant of love. But no one for a while, please. No more company, thinking, friends for a while. I have committed a sin and now want to be alone. I feel no easy pain—all this was committed in my mind long before she came down to the hotel in Washington.

Madison, Wisconsin: These beautiful lakes and the hill at the university. The sunlight. I sat near the lake all this morning, thinking, thinking.

\* \* \*

Paolo Milano is right—I am infatuated—hate it and hate myself. But yes, I am going through with Mary Lou. I am going through— I mean to see the final edge of the woods. Where is the meaning that is supposed to flow out of love? Asya is going away. There is a crack in me that I do not want to heal.

Countess Tolstoy comments in her diary on her husband:

A gifted man puts all his understanding and all the subtlety of his soul into his works, while his attitude to real life is dull and indifferent. It is the same with my husband, who is infinitely more gifted than Taneyev. What a wonderful understanding of human psychology there is in his books, and what an extraordinary indifference and lack of understanding in his home life. He neither knows nor understands me, or his children, or any of his friends.

Jan. 8, 1944: Goethe's poem—"Neue Liebe, Neues Leben." Whitman—

Surely whoever speaks to me in the right voice, him or her I shall follow.
As the water follows the moon, silently, with fluid steps, anywhere around the world.
All waits for the right voices. . . .

Living in a miserable room on University Place, the Hotel Albert. I heard once that the hotel was owned by the painter Albert Ryder's brother, who named it after him. Perhaps this is why I let myself come here. But the spirit of Albert Pinkham Ryder is not here now. I pray for a little rest here, and want to be quietly alone.

So glad to be out of Isaac Rosenfeld's apartment in Barrow Street, when I lived there with Lou. How much darkness is associated for me with those rooms and Isaac's crude orgone box, in which he sat like a man waiting in a telephone booth for someone to call him back. Endless processions of dirt that disappeared from one corner only to find new shape in another. Isaac the village philosopher. His special gift for humiliating himself and the world of nothing but ideas he lives in.

It is unpleasant to rent from your friends, to argue about money, to lend them money as if to stop their mouths about the lovesick ass you have become in their eyes. Which they have no thought of repaying. Unpleasant to learn so much about them from the objects they have indifferently handled—not knowing that the friend will come to live there only because he has gone gaga and has nowhere else to turn.

Swann—

What an abyss of uncertainty whenever the mind feels that
some part of it has strayed beyond its own borders; when it,
the seeker, is at once the dark region through which it must
go seeking, where all its equipment will avail it nothing.
Seek? More than that: create. It is face to face with something which so far does does not exist, to which it alone can
give reality and substance, which it alone can bring into the
light of day.

The Allies have landed in France, and I am in Pasadena, California, working on Blake for the Viking Portable and writing on Dreiser! I feel sick with shame, useless, and in total exile. Walking in the sun-drenched California streets on my way to the Huntington and its tinkle-tinkle "noiseless" typewriters, I confront the nothingness of my life here. The overbearing rich houses on every side of me, the solemn little academic specialists each full of his "field" (sometimes called "my area"), the void in which I live. Thinking of tormented Mama and all the ghosts with which I wrestle, I cannot thrill to the Shakespeare Garden and my first taste of avocado. I was accompanied by an armed guard when I went downstairs at the Huntington to study the magnificent original of *Songs of Innocence and Experience*. The guard kept his hand on his holster all the time I was turning the pages in awe.

A wonderful dream scene in something that actually happened a few minutes ago. I found out only after it had begun that a concert of recorded music was being given in the Dabney Hall of the Cal Tech campus here, the first number being Beethoven's Ninth. I rushed over, but on entering the hall found it dark and could see nothing but the the backs of chairs with figures in them. Beethoven's Ninth roared on and on over the weird silence of these figures so stiff in their chairs. There was no place to sit down, no one to join. They would have nothing to do with me, sitting with their backs to me, silently in judgment.

Went down to Hollywood. The Group Theater people are all here, enjoying newfound prosperity. Clifford Odets was sitting in his flagstoned patio with the twinkly Irish actor Barry Fitzgerald, listening with rapture to a new recording of Brahms's Third and waving his glasses up and down as if he were conducting the music himself. In his emotion he let the glasses fall on the flagstones, where one lens cracked. When I wondered what he would do now, he looked at me in surprise and said with a touch of pride, "Not to worry! I have four duplicates upstairs."

Dear Harold Clurman, always a favorite of mine, picked me up at my hotel and drove me to dinner at Musso and Frank's. I listened with so much interest to Harold's sardonic instructions in Hollywood protocol that it didn't occur to me to wonder why the drive was so short. Harold told me how important it was to the movie set to be seen driving a "really smart car" and to enter a restaurant wearing a very expensive-looking tie. A few nights later, taking a girl to dinner at Musso & Frank's, I discovered that the restaurant was exactly one block from my hotel.

Sylvia Sidney looked a little hung over when she opened the door. "So what brings you to California?" I explained that I was working on Blake at the Huntington Library. "Blake, huh?"

"Hey, Luther," she called to the next room, where her husband, Luther Adler, was playing cards. "Didn't we buy a print, something by this Blake guy the other day?"

Provincetown: another bedroom. I had followed Mary Lou to Monhegan Island; useless, since I no longer know what I want. The only joy sitting around a battery-operated radio on a table lighted by a kerosene lamp was hearing of the liberation of Paris. In Boston went to Dixon Wecter's in Berkeley Street and to bed. Just before walking that morning early I dreamed of Paul Goodman. He was walking with me somewhere, suddenly stopped, and with a malicious smile said, "Well, shall I start asking you questions about Blake now?" I awoke with a shiver, felt the old familiar panic—a fog sweeping in on me from an unknown sea. I lay in bed unable to get up, when suddenly I thought to myself, "No, no, it can't go on like this, I must fight it!"

I left Boston yesterday afternoon and came into Provincetown last night. Why did I come back? Because I was looking for Asya as we had been here, 1940, in the cottage off Priscilla Alden Lane rented to us by Varian Fry's English in-laws. Looking for our easy days together when, after work on the book, we went off to the great beaches at Race Point, Long Point, Highland Light in Truro. The great event was making our way over the dunes where Eugene O'Neill had lived for a season, and after him Edmund Wilson. At the end, the ocean, the Peaked Hills Coast Guard Station, the edge of the continent, the last of America. Nothing like Cape Cod, the farthest point out. There is nothing like reaching an end.

The tyranny of love in Proust; fills all the spaces once occupied by custom, law, religion. It is the private man's last expression of his finiteness and longing for the infinite. The irony he sees in his own suffering, at once so great yet trivial in its self-absorption. How profound—Proust describing Paris bombed in the First World War, the background for Charlus chained to his bed in the male brothel. The last of the aristocracy "until the day when this willing Prometheus had had himself chained by force to the rock of pure matter."

Black Mountain, North Carolina: Went last night with some girls from the college and soldiers from the neighboring Moore Hospital to a "folk festival" in Asheville, a three-days-running show. The MC was a fat, friendly little man in a white suit. The crowd was cordial, a little baffled, in quest of excitement—answered at the high moments with the Rebel yell. The "folk" dance was jived square dances; stringed strumming; a seven-year-old boy propped up on a chair next to a microphone singing "God Bless America" in a timid whine. The only performance that had any ancient "folk" dignity was a spontaneous dance launched by an elderly man with the seamed look of a carpenter and old black mustaches who stepped out onto the wooden extension of the stage under the high, blank light and tentatively, affectionately, tried out a few steps of his own. Then a man came out at the other end of the stage, duplicated and varied the steps of the first. The fact that he was wearing a dark city suit, collar, and tie made his dancing all the more vivid. Then another man, and still another, until there was a ring of them, most of them dressed up like city people, businessmen, but each doing his steps quietly and absorbedly in his own corner. Homesick beyond repair, I remembered my uncles flashing out at a wedding to join other Jews dancing in a ring.

I walked the Asheville streets with Mary Schmitt, waiting for the bus to take us back. Saturday night in Asheville—the leaky neon colors; the banned liquor among the soda-pop bottles; the soldiers drunk to madness propped up in front of cigar stores and ice-cream parlors.

Went to bed early last night and had a violent dream. It hurts to write this even here. I dreamed that Mama had fallen ill, somewhere in this region, and was being taken to the hospital on the top of an enormously elevated car or wagon. She lay there, the car moving heavily through the streets as if on parade. The scene was full of spectators! Suddenly she fell from a great height right into the street. My mother was dead. I was painfully, intolerably stirred; not so much from grief as surprise at such an event, surprise at my realizing (even in the dream) that I could accept this without horror.

My first impulse was to tell everyone within reach, to let it be known that Mama was dead. Entering a restaurant, I encountered Clifton Fadiman and a stranger accompanying him. He was in Asheville on a lecture tour or something. He was indifferent in his general attitude, and when I told him about my mother, he and his friend smiled coldly, as if amused by my feelings, and went off.

Talk about exile! Black Mountain has lost whatever faculty it has had—Eric Bentley, its stormy literary scholar, has departed for Fisk or something like—and depends on refugees who at the moment have nothing else. In painting, Josef Albers, from Westphalia, with a Jewish wife. In music, the conductor Hans Jalowetz, from Prague. In science, Dr. Erwin Strauss, a psychiatrist from Munich. He actually brought his heavy European armoire with him. I try to imagine it making its way from Munich over the ocean and mountains many. And I have one seminar in Blake, one in *Moby-Dick*, one in the Bible. I discovered that no one recognized any of the Old Testament references in the book.

All this for fifteen dollars a month and helping with the chores. Black Mountain is hobbled more by its lame ducks, as has been true of every American utopia, than by its poverty and its sentimentality about "community" and "liberation" in pathetic defiance of traditional education. But it is bracing to live in this mountain setting, and I am so glad to be teaching again—Blake and Melville and Job!—that it seems right to do it for nothing.

Primitive, magnificent country surrounds our pathetic idealism. The other day, walking in the back fields past the college, I stumbled on a chain gang! Overseer with rifle. Tall, hulking guard with prisoners all black of course. Walking in the early morning cold to my two slices of bread and one strip of bacon (the bread economically buttered with a brush), the mists ribboning the mountains, is as heady as a dip naked in a mountain stream.

Thank God for Wallace Stevens.

It is hard to think of a thing more out of time than nobility.
Looked at plainly it seems false and dead and ugly. To look at
it at all makes us realize that in our present, in the presence
of our reality, the past looks false and is therefore dead and is,
therefore, ugly. . . . But as a wave is a force and not the water
of which it is composed, which is never the same, so nobility
is a force and not the manifestations of which it is composed,

which are never the same. Possibly this description of it as a force will do more than anything else I can have said about it to reconcile you to it. It is not an artifice that the mind has added to human nature. The mind has added nothing to human nature. It is a violence from within that protects us from a violence without. It is the imagination pressing back against the pressure of reality. It seems, in the last analysis, to have something to do with our self-preservation; and that, no doubt, is why the expression of it, the sound of its words, helps us to live our lives.

The fall lingered on, but now the cold has set in. The grass I walk to the dining room frozen white, shivery in early morning light and the mist from the river.

Received news from the Rockefeller Foundation that they can probably get me over to England by the first of the year to document the popular education movement in the British armed forces and war factories.

Another letter from Bob Flint, Harvard's most assiduous recent intellectual, who loves to write me his reflections, letter after letter straight from serving a flag admiral in the Pacific Fleet.

*Every effort has been made to destroy the intangibles, but the fact remains that this war in the Pacific is one of the great explosions of pioneering energy in history, involving huge masses and breaking up the threads of social development like cobwebs in the grass. No one of us expects to return in less than two years, unless we have been wounded, and undoubtedly, we won't come back unchanged. Anything like a normal, predictable future seems like the remotest possibility.*

Thanksgiving Day, 1944: Enormous walk to the state road and by the back road back to the college. Saw beautiful black horse let out of the stable circling wildly in the fields. Wonderful sight. Saw feisty Airedale with black snub nose tearing past me on the road. Looked like the busy bureaucrat, sniffing the scene in disapproval of every dog but himself.

As you go down the main road, the houses you come to are on an incline, and so close to the path that it all looks like a tableau—log cabin, oxen, waterwheel, plow, farmers in ancient tattered straw hats.

Brooklyn to Liverpool on Liberty ship *Hart Crane* in convoy of fifty-three vessels plus Canadian escort vessels. Four civilians wedged together in hospital room stacked with bedpans for army. One Franciscan to replace ailing Franciscan in Liverpool. One Baptist missionary to France. One radio engineer who sleeps all the time. And Kazin.

Long straight lines of vessels in convoy make me think of ducks on parade—mother ahead, chicks plodding obediently after her but wavering out of line from time to time. If a chick gets too far out of line, it is in danger of being picked off. Second day stood watch with Ensign Petty, officer in charge of navy gunners on top bridge. Former math teacher in Liberty, New York, talked about how lonely it all is.

Ships in our line of the convoy, extreme right, went out of position during the night. Now we're last in our row again.

Bitter cold on bridge. Ocean the color of dirty iron. In Prescott's *Conquest of Mexico* description of Cortés's journey into the interior.

It was August 16, 1519. During the first day their road lay through the *tierra caliente*, the beautiful land where they had so long been lingering; the land of the vanilla, cochineal, cacao . . . products which, indigenous to Mexico, had now become the luxuries of Europe; the land where the fruits and the flowers chase one another in unbroken circle through the year; *where the gales are loaded with perfumes till the senses ache at their sweetness*; and the groves are filled with many-coloured birds, and insects whose enamelled wings glisten like diamonds in the bright sun of the Tropics.

\* \* \*

Snow. Icy cold. Falling asleep in my bunk over every book. "HURRY UP PLEASE ITS TIME." Time, like a broom, hangs over the dust of the days, to sweep it all away, and soon. Commodore of the convoy gives orders from a Dutch ship. Best thing in Prescott is the portrait of Montezuma, who felt himself "rebuked by the superior genius of his foes."

Steward, of French-Canadian descent, never shuts up. Subject this morning the *fucking* British Empire. Our ever-present sense of danger—submarines, storms, collisions in the dead of night, bombings. No joke standing watch four hrs at a time in this intense cold. General cynicism, but great individual pride in power material and military of the U.S.

Fair amount of damage from yesterday's storm. One ship in convoy drifting about in distress. Note of fatalism in old Aztec chieftains up against the Spaniards. Spaniards seemed "the great beings" whom the oracles had foretold. Aztec sense of historical inferiority *not* produced by the abstractions of Christian theology. The Western Hemisphere waited for the East to conquer it?

James Clark, the chief mate, was in a lifeboat for eight days in the Pacific until he was picked up. The third mate on the subject of Negroes and Jews: Negroes are prone to respiratory diseases because of the shape of their nostrils, which makes their breathing *different. All* Jews are used to a semitropical climate and become irritable when it rains.

Lifeboat No. 4 (*my* boat!) damaged badly. Men move from boat to boat with each voyage, and are often strangers to each other the whole voyage.

As the heavy metal door to the ship's "library" suddenly opened and then smashed shut with a terrible bang, sleeping men jumped out of their bunks yelling that we were under attack. We are in the danger zone approaching the Irish Sea. One depth charge after another hurled overboard. Can read nothing but detective fiction, and as usual I am fascinated by the totally sexless, imperiously detached Buddha brain presented by Poe's Dupin, Sherlock Holmes, Hercule Poirot, even ridiculous Nero Wolfe. Stooge Dr. Watson on godlike Sherlock—

> It was not that he felt any emotion akin to love for Irene
> Adler. All emotions, and that one particularly, were abhorrent
> to his cold, precise, but admirably balanced mind. He was, I
> take it, the most perfect reasoning and observing machine
> that the world has seen; but as a lover, he would have placed
> himself in a false position.

It is just this "saintliness" that puts us in awe of Sherlock, gives us our confidence in him. Only evil engages his interest. Like Hitler, but on our side.

At daybreak saw lights around dark water. English pilot at breakfast wolfing down bacon and eggs with a great smile. Cleared by 5 A.M., couldn't wait to see Liverpool, my first sight of Europe.

In these wretched, much-bombed dock areas of Liverpool thought of Melville landing here a century ago for *his* first sight of Europe. Have never been able to forget the lacerating chapter in *Redburn: His First Voyage*, "What Redburn Saw in Launcelott's-Hey" describing the indifference of Liverpool to the starving mother and baby in the narrow street of old warehouses. Or his patriotic enthusiasm at seeing so many emigrant ships setting out for America. "You cannot spill a drop of American blood without spilling the blood of the whole world."

Drab painted signs along the docks: HANDS OFF GREECE. Clergyman in cafeteria, still looking entirely correct as he carefully shovels beans into himself off a knife. My first view of the most destroyed bombed areas. The astonishing delicacy and courtesy of the exhausted girls in the shops. In the train to London, corridors dripping water, a fashion buyer lady who travels all the time between London and Liverpool confronted me with *"your* Negroes." Wanted to know if because of their oppression they are allowed to pay less income tax than other Americans.

Lunch with Office of War Information people, agreed to consult, give talks on American writing. The streets full of whores, GIs milling around them. Lunch with sociologist, now a member of a royal commission on population, who was most charming in America but in England has nothing to say about us that is not poisonous. Wife a German refugee, rapturous over Soviet military govt beginning to be set up in Germany. Such a fellow traveler, she burst out at me when I mentioned Stalin's murder of the Jewish Bund leaders Ehrlich and Alter.

Walked out of the blackout into Laurence Olivier's *Henry V,* overwhelming in its golden coloring after the hooded streets. Cutting and varnishing of the play to meet the present hour cleverly done. The audience laughed and applauded when Olivier, shining in armor, urged on his troops with "For England and Saint George!" Then back into the cold and blanket darkness of the streets, leaving me homesick.

Food on everyone's mind. Sugar scarce, and when it comes, looks battered. Dirt on dishes. General subdued feeling that some big push is coming.

So many old gentlemen with wing collars. The style persists after the power is gone. General appearance of people better than I had anticipated, but so many shops boarded up. Protective shields of stone and piled-up sandbags in front of Tube stations. Rosy-looking children (they alone get orange juice and vitamins) playing in the cold, dead twilight along the alleys. Low, massive palaces. Royal Academy rooms at Burlington House: chipped statues. General feeling of grime, fatigue, but inner determination and cheerfulness.

Great question in my mind how they keep from hating us. A hot-shot American pilot waving a long, white ten-pound note like a scarf to get a taxi, and when it rolled up was heard to say disdainfully,

"What the hell can you do with a broken-down old flivver like that?" Indignant English girl—"*You* would either drink it or fuck it!"

GIs lined up by the dozens in Piccadilly Circus; always in front of American movies. I hear that on their tour five American senators were most anxious to be photographed with Bob Hope. One or two actually invited Hope to accompany them to 10 Downing Street. Ambassador Winant had to whisper in their ears that it isn't done.

Uniforms, uniforms; all the English and Scottish regimental tabs. Privates in drab khaki buttoned up to the neck, while the officers look sleek and cool. Really quite grand looking compared with our aggressive lawyer-turned-major types. I am propagandized to death by government press officers that there is more democracy in their army than was conceivable before the war, that it is possible to "rise from the ranks." But imagine an American officer saying to another, as I heard one British officer the other day say to another on a railway platform in the Midlands, "Oh dear, I do hate to keep troops waiting." Americans feel superior only because we have *more*. Sailors in Chicken Coop restaurant deriding bare English diet. Hilarious sight of American lieutenants in Tube blowing their bubble gum in unison.

Heard V-2 go off my first night, but tight restriction on all news of the V-2s. Searchlights endlessly combing the sky from or around Hyde Park. All American talk around me superficial—differences between *us* and *them*. In wartime the basic category in which people think politically, spiritually, emotionally, is the purely consensual notion of the Nation.

Thrilled to be walking the London Blake walked.

The fields from Islington to Marybone,
To Primrose Hill and Saint John's Wood,
Were builded over with pillars of gold;
And there Jerusalem's pillars stood.

Silence of streets at night eerie. Hard to tell if people have abandoned all these blitzed-looking houses or still live in them.

The hill of subway sleepers on the platform of my Tube station, Marble Arch. Old lady with glasses sliding down her nose perched on the highest bunk, and with her head way out of the bunk to catch what light was there to read by, reading the *Church Times.*

*The Circle* (W. S. Maugham) at the Haymarket. The audience roared when Lord Porteous, red in the face, said, "The damned radicals can say what they like, but after all, a gentleman . . . damn it all, a gentleman is a gentleman." The play, circa 1912, a satiric comedy of manners, tinctured with Maugham's light cynicism and his easy pity—a pity that is Maugham's usual excuse for saying everything is just rot. Company openly laughed at the lines, as if the play with its once "amoral" conclusion had not already enjoyed the disintegration of the old order. Play now a costume piece.

Tour with OWI people. Touched briefly on the East End. The chauffeur, hired with his car for the occasion, quite a snob. When I pressed him to go on to Whitechapel, he explained there really wasn't much to see there—just "lower-class dwellings."

The Nazis went after the East End? Whole blocks of houses eliminated. What I saw was a dirtier, grimier, emptier, seemingly abandoned Lower East Side.

Lost my way on the subway and then on the bus trying to get "home" to the American billets on Great Cumberland Street. Overtaken by terrible depression. Went into a fog. Dinner at the billets and stayed for the movie. Lana Turner. How we all loved seeing our natural resources so generously displayed. Our homesickness could have been cut with a knife.

Rain pouring through the blackout made a beautiful London vignette. Over and again, walking about in the evenings, I have the misleading sensation, looking at the completely blank-seeing houses, that no one is living in them at all. Even in the daylight many houses appear so battered and decayed that one supposes them vacant. The unbelievable emptiness makes me so much lonelier than I already am here that I want to yell, "English! Where the hell are you all?!" But the town is crowded.

The shortage of foods easy to get at home very acute, but what is available is distributed more equably. Three weeks' ration of chocolate, three-quarters of a pound. A lot of eating on the run. Sandwiches and cakes eagerly bought in refreshment buffets at dinner. Communal kitchens a great comfort to the bombed-out.

Harold Laski's open night for Americans at his bomb-damaged house on Addison Bridge Place. He is in evening dress, tassels on his evening dress slippers. I am surrounded by Americans in uniform, correspondents, folks from the embassy. In New York in 1939 I heard Laski address the teachers union fervently on the necessity of socialism, and he is still at it. Profuse compliments on *On Native Grounds*, but nerve-racked me by name-dropping—"My old friend *Frank* Roosevelt!"—and shocked me by saying he was a "realist" on Poland, must accept Russian demands, etc. I recognize the difficulty of the situation, but Laski is so cheerful about it all. Told us with feeling that he was awaiting a nephew of Justice Brandeis, now in England with a Justice Department team. The nephew, to Laski's intense chagrin, proved to be coldly unresponsive to Laski's florid praise of "my good friend the Justice."

Letter to the *New Statesman* complains that while the paper approves Churchill's offer of British citizenship to those Poles in their exile army who may not wish to return to Poland, Austrian and German refugees in the British army have not received such offers of citizenship. *They have just been allowed to adopt English surnames.*

\*   \*   \*

The beauty of St James's Park at a twilight hour still soft with light. Walking across it to dinner at the Pep Club I was staggered by the scene—it bespoke another century, tranquillity and peace—made by the bridge and the palace at the far end of the water. But the night was horrible. Chambermaid told me this morning that the rockets sounded so close to her, she fainted while lying in bed.

Twice now I have been awakened before daybreak by a vast hollow boom in the center of town. Oxford Street gets it again and again. Long line in front of shop that had all its windows knocked out. To pay tribute?

A soldier angrily speaking up in an army discussion group: "By politics *I* mean the way most of us have to live."

Officers refer to their troops as "bodies." Reminds me that in Melville's *White-Jacket*, officers in the American navy, 1840s, referred to sailors under their command as "the people."

Major in the Education Corps tells me that after 1870, when the first big Education Act was passed, giving children a few more years in state schools, the birthrate went down. Children, now forced to go to work later, were thought of only as economic assets. With all this new education reform building up, one wonders if birthrate will go down farther.

God, how hidebound they are in the smallest things, while talking so grandly and even fiercely in army and factory discussion groups about the "new Britain" after the war! Visceral conservatism of officers, indifference to Europe, paternalism not lacking in their mixed attitude toward their people. Pride in their holding out but impatient with troops for "softness toward the Germans"—for wanting to get out as soon as possible. Contempt for the Negro with us; for the "Oriental" with them. Who in England first said, "Niggers begin at Calais"?

At army brain trust I was informed, "Semites write from right to left and *think* from right to left."

Where else in this world at war would I have had the bliss of hearing Kathleen Ferrier sing Handel and Glück in a war factory to hundreds of workers joyously massed together at the lunch hour to hear her? Where else would I have been able to hear Myra Hess, bundled up against the cold, playing Schubert in the National Gallery—divested of its pictures but massed with people, many of whom had waited an hour to get in, and only when they sat down had the chance to nibble at their little sandwiches? What a scene! What a people! And they *are* a people, solidly together to preserve their existence, in a way that moves me every time I find myself in the middle of them.

The "interior court" where the concert was held now as grimy and empty as all the great houses, museums, etc. But with that high regal look the great squares keep even with their iron railings removed, melted down for war matériel.

In the evening after dinner the new double-daylight-saving time gave us light, and Ruth Hooper and I walked to Waterloo from Park Lane—through the Green Park and St James's to Westminster—and so on to the border of the East End. In this subtle light prolonged into the evening I saw London as I had not seen it before. Walking through the quiet and leafy park I felt that the light was renewing itself hour by hour.

*   *   *

Went down this Friday afternoon to the East End. In one not-blitzed section the street is lined on both sides of an alley with houses dark, small, and leveled together in a brown mass where nothing stands out of itself. I almost wept on seeing the street itself half filled, every ten yards, with shelters that took up whatever air and space were there before. Tyne Place, Aldgate East—worse than New York's old East Side, and everything shuttled together by the bomb-ings. . . . Scooped-out squares are now storage tanks; only faint structural supports left. Bombed buildings make one arch after another you can see through if not pass. Liverpool Street station murkily beautiful this afternoon; half the old glass roof is out, as in so many London railway stations, and the light fiercely reflects the hurrying crowds, the tea wagons, and the dirt.

British officers do not take an oath to the king. They are his "friends, . . . looking after his troops."

They say . . . they say. . . . Speech changes in Britain every thirty miles. Commanding officer of Dorset regiment tells me most of his men still speak dialect.

First-aid station, Walthamstow, London, running full blast despite bombing lull. People still serving twenty-four hours on twenty-four off. Hot-water bottles still being filled for shock cases. They miss the feeling of danger and of "being together."

"Adult education with us now, what religion used to be." A long-deprived people, always talking about "a better England."

The President is dead. Great wreath outside U.S. Embassy—ENGLAND MOURNS ITS BEST FRIEND AND HUMANITY ITS ELDER BROTHER. Embarrassed as the only American at Toynbee Hall meeting to be addressed from the chair and told of English sorrow. In the emotion of the moment breakfasted with a group of

Americans, among them the composer Marc Blitzstein, who was reading a newspaper as we ate. He suddenly became heated at something he read unfriendly to the Soviet Union. Shouted "Outrageous! Slander! This should not be allowed!" To our astonishment he got up from the table in such a frenzy that he tipped it over.

Interview with T. S. Eliot at Faber & Faber, ostensibly on official business. In his first years here Eliot, active in popular education, taught for the Workers Education Association and in evening classes sponsored by the London County Council. He must now be fifty-seven. Face has aged and relaxed greatly, so that one's first impression of him physically is of a rather tired kindness as opposed to the feylike removal in his early photographs.

He was extremely kind, gentle, spoke slowly and hesitatingly. Livened up when I pushed the conversation to poetry. Looks like a very sensitive question mark—long, winding, and bent. Gives the impression that his sensibility is in his long, curling nose and astonishing hands. I was afraid he would be standoffish and nervously yammered on, but to my relief he kept bringing the conversation back to America, asking questions. He just verged on "you Americans." To my astonishment he asked, "By the way, what's this Truman like?" In the nick of time I replied, "You ought to know, you both come from Missouri!" He grinned, brightened up considerably, and asked if I was a Harvard man. His office is full of Harvard mementos.

Prostitutes are as established a part of London life as buses. The ones I see in Piccadilly, where in the blackout GIs are always flicking their Zippo lighters to get a better look, are young, brassy and sharp. Imagine my surprise when, on leaving Julian Huxley's talk on his meetings with Russian scientists, I was accosted by a sweet old lady in a coat with a rabbity collar. Friendly as could be, she asked, "Want a little pleasure, dearie?" It was noon, the sun was shining bright with all its might. Not knowing what to say to a whore who resembled my tedious Aunt Sarah, I came up with: "But it's so early!" Whereupon she tittered, "Easier to see your way in!" and marched off looking pleased with herself.

My heart sinks whenever I am handed one of those British government much-reused tan envelopes with a British stamp. I go to our army post office every free moment for V letters from Asya and her news of home. Dick Hofstadter's wife, Felice, is dead.

Asya's letters are friendly but careful. The English are the most civil and admirable people in the world, especially in wartime. It is an education in otherness getting away from rambunctious *us*. But Asya is home and I want to go home.

For months now, living in the billets in Great Cumberland Street, I have encountered every day a young man my age whose name is really Johnnie Smith. He is a kind of assistant porter or general utility man, and he talks very broad Cockney. Johnnie does not know that I am a brother to him and as scared as he is; he always calls me *sir*. Not *sir* at the beginning or the end of a sentence, but *sir* as a constantly intervening part of speech, *sir* as preposition, noun, verb, adjective. Well, *sir*, yes, *sir*, how do you do. If you like, *sir*. *Sir*. He stammers, is crestfallen, and in his recessive speech is all the plaintiveness of all the poor and frightened in the world—not to forget my dear mother trying to talk English and my poor father talking anything. Once, when I was shaving, Smith called me twice to the telephone, and with my usual impatience I must have sounded cross.

His face flushed, and he actually fell back before me. How ashamed I was—not merely because I had frightened him but because he really seems to believe—Jesus almighty!!—that we are master and man.

This morning, after apologizing, I requested him not to "sir" me. He smiled sheepishly but looked a little suspicious.

A British medical detachment in the North German woods has reached the Belsen concentration camp. Forty thousand sick, starving, and dying prisoners on the ground. The report in the London *Times* begins: "I have something to report that lies beyond the imagination of mankind."

Peggy Ashcroft in *The Dutchess of Malfi*—trembling, innocent, fragile, so vulnerable, making me tremble as she was strangled before us. I was staggered by the perfect application of the words to humanity May 1945 when Bosolo came out with:

A long war disturb'd your mind;
Here your perfect peace is sign'd.
Of what is't fools make such vain keeping?
Sin their conception, their birth weeping,
Their life a general mist of error,
Their death a hideous storm of terror.

. . . . . . . . . . . . . .

'Tis now full tide 'tween night and day;
End your groan, and come away.

Can a Jew still believe in God after reading the report by the Parliamentary Commission on Auschwitz? Four million deaths. The crematoria had a total capacity of five and a half million during the time they functioned. The commission investigated conditions at Maidanek, Treblinka, and other annihilation camps, but described Auschwitz as the worst in its experience.

Theses were published on the experiments performed on human beings.

Seven tons of women's hair were found ready for dispatch to Germany. Human teeth, from which gold fillings had been extracted, were piled several feet high. One hundred thousand children's suits of clothes.

Can a Jew still believe? But who ever said that "the Eternal Blessed Be He" could be distracted enough from whatever it is that occupies Him in Heaven to look down long enough to save a single infant from Hitler?

It is not the God of the Jews that holds me but my fellow Jews, faithful to the end. Waiting out the rain in the entrance to a music store just as the radio is broadcasting the first Sabbath service from liberated Belsen, I weep with them as they say the *Shema* and say it with them. "Hear O Israel the Lord Our God the Lord Is One."

I did nothing to beat Hitler. I saved no one.

"Grandpa, what did you do during the war? What was your worst experience?"

"Surviving the martinis at the Hotel Connaught as I sat facing the monumental portrait of Victoria, Queen and Empress, and her 'immortal' words during the South African War: 'There is no pessimism in this house and there will be none.'"

Waiting in line at our army PO, hoping for a letter from Asya, I find that I am of some interest to a large handsome girl with brilliant black hair who is standing right behind me. She does surveys of English public opinion, she is from Madison and Seventieth, she is so sophisticated that she takes me in hand and without my quite knowing how all this got started so fast, I find myself in bed with her and enjoying her directness. Caroline says with a smile, "Isn't

46

it amazing? A nice girl like me can end up having had as many men as . . . !" When I tell her that I am about to leave for Paris, she replies with the total self-assurance with which she regards everything, "I'll see you when you return."

How right she was. When I managed to get on the *Queen Mary*, packed with returning troops, she was there. When I discovered that Asya had fled our old apartment, and in the ghastly housing shortage I ended up in a painter's rickety old studio on Pineapple Street in Brooklyn Heights—at least it was Brooklyn Heights—I returned late one night from a party to find Caroline sitting on the steps, waiting for me. Not that I minded; everything from that point on was all so delicious, rich, and new. But I never really felt I had a choice in the matter.

# PART TWO

1946-1950

*E*very time I go "home" of a Friday night to Brownsville, it all feels like a foreign country. The old immigrant Jews remaining, my parents—all these old Jews are my parents!—may *look* like the inhabitants of the country where I live, but have stubbornly, slyly kept some rich difference in their speech. Under the plastic aprons, the "Yenkee" dresses and suits, the Woolworth tchotchkes in the kitchen, the old, deeply resistant Jewish life goes on and on.

Only the bodies are in America. Their inner lives are still in the caverns of Russian memory and grief.

As always Mama and Papa are stuck fast, unable to change, getting old. They break my heart. Mama, stooped from a lifetime bent over the sewing machine, looks a wreck, still weeps over Asya. Stares at me as if she no longer knew me. "What happened? How could it have happened? What did you do, what did you do?"

As the Jews move out, the blacks move in. Brownsville is now more than half black. Papa, the good socialist, timidly confessed his outrage with black house painters. They work for less than the union scale, cutting out the old-timers for whom solidarity with the union is sacred.

Pineapple Street off Fulton, a decaying old three-story Brooklyn Heights brownstone sadly fallen, broken down in every respect. As you make your exit down the once-elegant steps, a smell of smoke.

The painter, a friend of Saul Bellow's, has left me his workplace, a skylight, and some terrible pictures of concentration camp prisoners with violently suffering eyes that stare at me every time I rest my head on the couch. I cannot get myself to move these damned pictures.

Brooklyn Heights, 1946, my postwar home. Quite a change from 1938, that studio apartment in a newly opened apartment house on Remsen at Clinton that enchanted Asya and me, the freshly married couple. Now I am no longer even married, and despite our five years together, officially never was. Asya, all on her own, has amazingly and most generously managed to procure an annulment so as to avoid the pain and "disgrace" of divorce. It's all unbelievable, unreal, and somehow wrong. What a love. Truly, "the pleasure of love lasts but a moment—the bitterness all your life."

I am stuck with myself as never before. Midway in the journey of our life I find myself in a dark wood where the straight way is lost. But listen, dear Dr. Janet McKenzie Rioch. I think you're smart, warm, *sympathisch*. I am inexpressibly grateful for giving me some objectivity about things, parents, old loves, I've never had before. After I leave your office I sit over a cup of coffee on Sixth Avenue going over it all, glad to discover that I am just another case, not the center of the world.

But this *is* my life, and while I shall always be more a mystery to myself than others are to me, I know for sure that the disorder in my soul is not altogether covered by the deficiency in "interpersonal relationships" I hear about three times a week. When I mentioned my violin and my obsession with music I keep hearing in my head, I had to laugh when you said in all solemnity, "Some of my colleagues worry that the solitary enjoyment of music can be carried too far."

It is all so easy, so shallow, so ignorant of my tumultuous life as a Jew among Jews who never cease to press their lives on mine.

Gussie Kazin instilled the history of the Jews in me with her milk. Rioch grew up in India, the daughter of medical missionaries, and while she knows my mother's racked character by now, anxious and so unyielding, she can't know why I can never look at the letter *ayin* in the Hebrew alphabet without seeing my mother's face.

As Max Schmeling's manager, Joe Jacobs, said, "We wuz robbed. We shoulda stood in bed."


Writing is my life, the one steadiness I have. Yet at the moment I am out at sea trying to write something entirely new for me—a book about New York. I don't seem to convey the worry and exaltation of what that is like. *That's* my secret life, not the silky evenings with Caroline!

Ever since *Harper's Bazaar* gratified me beyond words by assigning me to work with the photographer Henri Cartier-Bresson on a piece about the Brooklyn Bridge and the different worlds at each end of it, I have wanted to write about the city. Cartier-Bresson is an aristocratic radical—laughs, "I was official photographer for the Resistance"—is gently disdainful of the new mass housing projects crowding the view of the Lower East Side from the bridge. Most of them named after labor and socialist heroes my father worships. But old New York, still visible in 1946, gives particular pleasure to Cartier-Bresson's genius eye as we walk down the center of the bridge.

"It breathes!" Cartier says happily about this central promenade. "See how it breathes!" With his devastating clarity and my zeal for these leftover streets, we bring home the Brooklyn Bridge still anchored in the Iron Age, the "Swamp" district of leather factories, old gold assayers' shops, dealers in perfumes and wines, the ornamental fire escapes still sculptured with John L. Sullivan prizefighters out of the old *Police Gazette*. Cartier-Bresson and I get on so well that we think of doing *tout New York* in a book. But Paris is his world, and New York is mine.

Waking up uneasily every morning in Pineapple Street to the glare of postwar New York, so different from the depression thirties and my early working-class life in Brownsville, I am now on my own, trying to do the city at large in a way that will do justice to the color, the variety, the imperial range I absorb walking the city every day. I dream of capturing what Whitman in the greatest New York poem, "Crossing Brooklyn Ferry," called "the glories strung like beads on my smallest sights and hearings—on the walk in the street, and the passage over the river."

"The glories" are not much in evidence when Cartier-Bresson insists that I show him Brownsville, at the far end of Brooklyn. Brownsville, the road every other road in my life has had to cross. Brownsville in dead winter. We walk about most of the morning and early afternoon in the cold. I hadn't before seen so much of the Negro section that now dominates my old neighborhood, and am stunned by the emptiness of the faces, the drunkenness, the kids playing in the dirt, the yards dark with rubble.

Henri stops to snap some cute little boys, and a woman comes rushing out of the yard—a demented face, eyes rolling in her head like a violently beating heart, screaming that she knows what we is doing, all right, couldn't fool *her*. "Are these your kids?" I ask. "Yah." "Is your husband around?" Grins. "I'se married to everybody."

What pictures in the empty afternoon air, with the winter sun showing the emptiness. A Negro man, about fifty, sits in front of his house just staring ahead; a pregnant woman, drunk, with an Empress Eugènie hat, feathers and all, perched on her head; a man stomping about on a wooden leg.

When I walk with Cartier-Bresson I take his kind of picture in my mind.

"Europe-America groups," a bunch of us "New York intellectuals" still vaguely radical in this postradical period, brought together to send food and clothing to French intellectuals in distress. Dwight Macdonald a leading spirit, just as his humble wife, Nancy Macdonald, is still raising funds for Spanish Republicans who managed to get to France after Franco's victory. The monster in power with the aid of Hitler and Mussolini and the blessings of the Holy Church is still shooting survivors of the Republican Army who could not escape.

To my astonishment Simone de Beauvoir was present at this meeting, looking pretty but immensely reserved. She will have a lot to tell Sartre about these once-radical Americans who spend so much time together berating one another for their "mistakes." Sidney Hook cut Dwight down with his usual show of merciless logic. Hook is now completely out of the Communist orbit and in fact bitterly anti-Communist and aggressively patriotic. At one point he labeled Edmund Wilson "anti-American." But he dominates with the same awful self-assurance he had when he was writing *Towards the Understanding of Karl Marx* and hoping to found still another splinter group, called the Workers' Party.

At seventeen, a City College sophomore, I heard Hook tell the Social Problems Club that no, socialism was not "inevitable." The Stalinist audience was outraged by such heresy. I thought Hook's skepticism entirely sensible, but he was so superior I wished I were somewhere else—or that his position came from the mouth of another man.

Dwight is always in a state of intense political evolution—from Stalinism to that high-principled murderer Lev Davidovich Trotsky (né Bronstein) and as usual, is as combative as a cat in heat about his latest "position," anarchopacifism, with many a slam at "mass culture." This is probably his rationale for the failure of socialism to attract the masses in the United States. Dwight is your old-fashioned American protester. He advances from position to position not because he is fool enough to think the world depends on one (unlike the messianic believers from the slums ranting in Union Square, who judge everything and everyone by adherence to the world's total salvation through revolution), but because he always wants to think *right*, to be right with himself—his personal integrity is always the issue.

Which makes him as arbitrary as a spoiled child. During "the worst episode in human history" (Churchill) Dwight followed Trotsky's superrevolutionary line. No difference between the Nazis and ourselves, imperialists all! As a Russian Jew said of the Bolshevik Revolution, "The Trotskys make the Revolution, and the Bronsteins pay for it." Facing the inevitable collapse of Europe after the most total war in history, Dwight jeers in *Politics*, "So what did you fight for?" Missing the only point involved. Listen, Dwight, we did not fight "for" anything—we fought to save the world from the worst killers in modern history.

But in moving away from *Partisan Review* to found his own journal, *Politics*, Dwight has done something altogether splendid—and moving in, getting to clean new moral ground away from Leninism, Trotskyism, the usual hates and polemics of the Left. I owe to *Politics* my discovery of Simone Weil, whose essay *The Iliad: Poem of Force*, astonished and moved me at the end of 1945 by removing the stage heroics from the Trojan War and presenting the true horror of war, death by death by death, as the submission to merciless impersonal force that was the fate of innocent millions during Hitler's war:

> The true hero, the real subject, the core of the *Iliad*, is force. The force that is wielded by men rules over them, and before it man's flesh cringes. The human soul never ceases to be transformed by its encounter with force—is swept on, blinded by that which it believes itself able to handle, bowed beneath the power of that which it suffers.
>
> Force makes a thing of its victims. There where someone stood a moment ago, stands no one.

The piercing simplicity of Simone Weil's style went to the heart of the lasting fear of the war, of the Holocaust, of the forgetfulness it made imperative for so many people. The simplicity was what was left after war—it was elemental, absolute in its sense of what was true, the final truth, about war. As I read it I thought of a photograph taken by Germans themselves during the war. A helpless Polish Jew in rags, reduced to total helplessness, rigid with terror, utterly at the mercy of these soldiers in battle dress *laughing at him*, waits for whatever *more* it is they want to inflict on him. So another Jew was mocked by Roman soldiers.

Simone Weil, a Jew, had been deprived of her lycée teaching job because of her "race." So ordered by a good French Catholic whose middle name was Xavier. She had written *The Iliad: Poem of Force* in Marseilles while waiting with her parents to come to the United States. Refugees all. Surely it was the fate of the Jews—proscribed by Vichy's own clerical fascists, whose police rounded up more Jewish children than the Nazis demanded—that had led her to describe so trenchantly the domination by force?

I couldn't have been more wrong. She was Jewish and looked it, but was obdurate, half manic in denying the Jewish sources of Christianity. She saw nothing in the Old Testament but the wars waged by the ancient Israelites against their national rivals and their extermination. Simone Weil, born in Paris to a Jewish doctor of Alsatian background and a Jewish mother born in Rostov-on-the-Don, despised herself for being a Jew. Being labeled a Jew by her own people, the French, apparently troubled her more than the chance of being murdered *because* she was a Jew. "Assimilation" never saw a Jew more eager to deny herself. She declared herself so entirely French that she boasted she had learned to read in texts by Racine and Pascal.

Reading this, I remembered wandering into the Church of Saint Germain-des-Prés in July 1945 and discovering on a wall the lines that Pascal had feverishly scribbled in his "night of vision"—a paper discovered only after his death, sewn into the lining of his coat:

From about half past ten in the evening until about half past twelve—FIRE.
God of Abraham, God of Isaac, God of Jacob, not of the philosophers and scholars.

Certitude, certitude, feeling, joy, peace.
*God of Jesus Christ*
Thy God will be my God.

Thanks to the school edition of Pascal that had been presented to me by French professors of English after my lecture, I was uplifted. This was truly a gift for life. Pascal combined the greatest possible intelligence with the most acute need of God. In a style that already astonished me by its perfect transparency, he brought me to my knees—this in the universe of death that was the war world of the Jews:

*Advantages of the Jewish People.* In this search the Jewish people at once attracts my attention by the number of wonderful and singular facts which appear about them.

I first see that they are a people wholly composed of brethren. Being thus of all one flesh and members one of another, they constitute a powerful state of one family. This is unique.

This family, or people, is the most ancient within human knowledge, a fact whch seems to me to inspire a peculiar veneration for it . . . if God had from all time revealed Himself to men, it is to these we must turn for knowledge of the tradition.

None of this appears in Simone Weil, who coupled Pascal with Racine—from whom she had "learned to read"—and in whose names she demonstrated her cultural reverence as a French patriot. She hotly denied the Jewish roots of Christianity, to the wonder of Catholic friends impatient to see her in the church; saw the Jews as the "impure element" that kept her out. She liked to recite the Lord's Prayer in Greek, but made nothing of Jesus praying to Our Father and in the Gospels reiterating *My Father, Our Father.* She called herself a Christian, in her extraordinary notebooks described herself as a tormented pilgrim coming close to the church but never able to join it. Living in New York (on Riverside Drive), she permitted herself to enter one synagogue—in Harlem, attended by Ethiopian Jews. Her loyalty was to the downtrodden, the poor, the eternal victims—"afflicted" like her, therefore desperate for a new and truer world in which justice alone would rule.

What a tormented, gifted, madly aspiring creature! Extremes were all. In the thirties, on the surface still another leftist Jewish intellectual, she was briefly in the Spanish Civil War, with an independent radical brigade (not Orwell's). Maladroit in everything, the world external to her, she managed to get her foot into a pot of burning oil. Papa the doctor had to bring her home. Constantly attended and protected by her parents, obsessed by what she considered the superior gifts of her brother André (soon to be a world-famous mathematician at Princeton's Institute for Advanced Studies), she was truly of "immoderate Jewish temperament." (This said by a Catholic who protected her even as she alarmed him.)

But in her Jewish excess of zeal, she was as bold as Orwell in denouncing the crimes committed in Spain by Loyalists. I discovered in Ignazio Silone's beautiful autobiographical essay on how he went from the church to the Communist Party, "A Choice of Comrades," the astonishing letter Simone Weil wrote in 1938 to the novelist Georges Bernanos on her experiences in Spain. She wrote because Bernanos, the passionate Catholic, had denounced the horrors of Franco's rule in Majorca in his searing *Les grands cimetières sous la lune.*

*I have never seen, either among the Spaniards or among the French who have come here to fight or to amuse themselves (the latter often being gloomy, harmless intellectuals) anyone who expressed, even in private conversation, repugnance or disgust for, or even only disapproval of, unnecessary bloodshed. You talk of fear. Yes, fear has played a part in these killings; but where I was I did not find it played as large a part as you ascribe to it. Men to all appearances courageous, when dining with friends, would relate with a warm, comradely smile how they had killed priests or "fas-*

cists"—*a word of elastic meaning. I felt that whenever a certain group of human beings is relegated, by some temporal or spiritual authority, beyond the pale of those whose life has a price, then one finds it perfectly natural to kill such people.*

*When one knows that one can kill without risk or punishment or blame, one kills; or, at least one smiles encouragingly at those who kill. If one happens to feel some revulsion, one hides it, one stifles it, fearing to be seen lacking in virility. There seems to be in this some impulse of intoxication which it is impossible to resist without a strength of mind which I am obliged to consider exceptional, since I have not found it in anyone. On the contrary, I have seen sober Frenchmen whom I had not previously despised—who of their own accord would never have thought of killing anyone—plunging with obvious relish into that blood-soaked atmosphere. The very aim of the struggle is blotted out by an atmosphere of this kind. Because the aim can be formulated only in terms of the public good, the good of human beings; and human beings have no value.*

Tubercular, she left safe refuge with her parents in New York to join the Free French in London. She had a fantasy: to be parachuted into France to serve as a nurse right in the front lines. De Gaulle thought her nuts. She was shunted off to write a program for post-war French recovery, *L'Enracinement* (The Need for Roots). This extraordinary document was not exactly what French politicians had had in mind.

Inflexible in everything, she would not eat more than the French were getting on wartime rations. Extremely ill from tuberculosis, she now literally starved herself and died in England at thirty-four.

Weil could not say, like many another Jewish prophet, "Zeal for thy house hath consumed me." The Jews were not *her* house. Neither was the world itself. But zeal for the divinity she absolutely believed in certainly consumed her. In the ghastly trial of humanity that was Hitler's war, she too would have been obliterated if her posthumously published notebooks had not revealed her, in all her excess, as a genius of the spiritual life. Representing nothing and no one but herself, she was no more with the church than she was with the Jews. As William Blake said, "Organized religion: an impossibility." Like so many homeless believers before her, she was speaking as "the Alone to the Alone."

But apparently the spirit shows itself, even if it is not passed on, in writing like Weil's—breaking through the crust of convention, "final"-sounding, naked and desperate. The sense of affliction that dominated her was really a kind of gift. It made her see the world in the severest light. I finally understood her when I realized that her demand was less for God than for total justice. *That* was God. And the demand, the quest, the inability to give up *anything*, did drive her nuts.

The only real question to be asked of another: What are you going through?

Attentiveness without an object is prayer in its supreme form.

Christianity is, in effect, apart from a few isolated centers, something socially in accordance with the interests of those who exploit the people.

What we love is joy itself. When we know this, even hope becomes superfluous; it no longer has any meaning. The only thing left to hope for is the grace not to be disobedient here below. The rest is the affair of God alone and does not concern us. That is why I lack nothing.

Those who are unhappy have no need for anything in this world but people capable of giving them their attention. The capacity to give one's attention to a sufferer is a very rare and difficult thing. It is almost a miracle; it *is* a miracle.

We do not obtain the most precious gifts by going in search of them but by waiting for them. How can we go toward God? Even if we were to walk for hundreds of years, we should do no more than go round and round the world.

Even in an airplane we cannot do anything else. We are incapable of progressing vertically. We cannot take a step toward the heavens.

The Polish ship *Sobieski*, bound for Genoa, carries the newly married couple, husband and wife both limping slightly after the glowingly handsome and usually efficient bride—suddenly uncertain about me after courting me from London to Brooklyn—drove into an intrusive hydrant right on our wedding night.

Also on board is a young Pole who, proud and excited as he ran across the gangplank, told anybody who could hear him, "I am returning to my country where we will now build socialism." Think of that!

The upper deck is lined with tough Italo-American types from the Village loaded down with cameras, radios, and other hard goods to be picked up for sale in war-wounded and deprived Italy by the Italian branch of Lucky Luciano's gang. They wear their heavy, dark city suits no matter how hot it gets on the upper deck, ignoring everyone else as they sit enjoying their own company and laughing heavily at their own jokes. Apparently they expect big, big returns.

As we entered the Mediterranean they arose as one and cried *"Bella Europa!"* I was so fascinated standing between Europe and Africa that I brought up a map from our stateroom to make sure of every landmark. This irritated Caroline mightily.

We are indebted to the wonderfully bright and engaging physicist Professor Mario Salvadori of Columbia University, exiled by the Fascist racial laws though only partly Jewish, for telling us what is going on among the Italians on board. He is our *cicerone*, our guide to the Italy I have never seen, and is so delightful and brilliant that he confirms for Caroline (to my wonder she was Italy-struck as a student and privately rich enough to visit Italy in Fascist times, before the war) her rapture about Italians and all things Italian.

How lucky I am! The only reason I am getting to see Italy just now is that I am married to Caroline. No other place on earth would do for a honeymoon year, helped out by my second Guggenheim. Her feeling for Italy is certainly intense. Italy and Italians sort of make a third presence in our marriage.

The story of Giuseppina Salvadori, whose parents under the pressure of Fascist race laws consented to be baptized while Giuseppina proudly refused, interests me far more than it does Caroline, from "Our Crowd," Seventieth and Madison. For Caroline being Jewish is a technicality that need never come up.

This makes for some difficulties with a Jew from darkest Brooklyn, who for all the pleasures that come with his new life is driving himself crazy trying to write a book new for him, a personal book about walking New York and summoning the city up for *him*. To say nothing of the anxiety that drives so many days and nights. "Always taking things hard," as Scott Fitzgerald lamented, "the stamp that goes into my books so people can read it blind like braille."

I laugh without mirth at the change in my circumstances, beguiled by the finger bowls, whenever I "dine" in the vast apartment at Seventieth and Madison. The parents are so careful to avoid a lapse in taste, anything that might be considered vulgar, that there are no pictures in their apartment—none at all—except those of the ancestors from the Rhineland who gaze down at us as we sit at table.

Mother is a collector of celebrities. At dinner I met the sumptuous Alma, who rolls into the room like a Valkyrie and who was successively married to Mahler, Werfel, Gropius and was much involved with Kokoschka. The mother is ripely sensuous, eager, related to Wertheims and Morgenthaus, thinks of herself as a leader in New York society. Drove Caroline through the wringer in her adolescence by being much occupied with a British lady literary agent in Manhattan. The father, a distinguished physician and pioneer in diabetes research, born in 1877, was either too old or too stiff to notice what was going on. His best friend was Judge Irving Lehman, brother of the governor and head of the New York State Court of Appeals. Caroline squirms in protest when the doctor tells the kind of joke that apparently rich Jews amuse each other with in "our crowd": "Messenger comes to the door, announces, 'I am the coon from Kuhn and Loeb.'"

Caroline came out of it all intact all right, but for all her physical presence—Mario Salvadori admiringly calls her "elemental"—hidden, tensely shy, and amazingly private—at least with me, her second husband. I gather the first was abruptly dismissed.

Only Italy brings her out—so in addition to these velvet nights and her luxurious body I am positively in love with her for having so much feeling for Italy's fabled landscape.

*Kennst du das Land?* Do you know the land where the lemon-trees blossom, where the golden oranges glow in the dark foliage, a soft wind blows from the blue sky, and the myrtle stands silent and the bay tree is tall? Do you know it perhaps? It is there that I would like to go with you, my beloved.

That's not Goethe any more, it's Caroline! O beloved Italia, Italianità, O Italy, how you complete our sensuous union.

Genoa: Getting through customs with all these trunks a joke to the officials, not one of whom wears pants that have any relation to his jacket, and all of whom are amused by our many encumbrances. Mario Salvadori helps at every point as we "do" Genoa. His grace and knowledge are irresistible to us both.

Terraces in sun, sunlight on the roofs of the city, birds everywhere flying in the water-flung air. Genoa a funicular city, the beauty of a tower that seems to float above the water. The symmetry of all these staircases. On the heights above the port, I think of Nietzsche once prowling the hills here, looking *down* for the perspective that allowed him to despise the bourgeois Christian world and to venerate the mountain seeker Zarathustra as his self-sufficient prophet. Actually, Nietzsche was here looking for *health!* Italy was his sanatorium!

The beauty surrounding me of these centuries here, while all the time one never knows from hour to hour what one's money is worth. Lire today 650–700 to the dollar. Sunday it was 950.

On the steeply terraced hills overlooking the harbor, the Communist Party has changed Piazza Ferrari to Piazza Matteotti. A socialist kid in working-class Brooklyn, I grew up with the image of Matteotti, murdered by Mussolini in 1924, as a Socialist Party martyr. And here the Communists have taken him over, as they have everything else on the Left. It seems that every single Communist in Italy was in the Resistance.

All our baggage crammed on top of it under a billowing canvas whose struggle with the wind we can hear below, the madly pacing bus (too many railway tracks destroyed by war bombing) careens up and down mountains at a hairsbreadth distance from the edge. Overwhelming impression of incomparable beauty and ruins at once—the strictly cut terraces, the hills topped by cypresses standing up there, hill on hill, like the flags of a besieged country. So many private houses eviscerated by bombs. Senseless.

Lucca: dusty ugly baroque church, a town that put a cold finger of fear down my spine. And now Florence. I seem to remember that

D. H. Lawrence went straight from train to hotel here, and when asked why, having just arrived, he was so intensely writing, explained he was writing his "impressions of Florence."

I have to look around first, and oh my Lord, *am* I looking! I have never seen anything like the Lungarno, the Ponte Vecchio, the hills taking us in from the other side of the river. Caroline, because she had been there before, led us confidently to the Berchielli and asked the manager if he had room for us. He laughed: "What will you have? The place is empty!"

The nightman at the hotel desk is a wizened, fatherly hunchback, with a face that belongs with the insignia ("*sono concierge*") of little keys fastened to the lapel of his official frock coat. In the hot and windless night, while tribes of green insects buzz around the flickering street lamps along the Arno, he bustles behind the bar, amused at our thirst, gently lifting stoppers from decanters and bringing up green and purple bottles from some mysterious bin right under his feet. An old magician doing his act for spellbound children, he first pours out a little of this and then a little of that, pretending to look amazed at their instant transfusion. Then, as he swiftly squeezes soda over the highly colored surface, he cries "*Eccolà!*"—but with a patient solicitousness that says plainly that while nothing will relieve our thirst if we insist on it so impatiently, he will go on inquiring into bottle after bottle, if we wish.

Beggar after beggar. With seven lire to a penny, it is easy to be bountiful, vaguely disgusting as it is to play the rich foreigner handing out money that is contemptible to you—and this to people with whom you have not the slightest human contact. Yet how beautiful and dignified so many of the faces are. The man lying at the entrance to the makeshift iron bridge that has replaced the Trinità, just lying there, has given up—a face out of a devotional painting in the Middle Ages.

How English and Victorian the lounge, an old family parlor, with the rubber plant on a doily over the upright piano, heavy brass-framed pictures of hunting dogs and "The Stag at Eve," plus old copies of the *Illustrated London News*. A withered English blond sits in one corner, reading the *Times*, and from time to time calls across the lounge in a piercing accent, recounting to another *inglese* her difficulties with the Italian law, "so fearfully complicated." She has come back to reclaim a house bought before the war. In another corner a man with the burned-out face of Oswald Spengler: head completely shaved, a fierce, wide scar running across his left cheek and deep into his neck like a singed envelope. Junker face, haughty with suffering: He never looks at anyone, prowls around the lounge smoking cigarettes through a long jeweled holder.

All signs are first in English, then in French, occasionally under-written in Italian. The atmosphere is that of a provincial British hotel in an eternity of Sundays, though *they* "no longer come to us as they used to. The English, too, are passing through difficult days." Americans, we are smiled on, are wonderful—so gay, so young, etc. But the manager's daughter, whose English was learned in wartime from the BBC, pouts that her friends laugh at her—"My accent has become a little coarse"—since the GIs were here.

The gallery that led from the Uffizi Gallery to the Pitti is broken in the middle. On both sides of the Ponte Vecchio a jagged heap of ruins, lit up by a solitary streeet lamp, has that crumpled look of scenery the minute the footlights are turned off and the play is over. In the daytime the ruins of war-blasted Florence are as incongruous as a tabloid headline in an illuminated manuscript, against the round towers and the slender cypresses, each cluster of them supreme on its hill. The Germans were on the other side of the river, the Americans on this. Florence was fought over right on this street.

At the noon hour an old man in an old boat, moored in the middle of the Arno just below our window, patiently dredging up mud from the bottom, hour by hour, which like a beaver he as patiently packs up on every side of him. Across the way a little boy swimming off a little delta that has formed in front of his house. A scull shoots by, propelled by a young man in tights and blazer and wearing that smart little beard—shades of Dino Grandi, Italo Balbo! Why did I think it was worn only by Fascist aviators and ambassadors? Just below the embankment, on the other side of the river, the familiar whitewash slogan we saw on every wall coming down from Genoa: VOTATE PER IL P. COMUNISTA CHE VI DARA PACE LAVORO LIBERTA.

The artist Ramy Alexander, born Alexander Goldstein in Odessa, fled to Italy from Stalin, to America from Hitler, wound up in Denver with a case of TB. This landed him in one of those Jewish sanatoria in Denver that were first built for garment workers much afflicted with TB, "the Jewish disease" in the sweatshop days. No garment worker Ramy! But Jews being Jews, it is as Robert Frost said: "Home is the place where, when you have to go there, They have to take you in."

It was in Denver that I came across him when I was covering the local wartime scene for *Fortune,* and I was charmed by the drawings he did in bed, his reciting Pushkin in Russian and Dante in Italian to me with such rapture. A slight, lightly skeptical figure, a bit weary after everything he has been through, he is now a consultant to UNESCO on the reconstruction of museums and artwork damaged by the war, and says that living in Florence he has come "home." Sitting on the Piazzale Michelangelo overlooking Florence, he was so moved by the scene that he wrote a poem in Russian commemorating the afternoon. I love to walk with him in the countryside outside Florence, and to hear him in his soft Russian-accented Italian telling a young Italian girl who is reading *War and Peace* for the first time all about fabulous Lev Nikolayevich. I am moved by the sight of Tolstoy, open in Italian on the sun-drenched table. The intermingling of Russian and Italian seems right for Florence, as the money speculators on the Tornabuoni are not. In his homage to

Italian art and culture, his positive *gratitude* after a battered life for everything he has found to love here, the freshness of Ramy's love for Italy is quite a change from the flashy Americans I meet near the American Express. One of them goes around with great wads of lire stuffed into the kind of leather zipper bags that are sold at home for packing a bottle of whiskey in a suitcase. He describes postwar developments with a show of inside knowledge that does not hide his awe at my ignorance. After years of being a nobody at home, and no doubt a "Wop" to the Gentiles, he is now making the most of his Italian American background, and with the best will in the world does not seem to like the Italians very much. Says they simply have no character, and outlines the black market situation to me, specifying how the government does not govern, that the whole economy rests on private buying and selling. The political situation is absolutely hopeless, divided between the priests and the Commies.

Funny to see him standing under the statue of Lorenzo the Magnificent, the latest *New Yorker* in one hand and that moneybag in the other, looking like an Oklahoma Indian who has just discovered oil.

In the great Duomo, Santa Maria del Fiore, above the altar in the choir, Christ hangs on his cross, but wearing a golden crown that is much too large for his head. Whoever this Jew was in ancient Palestine, knowing only Jews, drawing his disciples and his first adoring, grateful public from other Jews, in this magnificent place, as usual in Catholicism, the Son has replaced the Father he was so obsessed with in life—"*My* Father, *Our* Father" always on his lips, the only figure he ever answers to. In death Jesus has become the only reason for believing in the religion that Saul of Tarsus, "of the tribe of Benjamin," founded.

But if it is preached that Christ rose from the dead, how is it
that some among you say there is no resurrection of the
dead? If there is no resurrection of the dead, then neither was

Christ raised. But if Christ was not raised, then our preaching is empty, and your belief is empty, and we are found out as false witnesses to God, because we testified against God that he raised up Christ, whom he did not raise up.

If, that is, the dead do not rise. For if the dead do not rise, then neither has Christ risen. And if Christ has not risen your faith is vain, you are still in your sins. And then also those who went to their rest in Christ are lost.

If by this life in Christ we are no more than hopeful, then we are the most pitiful of all people.

Here dangling on the cross, his knees are upraised, as if he is still struggling with death, and death had struck him where he fought. His whole body slopes downward with a weariness in which I feel the weight of the ages. Yet here he is Christ the King, and so named not by his enemies in mockery, "King of the Jews," but King of Kings to the church that in his name, by his example alone and his rising from the dead, rules millions of the faithful.

At the foot of the altar, a young monk sweeping the red cloth and smoothing out the wrinkles in it. How strange it is to look down the whole length of Christ's bent figure, twisted into the deepest suffering and hopelessness, so forlorn above the altar—how strange to realize that the sculptor perhaps overdid it. Here Christ looks not a king but a scarecrow. The crown, which slopes over his head, too large for it, expresses not so much amazement and homage before him who undertook so much as the condescension of authority to its own figurehead.

The faces of young monks, like the faces of young girls in the climax of adolescence—both meeting in the same corridor, but the one going back as the other goes forward.

\* \* \*

Ramy Alexander drove us out to Settignano to see the Bernard Berenson villa, I Tatti. In the courtyard, which might have been the entrance to one of the retreats at which the storytellers in the *Decameron* flourished during the plague, there was a row of neat little lemon trees, each set in its black bucket with finicky care. The lemons all drooped in a plane, exactly an equal distance from the ground—with what immense and induced art it was not difficult to imagine. The elaborated niceness of the symmetry introduced me to Berenson's mind before I met him.

The butler seemed uncertain whether to admit us, Berenson being away, but Leo Stein, Gertrude's brother, whom Ramy knows slightly, came out of the library and offered to show us around. Stein is a tall, gentle, gangling old man, now seventy-five, who looks like a Jewish Uncle Sam—very rustic, nervous, deaf, but full of talk and little wisecracks, all of them delivered in such a flat, uncompromised American twang after his thirty or forty years of Europe, that it was strange in Berenson's magnificent gardens to take in Stein's mussed blue serge suit and hearing aid, a little knapsack slung over one shoulder. The Steins were originally from Allegheny, Pennsylvania, and this Stein sounded as if he never left it.

I Tatti dates from the sixteenth century, is very beautiful, and so quietly massed with Berenson's treasures that I found it almost too exquisite to walk in. It is like a private chapel raised to the connoisseur's ideal experience, where every corner and corridor has been worked to make a new altarpiece. The smallest detail shows off the mind of a man who has the means to reject all intrusions of mere necessity. He has shaped the whole with an inflexible exactness of taste that is just a little chilling. Of course its greatest effect on me is not so much to lead me to its pictures as to shame me into a fresh realization of how awkward, soiled, and generally no-account any life can seem compared with a work of art. In the dim light of the shaded corridors Sienese saints gaze past you, lost in their irrecoverable time and interred in an oil gloss—their faces tortured with thought and goodness, and somehow looking *away*, bearing your praise and awe with equal indifference. What golden and mysterious fish!

I noticed how jumpy Stein became when we stopped too long before some pictures. Of course, showing his friend Berenson's house must have been a bore; he had been in and out of the place for years, and comes almost daily now to work in the library. Yet I was surprised, knowing of his lifelong concern with painting, to hear him confess that it was not the work of art that mattered to him so much as the mind of the painter.

He is very much preoccupied with all sorts of psychological questions and told us that he had just finished psychoanalyzing himself. The devouring interest of his life was to discover "why men lie." This evidently touches him most deeply. While he had been showing us pictures and rooms with a certain irritation, and made affectionate, mocking little digs at Berenson's well-known aversion to Picasso and other twentieth-century gods the Steins feel *they* discovered, he suddenly, in Berenson's study, went off into a long discourse on psychology and the need for scientific exactness in determining character.

He now spoke with a kind of uneasy intensity, as if he had been held in on this topic for a very long time, and wanted us to understand him—whether or not we "approved." It was of the greatest importance to him, this practice of lying. It could be a key to all sorts of crucial questions, if only he could get his hands on the solution; it was all, you might say, at the center of our ambiguity. As he went on he would look up at us every so often, pull irritably at his hearing aid, and grumble: "What? What? You think what? I can't hear you!" Thus riding impatiently over us and his deafness for standing in his way, and rearing up against our passing comments with a loud cry, very moving in an old man, which seemed to come straight from the heart: "It's important! It's the big thing! No one looks these facts in the face! Animals can't lie and human beings lie all the time!"

He was, however, very happy these days; had got over a bad illness and was just publishing a new book in the States—*Appreciations: Painting, Poetry and Prose*. There was a lot of work ahead of him! He talked about his writing with a mingled anxiety and enthusiasm, as if he were just starting out on his career. Though very frail, he presented himself as a young man speculating dreamily on all the books he is going to write.

I should have caught on sooner but didn't until we went into Fiesole to have a drink: He had always suffered from a bad case of being Gertrude Stein's half-noticed elder brother, and now that she was dead probably felt liberated to go on with his own career. The fat and the lean! Gertrude was very fat and Leo was lean. His resentment of her shone through everything he said, so it was not for me to observe how much they were both addicted to analytic psychology.

Talking about their childhood in Europe, when they had been trundled around by a father "who didn't think we could get any kind of decent education in America," he seemed to remember most how Gertrude had always lorded it over him. "But you know," he said simply, "she was the kind who always took herself for granted. I never could." And one saw that she had dominated the situation when they had decided to make their lives in Europe. And were together for nine years before Gertrude took up with Alice B. Toklas. "She always took what she wanted! She could talk her way into anything, make herself believe anything! Why"—discussing her pioneer collection of modern paintings they had bought together—"she never even *liked* Picasso at first! Couldn't see him at all! *I* had to convince her! And then she caught on and got 'em for practically nothing."

After all those years the bitterness rankled, keeping him sprightly. How often, I wonder, has he been approached only as a lead to his famous sister, and this by people who haven't the slightest knowledge of his interests—and how much he shares them with her? It must be this, added to his long uncertainty about himself, which lends that strangely overemphatic tone to his interest in "facts." Gertrude started that way, studying psychology at Harvard with William James, medicine at Johns Hopkins, listening to the servants in their bourgeois milieu for the characters she found in the tone of their voices for *Three Lives*. But with Leo facts became the masculine domain of elder brothers anxiously toiling away at "real" things like aesthetics and psychology, things that would *reward* what he called the "journey into the self." Where Gertrude, the mother of them all, took the geniuses under her wing—Hemingway, Picasso, even Whitehead!—thought she had them all tucked away as illustrations of her theories about this and that. Her biggest theory was that she was a genius. So she even put the English language in her lap like a doll, making it bubble and babble on and on, though only she could last the course.

"She always did as she pleased." Interesting to see him now, at his age, going back and back to the old childhood struggle. They had transferred the cultural rivalry in their prosperous Jewish family to Europe, and though millions of other Jews had died because they found themselves in Europe, Gertrude had friends in Vichy who protected her. And so she and Toklas were saved. Leo seems to have managed somehow. For the Steins Europe was still the expatriate life, making of Paris and Florence new outposts for their old ambition.

Leo Stein has suddenly died, just a few weeks after our meeting. Ramy Alexander says it was all the strangest thing. His body was deposited before the altar in the local church. "Looked as if the townspeople didn't know where else to put him."

Rome: I had missed Berenson in Settignano, but went to see him today at the Hotel Hassler just off Trinità dei Monti. It was very cold, and he sat in a corner of the sofa with a rug over his knees, precise as one of his own sentences. Eighty-two: delicate little *élégant* with a natty white beard, very frail, an old courtier in a perfectly fitted double-breasted suit, every inch of him engraved fine into an instrument for aesthetic responsiveness and intelligence.

He spoke English with such severe and careful diction, delivering himself formally of his words, one by one, that he might have been putting freshly cracked walnuts into my hand. What a superior act he puts on. But what a fascinator. I have never before Berenson come up against anyone with such presence. He studied me, then took me in quickly, quietly, absolutely. "Your name is of course Russian and no doubt you are a Jew? There seem to be so many young Jews writing in the States these days. How is that? Quite a difference from my time!" "Oh! and is there much anti-Semitism in the States these days?" Oh!

His manner could not have been more impersonal, but he was extremely attentive to what information I could give him about "young Jews writing in the States these days." It was all, one was left to gather, a distant but not uninteresting fact to him, himself born a Jew, "born in Lithuania, in the Jewish aristocracy, the old gentry," and taken at ten to Boston.

Berenson has become world famous since the war, and has been constantly presenting himself anew to so many visitors, from the king of Sweden to GIs and my new friends in Italy, that I have been reading up on his extraordinary life and have learned much about him and his background. At Harvard he became an Episcopalian, in Italy a Catholic. Leopold Bloom also converted twice to Christianity, but never had it so good.

Berenson was born Valvrojenski in the shtetl of Butremanz. In Lithuania his father was a failure in the lumber business; in Boston a peddler from door to door. I can hardly believe that Berenson called himself a "Jewish aristocrat" as an impecunious student at Harvard, who owed his presence there to wealthy Bostonians impressed by his gift for languages—Polish, Russian, Hebrew, Arabic. Still, his remarkable gift for reinventing himself has probably always been his *carte de visite* to the world outside Butremanz and the slums of North Boston—from President Eliot's Harvard to the rich collectors who made his fortune. This is still a way of gently dissociating himself from any possible entanglements he has incurred by asking me about Amerian Jewish life today. Being a Jewish aristocrat does not diminish one's foreignness but transfers it to another plane—like the American Negro who went South with a turban on his head and was welcomed everywhere as a foreign potentate.

Whatever Berenson's fame as a connoisseur and art historian, his greatest work is this creation of himself. Exactly half a century younger, another Litvak, I am so impressed—yes, fascinated—that in the flesh he seems to me as great a character as Gilbert Osmond in James's *The Portrait of a Lady*. On the basis of his taste, especially in marrying wealth, this American considered himself "the first gentleman of Europe."

"BB" reads everything. There was even a copy of that shabby little *Rome Daily American* on his lap when I came in. It is curious how much more interesting he makes anything so typically journalistic and American look in his presence, so unbroken is the effect of elegance he gives to any room he sits in. Every day he goes through at least one Italian, French, Swiss, and English newspaper; takes all the reviews and magazines, even *Time*. All out of an intense curiosity in the political behavior of the human animal. Remembering his extraordinary library, supposedly the greatest private library in Europe, which Harvard will acquire after his departure, I had a picture of him at I Tatti as another Voltaire at Ferney, a kind of European intelligence office. Yet subtly remote from the pressure of events, each of which he puts away in some chamber of his apparatus for meditation.

Though he was himself another Jewish fugitive when the Germans occupied Italy, he had nothing to say about the almost eight thousand Italian Jews murdered, nothing about his old friend the anti-Fascist historian Gaetano Salvemini, who has just returned to Italy after years teaching at Harvard. Instead Berenson kept coming back to Henry Miller, whose works he knows fully, and detests. He vaguely shared my admiration for that moving long story in *Sunday After the War* that recounts Miller's return to his parental home, but turned Miller into a dreary historian of the imponderable petit-bourgeois bleakness of Brooklyn rather than the "cloacal" and confused rebel he had just dismissed. He said "cloacal" in a way that made me see all the refuse coming up from the bottom of the Tiber and gathering itself into the collected works of Henry Miller. And of course I shared in the current illusion that Kafka was a great writer? "There is a very small light of reason burning in the world," he said. "Mr. Kafka tries to put it out."

He has exact, firm judgments on everything that crosses his path; his years, his fortune, his delicious snobbery, and his famous taste have given him a freedom in getting past current intellectual fashions that is highly stimulating if not very satisfying. I miss that quality that alone makes a thinker interesting—his commitment to the living. We were talking about the cultural inertia and provincialism that become felt after one settles even a little into Italy. Berenson thought the decline had set in with the Risorgimento—which is curious not because there is any lack of skepticism today in Italy about the vaunted traditions of the Risorgimento but because of the example that immediately came to Berenson's mind. One was left to infer that the cultural elite had surrendered its prerogatives. Why, in his first years in Italy one could still pick up from Roman pushcarts first editions of English eighteenth-century novels that had come straight from the old nobility! He finds Italians now lacking in individuality.

Curious to see how he touches on all these things quite outside the realm of historical development; he goes straight to fundamental themes of *style*. The long romance with Italy is probably over. Italy the aesthetic concept, Italy as he first knew it in truly another century and as he has retained it at I Tatti, has had to bear the burden of a certain jarring and even violation under the storm of recent events. Not Fascism but the war! Although he managed nearly to suggest without saying flat out that President Roosevelt was going to send some portion of our otherwise engaged army to guard this naturalized citizen who had not visited the United States for decades, the war certainly threatened Berenson's safety in the worst way. I Tatti did not escape bombing, nor did his own luxurious hideout in the countryside. To my astonishment he drew his American passport from an inner pocket and proudly showed it to me. There have been unexpected infringements on so exquisite an existence. How hard it is to possess fully everything we buy in this world.

We talked about his old friend Santayana, who is living not far away as a paying guest of the Irish Nuns of the Blue Sisters—they no longer see each other. Curious to think of these two old intellectual grandees finishing out their lives in Italy, the one a Spaniard and the other born a Lithuanian Jew, but both formed by their early life in Boston, at Harvard, and in Europe thereafter—Santayana always slightly ahead, as he was born two years before Berenson.

Berenson greatly admires Santayana, and it was only in discussing him that he seemed younger and less *distingué* than anybody you ever heard of. But they are estranged, and to judge from the oily and underhand tone Santayana takes to him in his remarkable *Persons and Places*, the relationship ended on his side, certainly not Berenson's! Santayana has been a great student of aesthetics, but philosophy alone is his life's treasure, thinking for oneself, not the *derivative* life of a critic or connoisseur, especially not one so busy piling up treasures in this world. And then, of course, Berenson is a Jew whom Santayana has known since the 1880s as a madly ambitious, pushing Jew. Philosophy professor Irwin Edman of Columbia, who idolizes Santayana, was astonished to find his comments on Santayana in the latter's volume of *Living Philosophers* dismissed for "racial" considerations. Santayana is famous for remaining the disinterested outsider, always above the battle except when he is supporting Franco and making sly excuses for the Inquisition.

In any event Santayana is a wonderful writer, Berenson a noticeably stiff and self-conscious one. So it is fatally easy for Santayana to dismiss Jews who do not know their place. Despite the magnificent presence, the soigné air, the echoes of Matthew Arnold and Walter Pater, the fortune built up by Berenson as a consultant to that *goniff* Joe Duveen, now Lord Duveen ("the pictures are all in Europe and the money all in America. I must bring them together"), the villa and the "Jewish aristocracy" of Lithuania, one is compelled by

Santayana, after sixty years, to recall Berenson as a young immigrant given his start by Mrs. Jack Gardner.

But how Berenson looks up to Santayana, and how he rejects the faintest criticism of a philosophic system that because of the literary grace Santayana brings to it fascinates many readers never quite sure what he is getting at! Berenson himself hadn't read the Santayana memoirs; his companion Nicky Mariano told him not to, he would be too distressed. And very pleasantly and understandably, he couldn't share my respect for Alfred North Whitehead—a thinker with a background in science and a passion for intellectual history. Yet I was not to offer the slightest possible irreverence on Santayana—my faint complaint being his addiction to pseudo-classic wisdom. In some way Santayana's life as a reclusive scholar has always been the life Berenson meant to live—or so, amid all the finery, he likes to think. A famously troubled conscience.

I asked Elizabeth Hardwick why Berenson interested her so much. "He's so unhappy."

Imagine trying to live as a work of art!

Café scene in the Piazza della Repubblica, which everyone absentmindedly still calls the Piazza Vittorio Emmanuele. In the moonlight hundreds of people sitting at those long lines of tables, row on row, between the hedges or rubber plants that mark off one café from another; an audience about to perform for itself.

Wonderful to watch the long appraising stares, like an expert judging horseflesh, with which these open-air troglodytes look each newcomer up and down. No one misses a thing. They may look bored and weary to death, with scales over their half-closed eyes, sipping indifferently at their minuscule cup of *espresso* as if there were all the time in the world and they had been sitting here, with that same cup of coffee, spoon, and carafe of water, since the Etruscans. But in the air the preparatory vapors of a seduction; these are buds that open only at night.

As soon as we walk into this lighted den, making the grand tour up and around the long lines of tables, faint waves radiate from brains chattering with malicious speculation. Ah, some more *Americani.* The waiter in his soiled and patched evening clothes grins and bows; the three whores glumly sitting together look at resplendent Caroline with unforgiving eyes like one of those electric signal boxes in a prison corridor that madly shriek in alarm if there is any metal on your person. The cigarette vendors come screeching around like a flock of gulls maddened by the smell of food off the ship's bow—old, young, sick, every age and human condition, each holding out a little suitcase like a tray. *Sigarette? . . . Nazionali? . . . Americani!*

Every five minutes a beggar appears at our table—usually old women wearing a black shawl and the look of the eternal mother of sorrows, leading little barefoot girls whose faces are so gray and bent with suffering, whose arms hang so miserably at their sides as if they had been scratching old sores, that you find yourself either responding to the situation or rewarding the impersonation.

Under the table more barefoot kids in discarded GI pants and American air force jackets, hunting cigarette ends and storing them carefully in little tin pails; it will all go to make "new" American cigarettes. In the history of Europe this age should go down as the Pax Americana—meaning the secondhand butt.

The beggars cover the café in waves; they make sure never to come up together or at too close intervals. While one makes his rounds the others stand at the hedge, like actors waiting to go on. Notice how the Italians give, every time. They may look indifferent and after the tenth approach exasperated beyond words, but after shrugging their shoulders or trying a frontal attack (*Signora!*

*Misericordia! Non sono la Banca d'Italia!*) they grumpily come up with a hundred-lire note, peanuts. The crucial test comes when someone at a table tries to look away. Useless. The beggar simply keeps turning with him and staring him down.

In the brilliantly humming summer night all these café dwellers, each moored in his cultural swamp, gently pushing at the world outwide like a fly trapped in a dish of honey. The faces lack the paunchy, pasty look of so many Americans; here you can actually see the bony structure brought into the world at birth. The general good looks are amazing: face after face with that focused sensuality that is the personal ticket of young actors and actresses. Most of them emptily looking at each other or engaged in a little deal.

The air is damp with sex, but you can hear sums being recited at table after table; the whole piazza is one great bourse for the black market. *Centotrenta lire . . . centosessanta . . . tremila quaranta.* A fierce-looking boy in his late teens rides up on a bicycle and unerringly goes straight to the Americans. "Will you buy American cigarettes—real American cigarettes, I swear, not counterfeit? Wanna change some money, mista? Hey, mista?" Will you for God's sakes *sell* him something? You think he hasn't got the money? Takes out a great wad of sweaty lire. "Listen!" he says in disgust, about to ride off, "I'll buy anything you got! *Anything?*"

Funny in that place to hear the long wailing singsong of the cigarette vendors, which as the evening drags on becomes simply "America!"

Salzburg, Schloss Leopoldskron, the Seminar in American Civilization for Teachers, Writers, and Intellectuals from Austria, Germany, Italy, France, England, Czechoslovakia, Scandinavia. Poles and Russians opted out at the last minute, charging that the absence of Upton Sinclair and other "socialist authors" from our reading list made their attendance impossible. They should only know how much F. O. Matthiessen and I are doing on Henry James, that "rediscovered" American. No socialist author he!

Vassily Leontief, the great Harvard economist, delivered the opening lecture on the American economy. A German proud of the English he had improved in a Texas POW camp turned to me and, laughing at Leontief's Russian accent, demanded, "Is that supposed to be an American accent?" "The very latest," I explained.

Vassily tells me that an aunt of his, arrested during Stalin's purges, was sent to a labor camp so distant from all metropolitan centers that she didn't know of the Second World War until she was released.

Salzburg is packed to suffocation. It is an American military center, army jeeps and trucks jam every twisted medieval street, and tourists from everywhere are screaming to get into the Salzburg Festival, the great cathedral, the Mozarteum, the Festspielhaus for the opera. I am told there are as many as two hundred thousand DPs in the area; hundreds are in barracks on the roads leading up to Leopoldskron, which housed Nazi prisoners, and in a sense they are still prisoners of the Nazis.

Overwhelmed by the crowds in town, on the roads, on the terraces, and in the gardens of Schloss Leopoldskron, I feel, as always when I am in Europe (more in Austria than elsewhere), that I am concentrating on some dramatic performance that America is too diffuse to provide. There is nothing at home like the staging before the cathedral of Hofmannsthal's *Jedermann*, when Everyman's earthly pilgrimage ends just at dusk, with all the appropriate shadows enveloping the audience. A marvelous spectacle, which Max Reinhardt thought up, and which is still presented as Reinhardt conceived it, though Reinhardt himself ("his real name was Goldman," as one Austrian here did not fail to remind us) departed for Beverly Hills before the Anschluss.

Much of the drama at the seminar is also provided by F. O. Matthiessen, who fascinates the European students, holds them in

his grip, through an astonishing personal intensity, a positively violent caringness about everything he believes in and is concerned
with that he cannot suppress in public. What drives the man and
torments him so?

It was nice of Matty to invite me and not another Harvard to
share the lectures here in American literature. And as someone who
has had to think of Harvard as the unattainable, it amuses me to
have Matty playing the rakish outsider, making little digs at his old
student and present colleague Harry Levin as we ride from town
back to the Schloss, perched on a load of potatoes, in a beaten-up
old hay wagon, for the seminar. Matty: "Can you imagine Harry
Levin doing this?" He recalls Levin as an undergraduate, already so
unbearably learned that as Levin's teacher "I would quail every time
he raised his hand in class, usually to correct me about something or
other."

I was not prepared for so much fire in this slight, bald, mild-look-
ing Harvard professor, a bachelor in his middle forties who in
Boston lives on Beacon Hill and is a believing Christian. He is quite
wealthy—his grandfather invented the Big Ben alarm clock—was a
Greek major at Yale, Rhodes scholar at Oxford, and, switching to
American literature, wrote a book on Sarah Orne Jewett. He is such
an advanced liberal that although his tastes are clearly all for epi-
cures like Henry James and Christian thinkers like Eliot, he is planning a book on Dreiser.

This I suspect for political rather than literary reasons. I quoted
Mark Van Doren to Matty—"Dreiser lacked everything except
genius," but Matty seems to think of Dreiser as socially benevolent
like himself. Dreiser died a member of the Communist Party and
the Episcopal Church, not forgetting to leave money in his will for
"Negro orphans." That was certainly nice of "Theo." And yes,
Dreiser always thought of *himself* as a victim. That was nonsense. As
a novelist he was a master at portraying the force of power-sex-
necessity over others. His power was animal from the bottom up,
like himself.

On Dreiser, Matthiessen leads with his heart, not his natural taste—and his heart is clearly in many places at once. Better not to ask just where some of them are, he is normally so closed up. But to hear him open up, in the grand salon that is our lecture hall here, on the intricate beauty of *The Portrait of a Lady*, and this to an audience of spellbound Europeans hanging on every word, so much had his tension communicated itself to everyone in the room, was to be present at something remarkable. He certainly loves James's novelist mind and strategy. So much so that he began with a laughing apology for James's opening line, "Under certain circumstances there are few hours in life more agreeable than the hour dedicated to the ceremony known as afternoon tea." Very genteel stuff, one had to admit, but see how James went on to write the lasting moral drama embodied in Isabel Archer's rising above the campaign against her by her husband Gilbert Osmond and his old mistress Madame Merle.

Matthiessen devoted most of his lecture to a close analysis of the novel in James's own terms, recalling from the preface to *The Portrait of a Lady* James's wonderful saying: "The house of fiction has ... not one window, but a million." Expanding this image, James added that at each of these windows hanging over the human scene

> stands a figure with a pair of eyes. . . . He and his neighbors are watching the same show, but one seeing more where the other sees less, one seeing black where the other sees white, one seeing big where the other sees small, one seeing coarse where the other sees fine. And so on, and so on; there is fortunately no saying on what, for the particular pair of eyes, the window may *not* open; "fortunately" by reason, precisely, of this incalculability of range. The spreading field, the human scene, is the "choice of subject"; the pierced aperture, either broad or balconied or slit-like and low-browed, is the "literary form"; but they are, singly or together, as nothing without the posted presence of the watcher—without, in other words, the consciousness of the artist. Tell me what the artist

is, and I will tell you of what he has *been* conscious. Thereby I shall express to you at once his boundless freedom and his "moral" reference.

I knew from Matty's book on Eliot and especially his grand work *American Renaissance* how much he saw American writing in terms of the artist's "craft"—a tradition linking James, Eliot, Hawthorne, really connected by the highly selective tradition of rising out of *poetry* Eliot had founded, and which certainly did not apply to "loose" novels like *Moby-Dick, Huckleberry Finn, An American Tragedy.* But Matty's wholly sympathetic reading of *The Portrait of a Lady* had extraordinary resonance for his European audience, he looked and sounded so committed to Henry James's view of his own practice as a novelist! Unlike F. O. M., I dreamily pictured Italy itself in *The Portrait of a Lady*, his marvelous gift for conveying the look of a street that immediately takes in the people walking through it, James's description of writing the book in Venice, the Riva Schiavoni, and in the "fruitless fidget of composition" appealing to "the waterside life, the wondrous lagoon spread before me, the ceaseless human chatter of Venice at my windows" for help on his book.

Matthiessen on *The Portrait of a Lady* was the perfect critic of what James sought technically for his book. I, longing for the Venice I was still to see, delighted in James's saying that reading over certain pages of his book

have seemed to make me see again the bristling curve of the wide Riva, the large color-spots of the balconied houses and the repeated undulation of the little hunchbacked bridges, marked by the rise and drop again, with the wave, of fore-shortened clicking pedestrians. The Venetian footfall and the Venetian cry—all talk there, wherever uttered, having the pitch of a call across the water—come in once more at the window, renewing one's old impression of the delighted senses and the divided, frustrated mind. How can places that speak *in general* to the imagination not give it, at the moment, the particular thing it wants?

Listening to Matthiessen with a divided mind, all right, but definitely not frustrated, and proud as the dickens that he was having such an effect on these Europeans, I was in for a shock. A young Austrian from the Leopoldskron staff came up directly to Matthiessen as he was speaking and told him there was a telephone call for him. I hadn't fully taken in just how tightly Matthiessen was strung, especially when talking about his idol Henry James, until he turned in a rage on the luckless messenger for breaking the sacred connection. He upbraided the fellow before us all. There was a terrible silence in the room until Matthiessen awkwardly got himself together and concluded the lecture.

The next day it was my turn to perform. *The Education of Henry Adams*, long central to my sense of American history, was unfamiliar to most Europeans, and my admiration for Adams as an artist in history meant nothing to people who didn't know Ulysses S. Grant from Charlie Chaplin. I talked about Adams as the prophet of American power in the twentieth century, but while this theme had a certain relish for a group just now all too conscious of Americans lording it all over Europe, the all-too-subtle Henry Adams from his grand perch in Washington was not needed to document the ruthlessness of American capitalism.

One person in the group knew enough of Henry Adams to know that he loathed Jews, and wanted to know how I could admire such a writer. Of course Adams was incoherent in his hatred, raged about "J. P. Morgan and other Jews." In the opening of the *Education* he grandly compared himself, deriving as he did from the most distinguished family in New England, to a Jew born in Jerusalem under the shadow of the Temple and circumcised in the synagogue by his uncle the high priest: "Under the name of Israel Cohen, he would scarcely have been more distinctly branded, and not much more heavily handicapped in the races of the coming century, in running for such stakes as the century was to offer."

This proved nothing, of course, except that Henry Adams regarded himself as "no ordinary traveller." He was a great historical imagination, I think the greatest America has known, a wealthy undersized overdelicate epicure definitely not committed to "the races of the coming century, in running for such stakes as the century was to offer."

Why did he take on so about the Jews? Why not, when almost everyone else does! And did, from the writers of the Gospels to Voltaire to the creators, in *La France Juive*, of a racial-political anti-Semitism that would no longer tolerate Jews even as Christians— and from then on just wanted them dead? The world is so full of Jew baiters and Jew haters, not to forget Jews ashamed of being Jews and fashionably putting themselves down, that I would have little enough to read if I excluded them all. It is boring just to praise ourselves as the heart of a heartless world. What, for heaven's sake, was the appeal of Henry Adams to so many Jewish intellectuals who were always writing about his spell on them and preparing to write still another biography of him?

History. *We* are history and always in some strange way, by no means happily, at the crosspoint of history. We are forever reciting our history in the act of worship, and so do the Christians in trying to explain how the Son of God descended from this people, its kings, patriarchs, and prophets. Abominate them as you like, for whatever new rage you needed this eternal scapegoat, you could not write history, ancient or modern, without dragging in the Jews.

More than a thousand displaced Jews are housed nearby. They have their own guards to keep off unfriendly Austrians, who are many, and the merely inquisitive, who to these tortured people can also sound like enemies. I went up to a guard wearing a brassard marked with the Star of David, explained that I was a Jew from America and wanted to meet with the people inside. He rebuffed me sharply: "Sightseers we don't need." With Leontief's hotshot assistant Carl Kaysen, who is from Philadelphia and like me brought up on old-fashioned Workman's Circle belief in Jewish solidarity, I climbed a fence to get in. And climbed right into Eastern Europe.

O misery, O Jewish brothers and sisters. Benevolent Americanos, we gave out our chocolate bars and bobby pins and razor blades and listened to a woman—said she was "eight and twenty" but looked anywhere older than that—telling again the story of the Nazis entering a Polish village, rounding up what Jews they could catch and leading them off to a ravine to be shot. Hearing her, now others took up the tale. It was like a Passover seder, one after another reading from the Haggadah, but the tale was not of the escape from Egypt but of the many varieties of hell the Germans devised for anyone marked in face or body or by name Jew Jew Jew.

After several visits from me Hershkowitz, the camp policeman, had become a sort of friend. But it was his wife, who had been his brother's wife and whom he had married (as Jewish law prescribes) after his brother was killed, who drew me most. A woman perhaps in her middle forties, not at all "Jewish" looking, stiff and proud in a black dress—skin strangely stained and marked, mouth tightly drawn—strong-looking type. "*Nu?*" she said to me in Yiddish, waving her hand at the room. "How do you like the way we live?"

Twenty-four of them in a room the size of a single bedroom at the Schloss. A narrow camp of a room, lined with wooden slats—dirty, unkempt, food dumped in pails or sizzling on little burners. Yiddish newspapers everywhere in piles, sent in from New York. One old man sitting in the open, peacefully reading the *Forward* of a summer evening, just as my father used to do on his return from work. Sick people on mattresses. Ten children or so. With the woman in the black dress (a characteristic touch, little curled gold earrings she had somehow saved from the Nazis) was a bent oldish woman in a housedress—a woman who might have stepped out of my old neighborhood in Brownsville—so much so that looking at her, and the Jewish *Tog* on a makeshift table, I was home, suddenly pictured Mama and Papa as prisoners of the Nazis.

The black dress was bitter, humorous, proud. I loved her spunk.

Her stained face looked cracked with inexpressible, useless defiance. "Everybody has gone home now," she said. "Only the likes of us are left. Only we have no home to go back to. You American Jews, you American Jews, do something!" But for herself she wanted only to go to Palestine.

The tailoring shop, the shoe repair shop, the garage for the American troops in charge of the barracks. The crowd around the American sergeant, the little DP with snow-white hair saying in perfect British English, "Why do we not get white bread anymore?" And the sergeant saying with great clumsy ease and good feeling (this surprised me very much and made me grateful) that it was difficult to get white bread now; it had become so expensive—imagine, twelve cents a loaf in America!

There are about fourteen hundred in the camp, some five hundred children—half are orphans. In the children's playroom pictures of Eretz Israel, photographs of Herzl and Chaim Nachman Bialik. Sorrowful broken-down look of everything. Little Polish Jew with traditional covering and beard, selling tiny green pears at a schilling each, pears he had bought in town.

So I returned from the DP camp and took a shower and got into my fine suit and went off in a jeep to the Festspielhaus to hear Wilhelm Furtwängler doing Brahms and accompanying Yehudi Menuhin in the Beethoven concerto. Displaced persons in the afternoon; Hitler's favorite conductor, Furtwängler, and Menuhin in the evening. How I do get around! And Hitler's favorite conductor conducted very well indeed. Hard to tell whether the dreary minute sounds that occasionally came forth were beyond his control, but the Brahms First held me—I never thought it would again. Furtwängler's conducting had great spaciousness to it, the whole thing was majestically designed.

As for Menuhin! He still plays with the nobility that was so astonishing in him even as a kid doing the Bach Chaconne. Unforgettable.

Jews from the transient camp down the road were furious with him for playing with Furtwängler, who had conducted the Berlin Philharmonic all through the war. They stormed Menuhin's hotel, called him down from his room as he was undressing after the concert. He was still in his brilliant white evening vest as he came down and waited on the steps under the light from the hotel entrance. The Jews, hardly in evening dress, muttered at him in angry restlessness. They had collected in the street and the street was dark. Menuhin, directly in the light, was a vivid figure with his tousled blond hair. He spoke to the crowd sweetly, softly, helplessly. They would not be appeased. "Yehudi, what are you doing here?" cried out one DP.

The long white road lined at one point by the Jewish DP camp, at the turning by the old prison camp that held some Nazi bigshots right after the surrender. Austrians and migrants walking up and down in the August heat, the dust stirred up by the wheels of American military cars blowing into their faces. Europe full of wandering herds of people, endless lines of the homeless, the displaced, walking up and down. The winter was the coldest ever, they say; this is the worst summer in many years. Elderly woman bursting out at me, "I don't have enough to live on!" Carlo Levi described with relish Nazi and American Negro deserters holed up together in the North Italian woods. In addition to the Jews huddling miserably together in the stinking barracks, the Latvian "displaced" girl who somehow got into our seminar with nothing and no one to sponsor her, and the White Russians from Yugoslavia—all of them living crouched, in absolute human insecurity, where everything is provisional, and where, as a wag said, Austria today is like a WC—"frei" yet "besetzed." While in the heat, the dust, the faces of the past—Baroque fortresses, our "castle"—look blankly on.

Long talk with Adam Wandruska, late of the Afrika Corps; Ph.D. in history, Vienna; smoothly double faced like the others but finally more honest and interesting than his compatriots here. Admitted the hypocrisy of the Austrians—What? *We* were Nazis? We were occupied! A glimpse of the Nazi mind. Looking around hurriedly to see if anyone was listening, confessed with an air of pain and in great hesitation that even he could not prove the racial purity of his immediate family up to 1800. He had a Jewish great-grandmother! Manner usually buttery, confiding, intellectual; in repose, the coldness of a Nazi officer in full charge of the situation. Appealed to me for "understanding" on the basis of Nazi inefficiency—"We were not supermen!" And well I know it. So what?

Almost liked him at times, he has so many sides to him. Went into Salzburg with him to see the bad opera Gottfried von Einem has just made of Büchner's *Danton's Tod.* Remembering the passion Orson Welles brought to his Mercury Theater production of the play in the mid-thirties, I shuddered at the political frigidity that the Swiss-born Einem made of one of the greatest dramatic works written on the French Revolution. The play heaves and tosses with all the hope, despair, and fright that Danton and Robespierre brought to their dialogue. The music was empty, brassy; von Einem did not have an idea. A. W. disagreed with me sharply; at that moment Smittal, the blushful little depth-psychologist, said the French Revolution simply had no meaning. To these Nazi-educated intellectuals it is only a spectacle like a Hitler rally. Interesting to see that they have no conception of the active role the French masses played. They love the power of leaders; how they shift from their old ambitiousness in the *Hitler-Zeit* to their present passivity. In the French Revolution they see not a political idea, only the ins and outs.

The great Italian historian and anti-Fascist Gaetano Salvemini spoke tonight at the seminar, saying with his famous forthright simplicity things about the political situation that are absolutely true, and so no doubt useless, but which at least point the way back to politics as a moral science. Looks like a kindly Lenin—the same boxlike bald head. But with scathing sincerity in every breath, with every movement of his hands, this unbelievably pure old-fashioned man denounced the evasions and cynical ironies of the Right, the false system-making that the Left has smuggled into post-Fascist thinking. Principles are principles, and Salvemini is the very soul of political principle. Talked with the vehemence of an immigrant just off the boat, as in a sense he is, back in Europe after decades of exile as De Bosis professor of Italian civilization at Harvard. And do you know that no one else here has been so full of grace?

Turns out that he stopped here before returning to Italy. "What? Not to see *The Marriage of Figaro* first?"

Conscious today more than ever how much I remain the loner moping over the book I am writing on New York, how little I have used my time here to meet all sorts of strange new people, how unwilling I have been to throw myself joyfully and carelessly into "Europe." Caroline is with people all day long, especially the irresistible Vittorio Gabrieli, a "Milton specialist" from a famous academic family in Rome and sterling anti-Fascist who spent time in Regina Coeli prison. Wonderful man, though I am jealous of the special atmosphere that seems to ensue whenever Caroline meets the latest interesting Italian. The morning wasted in resentment and in getting over it, sort of. How strange I am to myself. How strange I am, increasingly, to Caroline, who has suddenly terrified me by admitting she is never easy with me. I guess to her I am a nerd, a bookish noodle, not genially at the heart of things, like her admirer Professor Salvadori, physicist *and* engineer, who is always brimming with good cheer. The wife and I seem to meet only in bed. It is as Shaw predicted: "Young man, be sure of what you want, because by God you will certainly get it."

\* \* \*

Rome: Arrived on a sunny Sunday morning after leaving Salzburg late last night, shivering in the rain flooding the bombed-out station still without a roof two years after the war. Now it is as if we had crossed the border into another world—so different in weather, in the faces of the people, in the odor of the streets, in the flowers, the wine, the food, that I find myself breathing deeper, rejoicing in every footstep.

How I love Italy, and more particularly Rome. I find myself at this moment almost too full of satisfaction. Almost the first words I heard last night as we crossed the border were those of the sleeping-car conductor, replying to a young mother who had brought a whole brood of kids in with her—without a ticket among them—and was sending out a passionate aria in her own defense. "Signora," he said with evident pleasure in his wit, "as a man I understand perfectly. As an official, no!"

Lunch with Paolo Milano in the garden of the Pensione Villa Borghese, where we are staying at the moment. Paolo is the most dogged bibliomaniac I know, and as a friend said about him, "doesn't believe anything unless he has read it." Do you know anyone else who, as an exile in Paris, would name his son Andrew after Prince Andrew in *War and Peace*, is convinced that Giordano Bruno in England met Shakespeare because Bruno is supposed to have met Sir Philip Sidney?

Books are Paolo's life. He is the mildest and most amiable of men, and though he likes ex officio to play the the skirt chaser in public, his life is books, books, books. He moves from writing a book on Lessing, a study of Henry James pointedly called (by contrast with himself) *L'Esilio Volontario*, to the *Viking Portable Dante*. With his perfect German, French, Spanish, English, his assimilation of everything in Russian literature except the language, and his proud announcement that he is planning to learn Russian and Chinese before too long, he is the perfect literary critic for *Espresso*, with that audience practically an *uomo universale* and, back in his native Rome, no longer a proscribed Jew, is happier than I have ever seen him in New York.

He gives me a copy of Antonio Gramsci's *Letters from Prison* and is excited, patriotically excited, that the letters of a leader of the Italian Communist Party have been awarded the Premio Viareggio, with the blessing of Benedetto Croce and other Italian luminaries. These hardly share the politics of Gramsci, the imprisoned Communist leader and strategist who died in 1937, in his middle forties, after six years in a Fascist prison. But they have been understandably moved and impressed by the poignant simplicity of these letters to his family and the stalwart convictions of his extraordinarily fine mind.

The prize jury said that in Gramsci they found "a lucid affirmer and witness of the human condition." I can see why Mussolini said of Gramsci: "This brain must be stopped from working." What I was not prepared for is the last humanist in such an important Communist position, such passionate literary culture and humane understanding of his many opponents. How peculiarly right that this fervently honest and believing man should lie in the Protestant cemetery with Keats, and Shelley's heart.

An amazing document. In prison he was all mind, this Sardinian hunchback who was incarcerated in more than one sense by his removal from his family, from the official Communist leadership with whose Stalinist dogmatism he had subtle disagreements. In the years since his published letters and works have been posthumously published, he has become a hero to independent thinkers on the Left, though there is no evidence that he ever entertained a break with the Party. The human situation revealed in this Communist family is intensely moving, and I can see why Paolo and so many other Italians totally uninterested in Marxism and in their hearts dreading an Italian Communism feel that *Letters from Prison* has made it possible to feel a certain love for Gramsci. Alone and in bad health, almost crushed at times by the stifling prison routine, he comes off here as a man of extraordinary personal courage and devotion to his family, and as an intellectual of superb literary culture who depended on Canto X of the *Inferno* to keep himself from going under.

Led by Virgil, Dante amid the "Epicurean heretics" is addressed by the ferocious Farinata the great Ghibelline chief, from an open sepulcher. Dante belonged to the opposite party in Florence, and so invites Farinata's scorn. But what a man! "And he rose upright with chest and brow thrown back, as if he had great scorn of Hell." Gramsci took heart from such fantastic defiance—in hell! But he was equally moved in Canto X by the drama of Cavalcante di Cavalcanti, who, raising himself on his knees, piteously asks, "Where is my son and why is he not with thee?" and falls back again, "show[ing] himself no more," when he realizes that his son is dead.

O Italy, O history, everything beautiful and murderous. I have seen a film of Fascists, sentenced to death by virtuous Communist "people's courts," being drowned in the Po, one by one. The lord high executioner sits in a boat pushing down hard on the head of the man thrown overboard.

Paolo, whose father, Vitale, had been head of the Jewish community in Rome, proudly tells me the story of his cousin Enzo Hayyim Sereni, one of the first Italian Zionists, who settled in Palestine, then as a member of the Haganah parachuted into Italy to rescue Jewish survivors. He landed inside the German lines, was transferred from camp to camp until he died in Dachau, no one knows how. Giorgio Fano, husband of Paolo Milano's sister Nella, was one of the 335 men and boys, many of them Jews who happened to be in Roman prisons at the time, who in 1944 were shot in the Ardeatine caves off the Appian Way in retaliation for the partisan attack in the Via Rasella on a truck carrying SS men.

I went down to the caves with an American writer. Startling to see a photograph on each individual tomb. Such is the exalted level of taste among the Fulbrights in Rome, she pronounced the makeshift tombs "coarse," and lamented the "crudity" of their design.

*　　*　　*

Rome! Exuberantly round and well-padded Carlo Levi. His training as a physician seems to have had no cautionary effect on his appetite for food and women. He is just crazy about Caroline, manages invariably to sit next to her, so close that I want to knock him off his bar stool. Breathing heavily in her direction he publicly announces in a tone of comic surprise, "Dio! And I thought all American women were blond!"

At intervals he throws remarks at me purely for effect. "On certain nights one can still hear lions roaring in Rome." Reading his *Christ Stopped at Eboli* in New York, just as we were about to sail for Genoa, I included Levi among my anti-Fascist heroes—Silone in Switzerland, Primo Levi in Auschwitz, Salvemini at Harvard, Giacomo Matteotti murdered in Italy, the brothers Carlo and Nello Roselli murdered in France at Mussolini's instigation.

*Christ Stopped at Eboli* has made Levi famous. Few readers knew just how primitive southern Italy could be until Levi published this record of his life for a year in a region so poor and remote. Levi was imprisoned for his anti-Fascist activity in the 1930s. Shortly before Mussolini attacked Ethiopia, Levi was banished to the province of Lucania, in the deep south of Italy. It was desolate country, mountainous and arid, virtually unknown to other Italians. To a cultivated northerner from Torino like Levi, accustomed all his life to the metropolitan traditions of the Italy closest to Western Europe, this was exile to a foreign country.

As the outlying province of the Kingdom of Naples, run by the Bourbons, Lucania had decayed to the point where it could not be reclaimed by either the nationalist or the social movement of the nineteenth century. The two small villages where Levi spent most of his exile, Grassano and Gagliano, are bleak, isolated settlements, remote even from neighboring villages. They are so backward and impoverished that the peasants lament that Christ never came to them. Christ stopped farther north, at Eboli.

Levi's life among these people recalls Kropotkin's exile to Siberia, Dostoyevsky's prison life in *The House of the Dead*—and James Agee's passionate inquiry into the life of southern tenant farmers, *Let Us*

*Now Praise Famous Men*. Here again is the intellectual voyaging into the darkest land of his own people, seeking authentic relation to them, and converting what might have been a sterile temporary exile into a longing for human solidarity. But Levi cannot help sounding like an anthropologist "studying" a remote culture far from home. The real theme of his book is his opposition to the cult of the state, which he absorbed in large part from the autonomous life of the peasants. When he was amnestied after the Italian victory in Ethiopia, he felt more alien at home than he had ever been in the forgotten village of Gagliano. There he had been forced down into deeper sources of life. His opposition to all state power is visceral, proud, romantic. The corporate structure of the Italian state? Pooh to the corporate structure of the Italian state!

Levi's observations come from a rare and meditated experience— the most abandoned section of his own people. The best thing in his book is the detachment with which he avoids sentimentalizing the peasants and at the same time renders their undestroyed feelings for human values. Such people were indifferent to Fascist glorification of conquest and the state. They had no feelings against him as a prisoner, and welcomed him in an entirely nonpolitical spirit. To the peasants "Rome" was a name rather than a power. Just as the regime was indifferent to their fate, so it had no authority over them. And anyway, they needed a good doctor. For the rest, they had been bored so long that everything about the stranger, from his painting and his dog, Barone, to his mail, was a change.

Other political prisoners in the village were forbidden to meet; they were workers, and so did not count. The physician-painter-prisoner was a gentleman to the Fascist mayor and local schoolmaster, and so raised everyone's social standing. Levi's doctoring, which he reluctantly undertook only after desperate appeal, ceased to offend the local physicians, most of whom seem to have been stupefyingly ignorant, once he made it clear that he had no wish to undermine their precious prestige. This was all they lived for; their indifference to the wretchedness of the peasants was matched only by their struggle to look important. It was the Italian situation in miniature. On the world stage at Rome it had tragic significance for millions.

The church did not touch the peasants much more. In Gagliano, a sun-bleached ledge on a mountain, dullness and hunger had created a spiritual vacuum which the misanthropic and drunken priest could not fill. Under the surface of routine devotion the peasants practiced primitive magic. My new friends in Rome like to say, "Below Rome—all is Africa." The local image of the Virgin was a black-faced Madonna, a subterranean deity, black with the shadows of the bowels of the earth, a peasant Persephone or lower-world goddess of the harvest. There was no real religion here; everything was bound up in natural magic.

All this was reflected in an amazing vitality. The greatest of the earth powers was lust. No woman and man could be together without surrendering to its force. A woman almost ninety once offered herself to Levi; another, not much younger, trembled when she went into his house unchaperoned. Levi's sometime servant, Giulia, had had seventeen pregnancies by fifteen different men, had been a priest's mistress, and was deeply shocked by Levi's refusal to obey the convention of passion, which she so richly embodied in herself.

Levi admired the peasants and learned from them; in the end they begged him to stay and offered to find him a wife. These were people with wasted gifts. The kind of Italian Levi did not admire was the new priest assigned to Gagliano, "a face typical of his generation of Italians. The type was that of an actor, a prelate and a barber rolled into one." This type ruled Fascist Italy; the peasants and intellectuals of Levi's stamp were not its only victims.

Levi's counterstatement to almost a quarter-century of Fascist domination has had a great effect here. In the discipline of the writing, as in the purity of its opinions, can be felt the reaction of what is being touted as "the new Risorgimento" against the whole spirit of Fascism. What a laugh. Thanks to Levi's celebrity, the Communists—those well-known antagonists of state power—are pushing him for the Senate, just an honor, but one that will reflect well on the Party, now well ensconced as the party of the "resistance." Levi is no Communist, but at the moment he seems to be enjoying life too much to remember the young prisoner of Fascism who in Lucania was so vehemently against the almighty state.

No radical writer of the thirties ever meant so much to me as Ignazio Silone. That burning year 1934, when America was deep in depression and Hitler already threatening the peace of Europe, I was nineteen, a poor boy, and still a radical of sorts in a Brooklyn tenement. Even as I enjoyed the ridicule with which Silone covered the pomposities of the Fascist state and pro-Fascist priests, I read *Fontamara* in rage, in tears, not thinking beyond Silone's empathy (and mine) with his abysmally wretched peasants in the Abruzzi. They were not simply poor but the poorest and most backward village south of the dried-up lake bed of Fucino. Mocked by the townspeople, ignored by the church, robbed by the "Promoter," their women raped by Fascist squads when they protested, their cry, "What must we do?" became at the end of *Fontamara* a summons to action through love of the oppressed.

In 1942, when I was briefly literary editor of the *New Republic*, Malcolm Cowley showed me an essay Silone had written in French to fellow socialists in Europe on the political problems they would face after the war. It opened with a reference to Saint Bernard. Whatever Silone's creed, his opposition to one or lack of one, it is the separatist, the independent religious thinker (whose entire belief may be a mystery to himself) who invariably captures my heart. I had somehow recognized even in *Fontamara* that Silone was not a Marxist like other Marxists, that he was driven by a sense of the injustice committed against the poorest peasants, the *cafoni* (whose very name, which also means "boor," indicated the general contempt for them), by a belief less in a hypothetical socialist state than in the need to demonstrate the wrongs, physical and moral, committed every day by the "indifferent ones" in respectable society.

The English translation of *Bread and Wine* appeared in 1937, ten years after Silone had broken with the Communist Party—typically, he refused to sign a document attacking Trotsky he was not permitted to read. He had for some time recognized that he was becoming less and less "political." In the novel the anti-Fascist fugitive Pietro Spina returns to Italy disguised as a priest, to work in the undergound. His encounters with all sorts of suffering and difficult people surprise him into depending for personal sustenance more on his original faith than he expected when he was still in exile.

As this was indeed Silone's own case, the more I was moved by his struggle to be a Christian outside the Church, faithful to the primitive Christianity not recognized or tolerated by the church—and meaningless to his old comrades in the "movement," who at a time when his writings seem to be known and admired everywhere except his native land, made life in exile all the lonelier for this "oddball."

The war is over; Silone is a Socialist deputy in the Parliament, but while *Fontamara* and *Pane e Vino* still cannot be found in the bookshops, everyone goes at him constantly—as if he were not simply a legend brought from overseas who writes "bad Italian" but a convenience to everyone's sense of superiority. It is very tiring to hear him knocked down with the same contemptuous phrases by every literary creature one meets. Frances Keene, Caroline's college teacher of Italian, now has an Italian journalist for her third husband. Through Frances he is constantly subjected to the admiration for Silone among English and American writers in Rome—especially mine—and is enraged by it. He loves to discourse on the "outside world's absurd overestimation of Silone." This puts him right in style and gives him a chance to lecture me. "You people cannot imagine how crudely he writes," he begins; then, screwing up his shoulders to make the classic Mediterranean gesture that denotes resignation to intractable human error or folly, insists on the argument after everyone else at the table has given it up as hopeless.

"Silone! Always Silone! You people have never heard of anyone else!"

He writes it seems, badly; he is a "political," not really a man of letters—a deputy, an active Socialist, editor of his own weekly, etc. He does not shine in conversation, but is in fact a depressed and depressing character; his reputation is out of all proportion to the real stars of Italian writing.

These Italian intellectuals are not disposed to honor a novelist who has been pushed at them as a symbol of the "real," the anti-Fascist, Italy. Comic situation: On the one hand there is this defensiveness about serving a regime that only the boldest cared to defy head-on, but that, as is now said, "was after all not so bad as Hitler. You have no idea how easygoing it was. With us, even authoritarian government is a little bit of a joke." On the other hand, whatever moral debt some Italians may have incurred for Fascism, none of them feels any great repentance now, not after the misery into which so many have been plunged after being bombed, pillaged, and near-destroyed.

So even Gaetano Salvemini's return has aroused mixed feelings. "He criticizes too much." I went to see and hear Salvemini officially welcomed back to Italy. When the crowd rose in homage, he sat himself down for a moment and wept. Then, shouting, "Dunque!" he took an immense manuscript out of his pocket and, dropping each page on the floor as he finished with it, proceeded to read a fiery political lesson to the astonished crowd, detailing everything democracy is up against in Italy today.

Benedetto Croce's daughter Elena told me that *Fontamara* was a terrible book, and that the first she had seen of it was an Italian edition sent over especially by Silone's English publisher—not easy for them to take that! He is simply not a "literary" writer, a serious matter in a country where, despite the influence of Hemingway, a rich style works on writers like a narcotic. One said to me, "My greatest pleasure is spending a morning shaping my paragraphs."

Silone is disliked, Paolo Milano says, because he personifies the one type the Italians cannot stand—the moral dissenter. "He simply will not reduce everything to the canonical Italian level of the 'family affair.'" When Silone praises those "who do not betray," the intellectuals feel that he is making sour judgments on *them.* And he has gone through an intense religious evolution that is simply not understood in a man representing the Socialist Party in Parliament. "In an Italian, it is very queer to take Christianity that personally."

Leaving Italy. We are soon to have a child. Our last night, dinner with Silone and Carlo Levi in a sweltering mob at the Il Re degli Amici—accordion players, Neapolitan blues singers, a grotesque one-man band loaded front and back with instruments and beating time to the upward and downward surge of a rusty black derby squeezed over his eyes, wandering beggars and nuns collecting alms. Sociability unlimited, the café of all good Roman artists, Socialists, survivors of the wartime *Partito d'Azione, Justicia e Libertà*. The beautiful Italian bedlam and intellectual merriment, people calling and flirting from table to table: all one great family party. Always at such moments, as when I walk the streets and feel the relatedness of these people to one another, I feel that the family sense binding Italians together seems stronger than the personality of each one. And I am envious. America is not like this.

Even Silone looked almost gay tonight, though taking, advantage of Levi's valiant efforts to speak English, which Silone pretends not to understand at all, he put his face into a great mass of fish, meat, and greens, and remained alone with his own thoughts.

Levi, in his most resplendent mood and most carefree costume, in a crazy fur cap given him by a Florentine carriage driver and a long checked overcoat straight out of the Marx Brothers. Always grinning from ear to ear, the most pagan of the Jews. Has been reading up on Stendhal's *Roman Journal*. "The plant, man, is more robust and large in Rome than elsewhere." Paints in the morning, writes in the afternoon, rounds out his day with a cartoon for *Italia*

*Socialista*, and then makes his grand entrance here, an old stogie in his mouth, cheery as a congressman back home on Main Street—the pinnacle of Italian self-enjoyment. Reports that the people he described in his book have taken to wearing signs on their clothes reading, "I am a character in Carlo Levi's *Christ Stopped at Eboli*."

Curious to watch Silone and Levi together—men of the same generation, both formed outside the shell of Fascism, and better known in other countries than in their own, types of the writer *engagé*, yet so different in mind and temperament that the extremes of Italian character have been called on to produce them. Silone is battered ("He has been told so often that he is bad novelist, he is ready to believe it") by every tyranny eager to kill us, yet speaks for us "premature anti-Fascists" as no exhausted ex-radical ever does. Truly, the seed still waits beneath the snow. The Silone I revere is not to be found in a crazy-quilt evening at a pizzeria, but in his work, with its scruples, its awkward tenderness, and its primitive humor. And the work is no longer separable from Italy; it is one more chapter in the *inner* history of the poor. Whom you have always with you.

And afterward, toiling through the cold, stopping for an espresso, admiring the nymphs in the Piazza del Popolo, a bag of chestnuts from the old woman on the corner warming herself at the fire, while in the faint light of the lamps in the park, just beyond Michelangelo's gates, that Roman god and emperor whose name I have never learned still stands with his arm half-raised, beautiful and indifferent.

New York: Unto us a son is given, with a full head of hair, Caroline's beautiful hair. Caroline proposed either Peter or Michael, grimaced when I vetoed Peter as outside the Jewish tradition, and so we have Michael, from the Hebrew *Mik-ha-el*, "who is like God." My mother, in rapture and tears after waiting so long for this, went alone to *shul* to recite the blessing on the birth of a first-born. I have looked into books, and rejoice that in the Haggadah, Michael is "the constant defender of the Jewish people." What an angel! And the terrible Yahweh notwithstanding, Michael warned Abraham *not* to give up Isaac.

Exhausted and excited after greeting Michael, I return to find the Russian pianist from whom we have sublet this provisional little place on Park Avenue (!), hysterically hiding at the bottom of the chiffonier his "little Lenin library"—paperback editions of *The State and Revolution* and other such gems of monolithic thinking, violently attacking everyone on the Left unhappy with Bolshevism. Although my "landlord" can't even remember who bestowed Lenin on him and is concerned only with making a career in this pianist-infested city, he is convinced that the Police Department's anti-Red squad and the FBI will have him deported if they find the "little Lenin library" on the premises.

I am desperate for sleep but try to joke the fellow out of his panic. I bring out a bottle. Even when I finally get him to join me in a drink to celebrate the new babe, he is forlorn, near tears. "If they send me back to Russia, I will die."

"The people of the book" are now the people of the magazine. A new Jewish magazine, *Commentary*. I sold them "Encounter in Edinburgh," about the Polish soldier I met in front of Holyrood Palace near the end of the war. The editor, Elliot Cohen, is originally from the Deep South, went to Yale, has a psychiatrist brother named Mendel. Mendel and Elliot! Elliot had his Communist period and is now violently ashamed of it. A great friend of Lionel Trilling. He hides his insecurities badly—simply can't let any piece alone after he has bought it. "I wouldn't be the editor I am," he confided in a fatherly tone, "if I didn't show you how to make your piece even better than it already is." I managed to steer him off, but Harold

Rosenberg was so exasperated he had to tell him off. "Listen, Elliot, if you want to write, write under your own name!"

From the playwright Sam Behrman, relaying a message to me from Bernard Berenson: "Berenson has read your extracts 'From an Italian Journal' in *Partisan Review* and wants to know why you don't like him."

Dinner in honor of Rabbi Leo Baeck given by *Commentary* magazine. When Rabbi Baeck was asked why he is not a Zionist, he replied, "I am a Jew. I don't need another crutch." Remarkable, dignified figure, obviously full of inner strength. Was a chaplain in the Kaiser's army. I am told that when the Nazis came to power, Baeck proclaimed the "thousand-year" history of the Jews in Germany at an end, and as head of the representative body of German Jews, the *Vertretung der Juden*, devoted himself to protecting the rights remaining to Jews under the Nazis.

Deported to Theresienstadt concentration camp (the Nazis said it was for "leading Jews"), he refused several chances to escape, became a special kind of guardian to the Jewish prisoners, who loved him as "a witness of his faith." At the dinner he said that one of his duties in Theresienstadt had been to find priests there to say mass for the Catholics—all converts.

What luck. Hannah Arendt placed next to me at the dinner for Rabbi Leo Baeck, and I have sought her out several times since. Darkly handsome, bountifully interested in everything, this forty-year-old German refugee with a strong accent and such intelligence—thinking positively cascades out of her in waves—that I was enthralled, by no means unerotically. Her interest in her new country, its constitutional virtues, its political background, are as much a part of her as her passion for discussing Plato, Kant, Nietzsche, even Duns Scotus—but Kafka above all—as if they all live with her and her strenuous and Protestant husband, Heinrich Blücher, in the shabby rooming house on Morningside Heights.

At the Saturday morning faculty meeting of the New School, which these days is less redolent of West Twelfth Streeet than of Weimar (just before the ax fell), I was enthusiastically describing my first impressions of Hannah to the formidable dean, Clara Mayer, when I felt a hand on my shoulder and, turning around, was faced with a rather debonair chap who announced in a single breath, "I am Günther Stern and wish to thank you for speaking so well of my former wife, Hannah Arendt." This was such a change from the abrasive New York style in which men and women I know are glad to damn their ex-partners in public that I laughingly reported the incident to Hannah. She frowned. "But of course. Why are you so surprised? *Erkenntnis.* Recognition. This is an understanding between us, a tradition."


Hannah has been working for Jewish Cultural Reconstruction, which seeks to recover and return the vast store of Jewish religious and cultural objects stolen by the Nazis. She left for Paris in 1933 as soon as the Nazis took over, worked for the Youth Aliyah sending Jewish children to Palestine. No less than the Bluechers, I feel that Hitler's war has not ended, in one sense will never come to an end.

Bluecher, born 1899, from a working-class background (he likes to hint that though a poor relation he is not unrelated to Napoleon's nemesis *the* Marshal Blücher), was a teenage recruit in the Kaiser's army, after the war a Spartacist, and is a German who loves Jews—his first wife was another Jew. Likes to reminisce that in 1918 he heard wounded soldiers openly asking for Jewish army doctors—

"Jews are not interested in immortality. A Jewish doctor tries his damndest to keep you alive."

Compact, always wound up, a bit rough in manner but intellectually "pure," a prodigious autodidact and walking philosopher, always trying to make up for his lack of a university degree. Hannah started calling him "Monsieur" after they met in Paris. She sometimes refers to him as Socrates. Bluecher is certainly a change from the ex-Communists I know. But what a contrast to his wife, Dr. Hannah Arendt, prize student of Martin Heidegger at Freiburg, of Karl Jaspers at Heidelberg.

Bluecher is an unstoppably *mental* creature, orates without stopping in his living room on any "great thinker" who has aroused his attention—from Heraclitus to Joachim of Floris. I got the New School to try him out. He is so vehement a teacher, and he is such a hit with the culture vultures there who just have to *listen*, that he has already been called to Bard. Hannah says he is incapable of writing for publication in German or English. He certainly makes up for this by shouting philosophy at you in the sweetest kind of way.

Heinrich is given to fantasy and exaggeration, noble lies about his military knowledge. I am told that German Communists thought of Heinrich as their military "expert." But he is the kind of obsessively reflective, altogether human German I no longer expected to meet. My God, the Berlin he encountered in 1919 after the army! In the midst of revolution and counterrevolution, angry mobs all over the place, you could hear Wagner or Bach just by inserting a coin in a box standing on a street corner. Protestant German once-radical married to a Jew, he certainly surprised me by his concern and identification with Jews.

Nothing has so unhinged me from my piddling old "progressive" views as the destruction of the Jews. The "Holocaust," as they are beginning to call it, invades me in a way I never anticipated during the war, when—especially after discovering Shmuel Ziegelboim's suicide letter from London on the looming murder of *every* Polish Jew—I already guessed the full horror to come.

Hannah and Heinrich are close, close, in a way that exalts married love beyond anything I know with Caroline—they seem to have been driven onto each other by what Churchill called "the worst episode in human history." They are positively enclosed by what Hannah calls the "catastrophe." In their shabby old *driven* apartment on Morningside Heights, where the Bluechers are in such straits they have taken in a boarder, the reverberations of the Nazi experience never, never cease. Hitler may be dead and gone, but here the *shock* of him—for Hannah even more than Heinrich—is the air they both breathe. I was not surprised to learn that Hannah is writing a book on totalitarianism.

Let's face it: "Homeless" as she declares herself ("homelessness" is big in her existential analysis of "modern man"), Hannah is far more German than she is Jewish. She is stalwart in her acceptance of the name, the identity, the racial odium Nazidom imposed on her, in her commitment to a Jewish homeland. She directs "Jewish Cultural Reconstruction," which seeks to restore to devastated Jewish communities the religious and cultural treasures stolen by the Nazis. In Paris she labored for Youth Aliyah trying to get children into Palestine. But if the Jews are a tradition, she certainly does not love this tradition. If the Jews are a people, she does not love this people. Intellectually, like many another Jewish intellectual, she is indifferent to Judaism and (like so many of us) has been much more influenced by Christian thought. What she has canonized all her life—philosophy as a daily activity. She wrote her doctoral dissertation under Karl Jaspers at Heidelberg on Saint Augustine's concept of love, and never tires of quoting her favorite maxim from Augustine: "Love means: I want you to *be*."

Her conversation, unlike Bluecher's, is so much from what she has written or is planning to write that her gruff but most friendly voice seems always to be lecturing me, repeating her favorite themes and quotations. Her astonishing expressiveness as an expounder, authority, teacher in her new country is inseparable from her charm as a woman. This expressiveness, physical and tangible, is for me her greatest attribute. She is too reverential about the great thinkers to claim "originality": In philosophy herself, her distinctive procedure, which she must have learned in German seminars, is to circle round and round the hallowed names, performing a "critique" in their name even when she disowns a traditional position. In the kitchen, too, she sails into the airiest speculations.

The shock of Nazism in full power turned Hannah into a political philosopher. She is writing to uncover "the origins of totalitarianism." Rescuing some English sentences in her manuscript—she thinks in strongly knotted sentences that in a single gasp refute conventional wisdom and then positively set things right—I am struck by how German, how ultrapositive she is in thought, whatever her vulnerability as a Jewish refugee. She is full of mournful longing for friends left behind and can make appealing noises about her acute sense of "homelessness," the difficulties experienced as an alien. I am sponsoring her application for citizenship. But she is enveloped in a sense of intellectual hierarchy that, while it certainly fills out my education, can be staggering in its contempt for more empirical ways of determining reality.

Truly wonderful. Here is a poor refugee on the Upper West Side attempting in an adopted language to give us not just the absolute meaning of totalitarianism in Germany *and* Russia (even the ex-Leninists will not like that) but its "origins." For her it all starts with the Jews, whose "national religion" (as she disdainfully calls it) has no interest for her, and in whose social role, at least in Germany— "outside all classes," as she likes to maintain—she sees the reason for the odium heaped upon them.

I love this woman intensely—she is such a surprise, such a gift. I am a sucker for this kind of advanced European mind, so much better stocked and subtler than the exhausted radicalism of almost every Jewish intellectual I know. She has brought into my life so many unexpected traits and pleasures, like her intense love of poetry as a higher form of thinking. She gives me Hölderlin, I give her Blake. She is so fierce about Kafka as the one and only novelist of our age— a large photograph of him, looking sheepish in a derby, stands beside the front door—that I practically had to run for cover after admitting my admiration for Thomas Mann's *Joseph and His Brothers*.

Even her vulnerability is interesting; it is so much part of her determination to take on the Nazi horror in all its historical dimensions. And dare I confess it—I suspect her of having the rarest of traits in the American world—like Spinoza, another "pariah"—she has an *intellectual* love of God. You can actually talk to her about the literature of belief.

Though she seems to abjure what Santayana called "egotism in German philosophy," in favor of politics, the public realm, and is deeply steeped in the classics and fervently celebrates the Greek tradition of the *polis*, she is at heart no democrat. Ironic. She frequently tells me she has shifted to political thought as the crucial subject of our time, away from the unworldliness of German philosophy (Heidegger the sometime Nazi, for all his brilliance, is the most telling current example). In what I have seen of *The Origins of Totalitarianism*, she cites Montesquieu and Tocqueville as the truly wise men, but she prefers passing judgment on the "mob" to making the kind of empirical observations with which Tocqueville filled his great book on the revolutionary spectacle of "democracy in America."

She is a theorist, a German theorist. The habit of mind natural to Heidegger, Husserl, Jaspers, even the theologian Bultmann (she was one of two Jews in his New Testament seminar) haunts her. Although she sternly and courageously notes every parallel between the Hitler and Stalin bureaucracies—their arbitrary use of exclusion and terror, the central importance of the police—she has nothing useful to say about the actualities of czarist *society*. She details the social predicament of German Jews as basic to anti-Semitism and the rise of Nazism. But Russian anti-Semitism was basically religious and, even as "an outworn prejudice" among Communists, was murderous enough in Stalin and his dictatorship.

Her conception of totalitarianism as "the burden of our time" is powerful, a stupendous literary idea, like the structure of Dante's hell. No one else has recognized the essentially arbitrary, make-believe nature of the reality that Nazism and Communism alike have imposed on their submissive victims, and how much the essence of the matter is "total domination" (so much clearer a term than "totalitarianism"). Simply as a vision of the horror visited upon our century, admitting the selective nature of the phenomena that fit into her theory, the last chapters are overwhelming, apocalyptic. Nothing else I have read on the subject has had such an impact on me. Very positive about everything she thinks. Very. With Arendt you *always* know where you are. But you can't argue with her and the slightest criticism dumbfounds her. How dare they!

Queer, footloose days, reading all around for the Brooklyn section of my book, living between our rented quarters and East Seventieth Street: the baby with nurse, Caroline, and her parents, who keep congratulating me on having a son—"Isn't it wonderful to have a son! Isn't it wonderful!" But what with the baby and the nurse and all the equipment, they have no room for me.

Except for the baby I have no sense of direction or the peacefulness that comes with having done something. I don't seem to be anywhere—not with Caroline, who looks at me blankly now that I have done my duty. Full of anxiety and dread—so lonely that I seem to ache all over for someone, someone, but mope about with no particular desire to see anyone.

In the rainy silence tonight, alone, thought of that voice of perfect peace and love I heard in Pineapple Street when I was finishing the long introduction to the *Portable Blake*—and then again when I sat by the Delaware, thinking of my approaching marriage, and heard the voice say so clearly, Do it, do it—aim for the whole of life again.

A detail, possibly for my "Dialogue with the Dead" or even an opening scene for *A Walker in the City*. There is an oldish woman who visits Mrs. Rogers downstairs, and manages to ring my bell every time she also rings hers. When I look down the stairwell, calling, "Who is it?" I can see only her hand grasping the banister. The slowness and painfulness of her progress up the steps, step by step, and then that white hand, mounting higher and higher, are all I have ever seen of her.

The Republican Convention opened in Philadelphia yesterday. While cutting the pages of Maurice Chapelan's *Anthologie du Journal Intime*, which I had bought with great excitement at Brentano's—I am writing about Thoreau's complete journal, all fourteen volumes of it, for the *Herald Tribune* books section—I listened to Governor Green of Illinois deliver the keynote address.

Honestly, their enduring hatred of the New Deal, though Truman has not exactly followed it, is enough to make one vomit. Of all the thick-headed monsters of selfish self-righteous arriviste Babbitry, these Republicans are the worst. And now that they are sure to elect Dewey in November, they swagger as they breathe. Clare Luce's oily speech upholding all the right values was typical. What a self-righteous convert—in every sense—she has turned out to be. A current joke has the pope saying to her, "But my dear, I already *am* a Catholic."

City man. Limping about in the summer heat, he gazes absently, his eyelids flickering in feeble response, at the headlines in the afternoon paper. Dewey, the perfect careerist for our time—no convictions on any subject, no compassion, not the slightest warmth, only ambition.

In the cave of the subway car. If the heat gets any hotter all this iron, glass, and paper will dissolve into a thickly colored stream of debris and carry him out to sea with it. He sits there sweating and smiling for a breath of air, a ray of light—meanwhile crushing in his mind the thin silks and cottons of the girls' blouses, hoping that the car will sail out to sea so that he can dream hungrily on the body of the girl next to him. At East 125th Street he gets out. Iron, rust, cobwebs, Negro Harlem, heat. He inquires the way to the footwalk of the Triborough Bridge from the little man (blind in one eye) who keeps the newspaper stand in one corner. The twitch in the man's good eye and the coal burning at the end of the cigar clumped between his rotting yellow teeth make havoc of the day in its circling heat.

Which way? Straight ahead, my son. He walks on to Second Avenue, and enters in his slipshod way the curving footwalk of the bridge. Before him, high like the smoking beacons of an Aztec sacrifice, the aluminum-and-steel towers of the bridge. Left and right the city recedes in the summer haze. A riot of form, of lines violating curves, of curves receding, ending far away as lines.

Bridges, boats, the city islands below his feet. Younger sons, in white jerseys, wearing cigarettes in their mouths, carrying baseball bats and gloves, slop along with him. Thus, by slow steps, to Randall's Island he descends. The artificial park in careful ovals and parallelograms of green; its oases of water fountains; its stadia; the hot lover and loveress languidly stroking each other's hair as they sit under a tree.

He is now above the north center of the river. On every side of him the great monster, prettified in dull, straight meadows of city green, stretches its tentacles from island to island. He sits alone on a park bench, looking at the old house on Ward's Island, hearing the sounds of the city beating back on him from distant drums. A tug leading a scow turns from the Harlem River into the East River, slowly dragging along the channel on its way to the head of the island. What a variety of forms! What a multiworld of iron and steel, aluminum and rust! A young man comes along, wheeling a baby carriage and bearing in the crook of his arm a little radio, warm with the damp commercial maternity of Kate Smith.

\*   \*   \*

Our next president. My God, if only I had the talent of Daumier to draw the little man with that scientific smile, that careful nose, that "administrative" brain! The perfect managerial lawyer for a bureaucratic society—functions like a machine; never tires; always thinly smiling, but only for the right people and not too much of that either; knows how to please by reconciling his formidable reputation as a hunter-down of criminals with his skill in avoiding offense.

Has been running for office since he was eight. The crowd waiting outside his balcony was duly informed that he was putting in a call to his mother. "Was that all right?" he cried, when he apologized for having kept them waiting. "Yes!" it roared back. "Yes!" The key to his character is that ridiculous mustache, grown (despite warnings from his handlers that the American people do not favor hair on a president's face) because soon-to-be-President Thomas Edmund Dewey looks even younger than he is. But hard-driving youth for energy, maturity for common sense. As he sits for his official campaign photograph, he carfeully puts one hand on his thigh in a statuesque show of dignity, responsibility.

We moved today to Central Park West, way up there past One Hundredth Street. Enormous business of packing and unpacking the many books I have been carrying all my life. Back in 1938 the cartons I was carrying into my first married home in Brooklyn Heights burst open, scattering books all over the front hall. A life crammed with books, books, and more books. Lord, how I would like to get free of so many *things!* I will date my freedom from the day I see a book I can do without. "Simplify! Simplify!" But I am crammed with obligations—like the many books I had to leave behind in order to get into this sublet from Italian Jews who have kept two big rooms locked up. Every week there are more possessions crowding in on us. In this great echoing barracks of an apartment house, every real or imaginary requirement of up-to-date living calls for still more equipment.

The fifteenth floor. From my tiny study I look out on the incessant hideous windowed wall of an apartment house just like ours. When I go up to the window, I engage roofs and roofs—rooming houses, ancient brownstones in a drab triangle to the southwest. To the east, the park—at least the end of it. The view from our bedroom is wonderful. An apartment house in New York—and we are on the fifteenth floor—an office building for living. The constant collision with others and the absolute lack of meaningful contact. The infinite duplication on every side of the emptily vast Upper West Side halls—all collecting their mail and papers outside the back door at the same time, all putting out the garbage at four-thirty. Cell on cell of New York living.

But this building overlooking the park is a middle-class oasis compared with the dismal interval of the barrio you have to walk west to get to Broadway. The *alrightnik* quality of Central Park West—psychiatrists, psychoanalysts, psychologists, progressive educators a dime a dozen—all this changes sharply the minute you leave the house and walk the dismal intervening streets, all Hispanic, to Broadway.

A black cat frightened up to the top of a tree on Central Park West. While the dog waited, snarling, to get at it, the ASPCA arrived, police, cars stopped, a messenger service. Great show. A man with a coil of rope wrapped around him went halfway up the tree with a long silvery-looking rod to get the cat down. It danced up there, feeling its way along the branches, looking all around like a king surveying his awestruck subjects—then suddenly missed its footing and fell to the sidewalk. An ASPCA man took the cat in his arms and drove off with it.

I am like that cat—up a tree. And waiting to fall from this stupid life, this loveless life.

\*   \*   \*

On my way home about five-thirty stopped on a whim in Emanu-El, the Jewish cathedral on Fifth Avenue, and on even more of a whim found myself enduring an evening service in the chapel. The "chapel," if you please! They also have a "sanctuary." If there is anything more unctuous and boring than this high-church Jewish Reform service, I have never seen it. The "reader," a fat, oily businessman, Ethical Culture type, read out the words with such deliberation that whenever he came to "God" he would stop, prepare himself, mouth the word as if it had three syllables.

Six decidedly cheerless people coldly recited back to him the familiar litany of praise, praise, and homage. O Lord You who knowest best You who are the Mightiest. Praise and praise to the mighty Jewish Lord who apparently cannot be flattered enough.

I was so bored and distracted that when I rose to leave I realized that mourners were standing for the Kaddish, and that I was being taken for a mourner. And so, standing, listening to the majestic, the truly divine words of the Kaddish:

MAGNIFIED AND SANCTIFIED BE HIS GREAT NAME IN THE
WORLD WHICH HE HATH CREATED ACCORDING TO HIS WILL.
MAY HE ESTABLISH HIS KINGDOM DURING YOUR LIFE DURING
YOUR DAYS, AND DURING THE LIFE OF ALL THE HOUSE OF
ISRAEL, EVEN SPEEDILY AND AT NEAR TIME, AND SAY YE,
AMEN.

I felt it might just as well be said over me, dead in my own home.

Shaken and most deeply impressed by Bellow's *The Victim* (dedicated to our exile friend Paolo Milano), a book so far beyond the introspection of his *Dangling Man* that you can see how the murder of Europe's Jews has toughened and deepened the literary intelligence

I marked in Bellow's first stories in *Partisan Review*. If I am not mistaken, this story of the Gentile Allbee accusing the bewildered Jew Asa Leventhal of persecuting *him*, seeking to ruin *his* life, catches perfectly the subtlety of evil. The Nazis triumphantly portrayed the Jew as predator, ubiquitous evildoer, exploiter, racially motivated corrupter, rapist, usurer—dominator yet subhuman!—and so justified "extermination" as if the Jews were disgusting parasites. In Bellow's novel the Jew, depressed by his wife's absence and the enervating heat of a New York summer, is subdued, morally disoriented, half convinced that he is in some sense "guilty" of something. He allows Allbee to take over his apartment, in a sense to take over his life— until Allbee's cynically taking a woman in mocks Leventhal's temporary loss of his wife. This causes the true "victim" to revolt against the man who tyrannized him by seeming to know all the answers.

Three years after the harrowing summer, when Allbee is restored to his usual life, Leventhal, meeting his old enemy at a theater, cannot resist asking, "Wait a minute. What's your idea of who runs things?" A marvelous thrust—the Jew as victim, the mediocre man out of the crowd who has lost his way, seeks an answer, *the* answer, from the rejuvenated enemy who has just left him with "I'm not the type that runs things. I never could be. I realized that long ago. I'm the type that comes to terms with whoever runs things."

A searing book in every way. The writing, sentence by sentence, is remarkable in its severe, neutral plainness, the exactness with which it crystallizes the absurdity of situations once "unlikely." Bellow has turned the ironic reversal in Dostoyevsky's *The Eternal Husband* into a parable of what lay behind the victimization of the Jew. And he is not afraid to show how the Jew contributed to this by his submission, his obedience, his all-too-willing "assimilation" of the doctrines preached by the stronger.

Remembering here the outburst of Caroline's uncle Leo—his growling hatred of intellectuals as "thought-monsters," of social reform as "philanthropy wasted on garbage," of "goodness" as "self-indulgence." He was looking straight at me when he said all this at the family dinner, so I guessed he meant me, the inexplicable addition to this phalanx of solid burghers. No doubt a "disillusioned" liberal, and very ugly he is about it. I can see him in the well-stocked shelter he has built against an atomic blast, threatening with a rifle anyone who is afraid. Very much like that little newspaperman I met in Minneapolis when I was teaching at the University of Minnesota. Said he had tried being "good" and "social minded" but was now determined to live "for himself."

A lot of conversions these days. The other day, halfway through lunch with the *Commentary* assistant editor Irving Kristol, I was startled to hear him say, "I'm turning right." I didn't get this at first, and joked, "Are we in a car?" Irving, like his fellow assistant editors Clement Greenberg and Richard Clurman, is quite a contrast to boss editor Elliot Cohen, who packs a lot of hysteria behind his professional geniality. I hardly know Clem Greenberg, he is always dashing past me with an armful of proofs. Dick Clurman is blond, soigné, quite a change from his uncle Harold Clurman, the theater man, a favorite of mine whose Lower East Side background is so marked that a lordly WASP actress withdrew from a play Harold was directing complaining that he was "not toilet trained."

Irving Kristol carefully explained to me—his style is always careful, ironic, debonair in his sedulous way—that in the army he had learned that a show of emotion is usually unnecessary. Irving was an active Trotskyist in Chicago when his wife, Gertrude Himmelfarb, was taking her doctorate at the university there. Who was teaching whom?

Clever, worldly, immensely likable Mario Salvadori and I walking on Riverside Drive, Mario gently explaining where Caroline and I have gone off the tracks. "You have to understand that she is elemental, elemental!" And without anything further being said, that I, being what I am, am now without access to her. What Mario does not have to say is that sooner or later, probably sooner, I am about to be replaced. By him.

Michael, not yet two years old, looking at me from behind the glass door as I leave, not understanding. Michael, not yet two years old, standing behind the glass door, behind the glass door, behind the glass door.

# Part Three

# 1950-1978

Rain again this morning. A bad night, and finally gave up much too early—tired, miserable, tense—to hear the truck traffic off Fifty-eighth Street heading for Queensboro Bridge. But am coming back to myself as I write this after coffee. Am listening to the first Chopin concerto (Artur Rubinstein), and feel better. The cars skid and whistle in the rain. Glistening drops of champagne fall off the imaginary piano to my left. Now Frédéric is playful: the quick last movement. Rumble, skid, and whistle from the traffic in the rain. The tires go round and round and round. My heart leaps over the abyss of the night, reaching as on a merry-go-round for the ring that welcomes on the other side.

I go back to Michael once a week. We play, we romp together. We act out a story called Alphonse, Gaston, and Slimy Louie. It is about two funny (I hope) characters who are farcically polite but as soon as they encounter each other trip one another up in a series of accidents. Papa acts all three of them, falling on the floor at regular intervals. Michael has the courtesy to laugh between bitefuls of lunch. The playground across the street is great, full of modern sculpture—slides, ladders, wheels, and sandpiles. My son is too young to understand why I have to arrive at a certain hour, leave at an appointed time, even in the Dr. Seuss I am reading to him. I have to be fitted in.

\* \* \*

Mother and child are on a West Indian island where you can frolic in the sun while obtaining a divorce—no need to "sue" anybody for anything, no hard feelings, very few feelings at all! So I am waiting out this period at Yaddo, where the most urgent topic of conversation, for once, is not *my book, my work, my performance* but the infamy of the case against Alger Hiss, who is on trial for perjury in federal court in New York. To my surprise, the best-known left-winger at table, the novelist Josephine Herbst, gave me a wink in the midst of a tirade from a guy who triumphantly dismissed the case against Alger Hiss by quoting I. F. Stone—"Whittaker Chambers is a renegade!"

Abandoned years ago by John Herrmann, a novelist who gave up mere fiction for life in the Communist underground and skipped to Mexico before he could be exposed as a Soviet agent, Josie is alone, penniless, comes on as a sharp-tongued, politically exhausted relic, a wreck of an old woman (although she is not yet sixty) *who has been through everything.* But if you show the slightest male interest in her, she blossoms, a prairie rose. When not at Yaddo, she lives without indoor plumbing in the old farmhouse in Erwinna, Bucks County, she once shared with Herrmann. She is dominated heart and soul by a hesitant, by-no-means-altogether-truthful allegiance to her radical past. As with Alger Hiss, I do not altogether trust her to tell where the bodies are buried. It was awkward meeting her at first—in *On Native Grounds* I put down her "proletarian" novels of the depression period—but in my hankering after love I am fascinated by the passion she brings to every side of her life. It is such a wonderful American story, and these regressive days, when so many ex-Communists are as abstract in their enthusiasm for America as they were abstract about "socialist" Russia, Josie's touches me as the *last* American story of its kind.

Sioux City, Iowa, in the 1890s. The spunky and brilliantly independent girl went off to Berkeley for an A.B. as if college were a romantic adventure—and the year after, took the lifelong adventure that was already herself to New York. There she read for George Jean Nathan and H. L. Mencken on *The Smart Set* and began to form those friendships with writers for which she has a special and enduring genius. Hemingway, Katherine Anne Porter, John Cheever, Philip Roth, Saul Bellow—Sid Perelman, Nathanael West, and Mike Gold in the old days.

In 1921 she went to Europe, as so many writers of her marvelous generation did, yet typically got right into the heat of things political and literary: Weimar had not yet succumbed to Hitler. I listen with rapture to Josie's tales of the 1920s, when in person she was so much a part of the new American writing that was emerging in Paris with her friend Hemingway. Josie in the early 1930s was in her element, found expression for all her rebelliousness in being right on the spot to report what even the conservative pessimist Freud in Vienna called "the great experiment taking place in the East." And the nine Negro boys in the Scottsboro case, aged thirteen to twenty-one, condemned to death for gang rape on the testimony of the two white whores found with them in a freight car. And the struggling farmers of her native Iowa.

Josie was with Dreiser and Dos Passos when they went down to investigate the terror against the striking Kentucky miners, with the Cuban peasants during the 1935 general strike, with the first—socialist—victims of Hitler's terror right after he took power, when apparently it took some radical experience and radical imagination to guess at the potential horror of what so many bourgeois German Jews could not.

The Spanish Civil War was obviously the high point of Josie's existence; she reverts to it as a mother would to her child. She was there from 1937 on—and she was really there, steeped in the life of the frontline villages and, typically enough, getting desperately needed rations for her fellow correspondents in the Hotel Florida from her always-well-stocked friend Hemingway, from whose room the smell of frying bacon and other goodies would drive less fortunate writers crazy. And during the Second World War, Josie, who needed the job desperately, was of course fired from the government's early information service, later the OWI, then busily mobilizing American opinion against fascism, for having been a premature antifascist.

June 1950: Her books are all out of print, she is out of a job, out of cash, out of fashion, and might have been out of a home if it hadn't been for that old stone house in Erwinna—with its now legendary outhouse. And truth to tell, what remains of her fervent radicalism, so pitifully identified with John Herrmann, who ran away from her in every sense, interests me far less than Josie the survivor—so broke, bent, and backward in many ways that my heart is touched, if not my head. She is a believer, an American from another century. Typically, she is writing *New Green World*, about our great early naturalists John and William Bartram, and loves me, just loves me, because I lent her my complete set of Thoreau's *Journals*. She would remind me of another survivor, Gussie Kazin, at the end of her tether all *her* life long—were it not for Josie's midwestern feeling for physical space and her gift for putting her whole soul into a letter. You can still see the flaming girl who was always getting mad and made you see the fun of getting mad, always for a cause.

One day in that now-romantic long ago, when Josie and John Herrmann went fishing with Hemingway off Key West, Hemingway lost his temper at John for not getting enough ice to keep their catch fresh, and kept grousing at him until Josie broke in: "Hem, if you don't stop I'll take your pistol and shoot you." Hemingway seems to have been properly impressed. He later gave her one of his manuscripts.

She loves to write letters. The quotation marks seem to be missing from her typewriter, so that a quotation from *Pride and Prejudice* folds without warning into some wrathful statement about publishers and the state of her soul, which in a letter is usually lyrical. She has just learned that I am spending a week in Nanuet with Hannah Arendt and Heinrich Bluecher, so I am enchanted to find this:

# 1950-1978

*Erwinna, July 7, 1950*

*A tiny yellow duck broke loose from its mother and waddled down the hill to my back door—then began a loud squawk in terror and fearful recognition that it was lost, lost. I got it in my hand and it settled down at once—I could have held it like that forever until we both perished, two ninnies in bliss together while the world fell apart. I called up the farm, they came with a truck as if the duck were a cow to be transported only in a huge affair and took it away. I loved it madly—Russell writes Scribner's may do the Bartram book and that Hastings House are bastards. It will work out. I am glad to think of you with friends away from New York. Here it was divinely cool last night, a fire in the fireplace, two blankets on my bed, a late big moon and before that a night thick with fireflies. Some stars are pale green. Some icy blue and there are some as red as my barn. I finally cleared the house of company. Today I am myself. No quarter asked and no quarter given. No more company except what I can fetch up out of my own soul. I loved your letter. I knew I would get it. Let me blow off steam now and then. My rich friends have often surprised me, have given me gifts of worth, real money, but if only once I went like a mendicant to them or like a confident customer to a bank, all would be lost. When one wants grapes one goes to the poor. They will be willing to rob the birds but they will share with you, share and share alike. Hasta revista J*

Hannah Arendt has finished *The Origins of Totalitarianism* and I've been going over the manuscript to de-Teutonize many of the too summary sentences. Extraordinary book. It has really shaken me. But there is so much to rework in her English that I wondered how far I should go, and asked Van Wyck Brooks to look at it.

He lives in a stately old house occupying a principal corner of the main street in little Bridgewater, Connecticut. In the train going up there yesterday, I was fascinated by the succession of triangles intervening as they connected the electric wires on the Danbury line. How they swell in size as the train comes up to them, and how they shrink as the train rushes on. Watching them as they flashed by, I saw nothing but close parallel lines ending in these connecting triangles, but the lines themselves were continually shifting, bounding, thrusting—then diminishing again. The lines seem to be in continuous vibration, then are absorbed in the sensation of movement.

Such technical novelty is quite in contrast with Van Wyck Brooks, who still writes with a steel pen. "The Post Office is right across the street," Van Wyck says, laughing. "Most convenient." He is now at the last volume, *The Confident Years*, of the literary history that began with *The Flowering of New England* in 1936, and is surrounded by huge bottles of ink. He still exclaims, "Capital!" for something he admires—a word that hasn't been heard in the United States since he graduated from Harvard, still spells *labour* British-fashion, and with his hair cut *en brosse*, the tweed jacket and tie in which (I am sure) he sits down to write every morning, looks in this wonderful old country house the complete (if slightly debonair) man of letters. I half expected Oliver Wendell Holmes and Louisa May Alcott to appear at any minute.

To my relief Van Wyck finally said of Hannah's manuscript "It will do!" and trotted out the cocktails. When I admitted to my latest marital mishap, he looked positively rosy. "Goodness," he said. "I've never any trouble with *my* wives!"

*The Origins of Totalitarianism* has been rejected by the Boston publisher who had an option on it. The publisher of course did not look into the book himself but sent it to a Harvard professor of government. The verdict: I don't agree with it, send it back! Hannah distraught. Fortunately I am still a literary adviser to Harcourt

Brace; took the book to its chief editor Bob Giroux. He must have stayed up all night to read it, because he called me in the morning sounding reverential. "It's a great book. Of course we'll publish it."

F. O. Matthiessen has jumped to his death from a mean hotel in Boston opposite the North Station. Forty-eight. The Boston papers had been crucifying "this professor" for his "subversive" opinions. Much is being made of the fact that he carefully put aside his Yale Skull-and-Bones key before he leaped. He is being portrayed on the Left, especially in Europe, even by the anti-Stalinist Ignazio Silone, as "a casualty of the cold war," another victim of Joe McCarthy, though in fact he had been catastrophically lonely since the death of his lover, the painter Russell Cheney.

What a strange relationship Matty and I had—it was so curiously political. As a critic he was essentially formalist, but his wealth and his essential isolation as a much-tormented human being (at the Salzburg lectures he seemed positively wired to explode) gave him a guilt-borne sympathy for the losers in America. And he *was* "religious." He wrote books about Eliot and Dreiser, but it was Eliot he loved; Dreiser was just a symbol to him—his tenuous contact with lower America. He liked me without genuine interest in my work, invited me to replace him during the sabbatical year at Harvard in which he took his life, and astonished me by suddenly writing me about his father's death on a California highway. His letters were usually defensive about views of the Soviet Union and the American labor movement that I thought naive, totally abstract, patronizingly upper class.

But what extraordinary human interest he presents, like a tragic figure in a novel—what a compulsive personal history. However much one respects his criticism, it is impossible to think of him as just a critic, the gentlemanly Harvard professor on Beacon Hill. He *was* a "casualty," but perhaps less of the Cold War than of the mysterious inner self that caused him to explode into the rest of us.

\*    \*    \*

George Orwell has died of tuberculosis, forty-seven. What a loss, what a loss. If Kafka became the head and symbol of "the age of anxiety," Orwell was the hero of whatever fight literature in our ghastly time has put up against totalitarianism. In 1939 *Homage to Catalonia* overwhelmed me: Orwell still believed in the just society even as he was running for his life from Stalinist police in Spain. In 1940 *Inside the Whale* portrayed (and without animus) Henry Miller as the perfect example of insular literature in our time. When I finally got to England at the beginning of 1945 and caught up with *The Lion and the Unicorn: Socialism and the English Genius* and his trenchant reviews in the independent Labour *Tribune*, of which he was literary editor, I felt that thanks to him, there was still something to be said for the individual socialist conscience (if not for "socialism" in party terms).

Doctrinaires like Raymond Williams and sentimentalists like C. P. Snow of course hated *1984*. It was "opposed to the future." But the future was already here, despotism of the party in the name of the irreproachable "socialist" state. More than any other writer in English, Orwell knew that this suspicion and even hatred of individual rights *was* the darkness clouding our time. So of course even the Labour Party secretary in Limehouse dismissed Orwell as "not one of us!" when I interviewed him on Labour's plans for the "new" postwar England I was always hearing about. Everywhere in Orwell's writings there was a realism about Hitler the aggressor, a hot patriotic concern for the English people, that impressed me all the more because at home sour disabused radicals like Edmund Wilson and Dwight Macdonald insisted that Hitler's was just another imperialist war.

Orwell "not one of us"? Before the war he had written in *The Road to Wigan Pier*:

We are living in a world in which nobody is free, in which hardly anybody is secure, in which it is almost impossible to be honest and to remain alive . . . and this is merely a preliminary state, in a country still rich with the loot of a hundred years. Presently there may be coming God knows what horrors—horrors of which, in this sheltered island, we have not even a traditional knowledge.

And then came *1984.*

How I wanted to meet him! But every time I went to the *Tribune* office, he was in Germany or France or trying in some unlikely place to get the better of his lung disease. In his cubicle I could still smell the rough shag tobacco he favored in the cigarettes that helped to kill him.

Horrible *Commentary* dinner last night. Insufferable to be in that gaseous anxiously self-congratulatory atmosphere of Jewish radicals of the thirties prosperously reappearing in the fifties as ex-radicals. Ideologues in every generation, no matter what their latest cause, they have not the slightest interest in social evidence—in poverty, in race hatred (except when "they" turn on us), in workers found to be "unemployable" by the latest technocratic revolution. And now they have found their latest cause in another ideology they call "America." America is just as unreal to them as the Soviet Union was.

Wild with hunger, wandered in an orchard of breasts hanging like fruit, of bodies like knotted trunks in a jungle mad with growth, clinging vines, and wild underbrush below.

Minneapolis, the University of Minnesota: Just an hour ago, when the coffee began to perk in Barney Bowron's kitchen, and thinking, still thinking over the long voyage I had made in the night, one single stroke cut through the ifs and buts, and in a moment there flashed into my mind the first bars of the Bach E Minor Violin Concerto, my old nickname for Asya formed on my lips, and I was home, home in our old kitchen and its smell of coffee.

How glorious it was walking out this morning along these sandy baseball lots and long private green roads near the freight cars—took myself back, found the *Walker* again, it will be good. Glow of sun on my chest, the railroad bridge across the Mississippi rising and falling in its subtle grades. Emptiness and quiet of the Sunday street in Minneapolis. Sang to myself as I walked along, saluted the sun, gave myself the gift of myself, after all the boring distractions of people in the house yesterday. The long, absolute slant of mind in me cannot be deflected without trouble. But these are days, to be more so when I return to New York, of the most intense rejoicing and creativity.

The sun in Barney Bowron's study fills me with inexpressible joy. I am alive, alive, I am fully in touch goldenly alive this moment; it has never been more wonderful. Step by step and step by step, every hour is growth and learning. The sun at the windows makes me tremble with delight.

Gandhi—"I do not believe in people telling others of their faith, especially with a view to conversion. Faith does not permit telling. It has to be lived and then it is self-propagating."

In the train back to New York from Josie Herbst's, where I spent the day. When I went out in the morning there were great thick heavy clouds constantly moving; I felt as if they had launched me in movement.

Turn of the year, turn of the earth's wheel. Josie is sick, worried, more impacted than usual. She is to go to New York Hospital in three weeks or so (whenever they have a free bed) for an operation. A growth on her neck. The day with her was boring and moving by turns; as always, a little strange. Ever since I've known her (can admit this only now) I've felt in her a kind of inner panic, hypnotized by her own disintegration. Her genius is entirely as a person, from the heart. She is inexpressibly rare; you can depend on her for absolute spontaneity, goodness, considerateness. But years in her house alone, stewing over John Herrmann, have sopped her badly. With me she is painfully submissive and much too humble. But probably only because she is so scared.

Josie is a tragedy—the writer who is almost too nice within, too decent, altogether too womanly, without the assertive intelligence for balance, either as a woman or as a writer. As a human being she is all echoes of Sioux City long ago, of the "Valley of Democracy" that the Midwest once represented to its own people. Now she is frightened, penniless, very much alone in that house. The silence she lives with! Yesterday at twilight I sat in the middle room across from her (each of us staring without a word at the green outside the other's window). It twisted me to see her looking so yellow and sick—pale in the light—contracted within her own fear. But then I saw her face as a young woman, the chin squared, wisps of her blond hair, her absolute naturalness. It always repels me to see the way she sucks at a half-smoked cigarette. Every ashtray in the house is full of those wet pulps. Yet this, like the way she talks in her growling, tobacco-sputtering voice (just like the mad push and pull with which she drives), suddenly brought back all that archaic revolution-bent naturalness of the 1930s. Josie is the living ghost of herself.

Rotten day yesterday. Fussed about with the Summer chapter in the *Walker*, getting nowhere, so flew off to Ninth Avenue, all the lyric motifs of my inner life beginning again as I walk. Those unknown streets on the far West Side, midtown, charm me by their dusty obscurity. Red-brick houses, a woman fingering a flowerpot, a drunk in an open shirt lying across a cellar door. The modest little French restaurants on Ninth Avenue—the Brittany, the Paris-Brest. In the Fifty-seventh Street bus watched with fascination a slightly overripe woman done up in style—marvelous tweed suit, alligator pumps, a great thick bun at the back of her head, a jangle of frippery at her wrists and around her neck. She was obviously feeling good—Saturday afternoon, etc.—but not a hausfrau, certainly not a woman with children, to judge from the way she clucked a little too publicly at the babe in front of her. She was in an absolute idiocy of enjoyment: God, just to look at her, her body so soft and satisfied in her suit; one shoe dangling off her toes; her mouth so selfish but ecstatically pouting at the window for everything she saw.

To Hannah Arendt's for dinner with the Russian French historian of science and philosophy Alexandre Koyré. Heinrich Bluecher as usual greeted me with a lecture, making the same brilliant citations from others he always makes in his defiant way. But my lack of contact with him last night was my own fault. So drawn to Hannah these days that I resent him? I'm not in love with her, just enchanted with her learning and her depths of insight. Heinrich the veteran of the kaiser's army, the political refugee who was the German Communist Party's "military expert," is all autodidact—and never lets you forget a thing he's learned, though much of it must come from Hannah, with her classical scholarship. Mysteriously, Hannah in the manuscript of *The Origins of Totalitarianism* said the book owed everything to Heinrich's "political philosophy." I can hardly believe that.

The talk at dinner was not very good. Was surprised and a little nettled (decline of the idol?) by Hannah's eagerness to please Koyré, the historian, her compliance, and Heinrich's sudden flourish of "good manners." Returned to my room lonely and scared. I just wanted to weep. Got into bed, said I would live another day, and here I am. *I will not give up.* I will not give up on my book, my son, on all those people I love and who love me. I have work to do. I still have a whole life to live. I will *not* give up. God, my God, teach me to be patient as I have already learned to be firm. My real time is yet to come. God, my God, there is nothing to do with this life but to think, to understand, to be aware—to love the predicament of being alive. No miracles please, no shortcuts, no violations of the human connection, no anger at people for disappointing you, no disappointment with them for being only themselves, as you wish for nothing so much in this life as to be yourself!

Listen, the wind over the roofs bears good tidings. On this last breath of summer air . . .

Met Ann. She has just won the Dodd Mead novel contest for college students with a novel about a rabbi deficient in holiness, *Star of Glass,* and her editor at Dodd Mead, Elizabeth Stille, assured her at this Italian restaurant in the Village that I could be helpful to her career. Turns out her father is the rabbi of the Actor's Temple on Forty-seventh Street. *The* rabbi in her book for whom the Star of David is "glass"? Rabbi's daughter or not, she is a blond wisecracker who comes on like show biz and leaned on me very confidently in the taxi when I took her home—Seventh Avenue and Fifty-fourth Street, Times Square!

Yaddo. Elizabeth Bishop's hair is thick and rises electrically on her head. That crisply warm voice of hers moves in measures as careful as her poems, shyly picking out the syllables, and when it comes to something she cares about (Dylan Thomas a moment ago) the hair shoots up straight, connected node to node by sparks. . . . That upsweeping electric hair is the poet's helmet, his rooster comb. Used to notice it in Robert Frost, and in Cal Lowell—it is the shield on which they take their blows, but it is also the flag breaking out in excitement. The electric shock of it is what I love—straight up and down, calmly burning. But these sudden moods can be scary. In the taxi taking us to a bar down on Union Avenue, Elizabeth began to heave and choke with an asthma attack. She got the inhaler out of her purse just in time.

Before he began his great novel, Proust found a seemingly inexplicable pleasure in watching three belfries in the plain. They seemed constantly to alter their relations, one to another, in space. Suddenly he asked for a pencil, and at once composed a fragment that he later inserted, almost unchanged, in the text of "Swann":

> I never gave what I had written a second thought, but when I had finished setting down my thoughts, I felt so happy, so sure that I had satisfactorily disposed of those belfries and of the truth concealed in them, that, just as though I myself had been a fowl and laid an egg, I started to sing at the top of my voice.

William James—

> The reason why we *do* pray . . . is simply that we cannot help praying. . . . In spite of all that "science" may do the contrary, men will pray to the end of time, unless their mental nature changes in a manner which nothing we know should lead us to expect. The impulse to pray is a necessary consequence of

the fact that whilst the innermost of the empirical selves of a
man is a Self of the social sort, it can yet find its only ade-
quate *Socious* [*sic*] in an ideal world.

Have just come back from an hour-and-a-half's visit with my son.
Seeing him as I do once a week, for a romp in the park, and with so
long a period of absence from him ahead of me, I must think out
everything I can humanly do so as to make our relationship deep,
tender, and durable. He understands so much already, and we talk
so well to each other, that I must get over the strain of my own life,
sacrifice everything to clarity, tenderness, understanding.

He is now two and a half. His extraordinary buoyancy and direct
interest in everything! Whatever he likes to do, he does with his
whole heart. And if he has done it once, he wants to do it again and
again. I am so moved and excited every time I see him that it takes
an effort for me to be quiet enough with him, to let *him* play. I love
him with my whole heart and think every day how awful it is that I
never see him go to bed, or rise in the morning.

She was born Channa or Anna, is now Ann, is the baby of the
family, the prettiest, and as the only blond among so many dark sib-
lings is much cherished as "Honey," the family favorite and genius
who graduated from Queens College with highest honors and wrote
the prizewinning novel about a rabbi who does not live up to his
vows.

The dark apartment on Fifty-fourth off Seventh Avenue still
looks and feels crowded, though most have departed. Everyone is
positively nailed to the father, he is so dominant here. There is a
constant smell of cooking and more *Yiddishkeit* than I expected to
find off Times Square. The children have Yiddish nicknames, fall
naturally into Yiddish folk expressions they have heard from Papa

the rabbi. In my brief, recently terminated experience of married life on Park Avenue, Madison at Seventieth, Central Park West, the word "Jew" was never heard. Here everything is *Jew, Jew, Jew* wherever you look and whatever you hear. On one wall a reproduction of Marc Chagall's fiercely concentrated dark-bearded rabbi in prayer shawl and phylacteries. On another the drawing of a beshawled Yiddish mother still "over there," mistily reading a letter from America. Plaque after plaque from Jewish clubs, federations, and fraternal lodges acknowledging the rabbi's active leadership and many good works.

The rabbi himself is tiny, clean-shaven, agile, immensely intelligent, sharp-witted, and sad. So many sharpies and Broadway wisecrackers to manipulate here! Even on the surface he is so little a man of God that he openly reads the *Forward*, the Yiddish labor paper that in the right-hand corner of the front page still summons Jewish laborers (are there any left?) to socialism—"Workers of the world unite! You have nothing to lose but your chains!"

I can see where daughter got the ammunition for her portrait of a disappointing rabbi in *Star of Glass*. The Mogen David *can* seem like glass if you have wistful thoughts of religious transcendence. Among the Jews *I* know, "God" is not so much an object of belief or disbelief as a given, a fundamental part of the Jewish *experience*, our very oldest habit, and more to be argued with and on occasion blamed for our many misfortunes than adored the way a Catholic "adores" the Virgin Mary. He is all too familiar, the head of the whole strange project Jews have lived in history since God knows when. I have never associated rabbis with holiness. Observant, nonobservant, Jews sit at the same table, for we are more a family than a religion.

And this rabbi is all father, founder, protector of his flock—a poignant figure in some ways. He lost his first wife in the influenza epidemic of 1918, and with three little children on his hands married this rather primitive fat blond from the Ukraine who gave him two more daughters, but who is so inert and always at her food that the distraught rabbi calls her "Plumpy."

What it is to be a Jew in fear of his life! In 1915 this young immigrant from Brest-Litovsk, a graduate of the famous Slobodka Yeshiva, was in Atlanta without a pulpit, a fundraiser for Jewish organizations. Two years before, a fourteen-year-old girl, Mary Phagan, was found murdered in the basement of the National Pencil Company, where the Texas-born Leo Frank was plant superintendent. Frank was arrested the next day and charged with the crime solely on the testimony of a Negro employee, James Conley, who had been seen carrying the body of the murdered girl by an employee who was afraid to testify—Atlanta had been whipped into a frenzy against Frank, "the Jew."

Frank was found guilty and sentenced to death; people in the courtroom howled for his blood. In his magazine *The Jeffersonian*, Tom Watson, the Populist Party's candidate for president in 1904, repeatedly demanded the execution of the "filthy, perverted Jew of New York." Watson founded the "Knights of Mary Phagan," which sought to organize a boycott of all Jewish stores and businesses in Georgia. The governor ruined his political career by commuting Frank's death sentence to life imprisonment. But, goaded by Watson, a mob dragged Leo Frank from jail in August 1915 and lynched him.

Ann's father was one of many Jews who fled Georgia for New York. He eventually was made rabbi of the Actor's Temple. "Stars of stage and screen" came not only to attend services but to join the rabbi on the pulpit for an exchange of witty remarks. The rabbi is essentially a quiet man, not a wisecracker like his daughter, a man much tried by life and his present wife, but he wearily rises to the occasion, exchanging witticisms when Buddy Hackett is making everyone howl with laughter and Sophie Tucker is proudly pointed out in the congregation.

What a complex character Ann is—so critical of rabbis for not being holy enough, yet more show biz than her father. She is intense about *A Walker in the City*. We sit over the ms. in one cafeteria or another (New York's only real cafés, you can sit there all afternoon with Isaac Bashevis Singer at the next table. Bars are too dark to read and write in). She is editing it with the most minute care.


Key West: From her days with John Herrmann at Hemingway's in Key West, Josie Herbst remembered this funny old wooden hotel on the main drag. Here, at least, Key West is still part of some quiet edge of Latin America long passed up by the gringos. Ann and I feel lucky and happy in our torrid upstairs room. Though the hotel feels as shaky as the pitiful two posts on the street helping to hold it up, we have a balcony and a stained-glass window at the end of the corridor. I am getting very fond of that balcony. Standing there I can see into the little cigar factory across the street where humble old Latinos roll up cigars, finally licking the last leaf around them. They are read to as they work, as nuns are read to when they eat together.

Happy, loving days. Tropical languor even on this cold morning, with the sun shining in my eyes. The palm leaves bend under the weight of the suddenly loosed winds. Along the waterfront the ghostly red-brick warehouses patiently receiving and discharging. White paint splashed along the old houses. In the Gulf, where two fishing shacks are lazily half-keeled over, the sun falls directly athwart the peaked cabin.

Josie Herbst asked Pauline Hemingway to meet me when I flew down first from Miami. She drove me to the Hemingway house. I was bewitched by the road from the airport, green water at one side, palm trees nodding on the other, everything in bloom. Small, dark, penetrating, sleek as they come, Hemingway's ex-wife sort of bewitched me too as she sighed over our destitute, broken friend Josie Herbst: "A woman shouldn't be that poor." Pauline certainly isn't. The house is wonderful in its sprawling, leisurely way. People talking slowly together in the heat, very slowly. Among them Joyce's early antagonist in *Ulysses,* Dr. Oliver St. John Gogarty, Buck Mulligan himself. And living up to form and his reputation for malice, he was actually gossiping about Joyce, his *carte de visite* to every literary home in the Western world. What a fellow! I actually heard him sneer, "Joyce and Nora didn't even marry until their first grandchild came along!"

Aboard the *Île de France.* Ann has won a Fulbright to Paris to write about Scott Fitzgerald and Zelda. She doesn't read much, but identifies furiously with literary characters out of the twenties. I refuse to play Scott Fitzgerald, but how intensely she can do Zelda.

I am to lecture on American writers at the Salzburg Seminar, the University of Cologne and Cambridge. Nothing like working your way through Europe on the strength of *On Native Grounds!* The fog horn blasts and blasts, and the sea outside and the air and the planks underfoot are all very wet. Long peaceful days on board with Ann. Have never known such uninterruptedly happy days, and even in separate cabins such electric joy.

George Woodcock, the Canadian anarchist writer, is on board with his wife. They took pity on our separated state, lent us their cabin for the afternoon.

We were in that little restaurant overlooking the Seine just off the Quai Voltaire. A day of rain, the gray stones of Paris older and more plaintive in the rain. You could hear taxis skid, wheels tracing invisible figures in the stones, see the young men in their ponchos crouched behind the pedal bars of their bicycles furiously wheeling through the traffic. And suddenly I found the tone, the full opening note for the scene in Forty-second Street I want for *The Open Street.* Rain in the city, the heart turns inward, and the mind laps comfortably at study. Safe and snug in the restaurant between the potted palms I thought of all the days of rain I sat through in the library for my first book, seeking *the inwardmost place.*

I am too much concerned with the small, pettiest details of life abroad; no French person ever understands my French; but before me, from the seventh (much despised) floor of the Lutetia, on the Boulevard Raspail, I study with rapture the chimney pots of Paris, the gray, dark sky. Rain, rain, let it rain, I am *inside*, I am following to the end the trail through the labyrinth of the city's unrest.

The bells of Paris. As I lay in bed listening to them, my first thought that someone in the city was striking at random tin plates. On the roofs, the chimney pots, the cobblestones. The bells could have been any sound. And thinking of the ghostly sighs, wheezings, and and rumbles of the buoy bell in the harbor at Le Havre as we were coming in after a night dancing on the glass floor of the main salon, I went on with my thought—some great bell ringer willfully hitting, up and down the city, anything he could lay his hand on—his clapper.

At Kappy's, H. J. Kaplan. You have to be from Newark to get this addicted to France and the French, but the impersonation is getting better and better. When I met him in Paris in July 1945, the first day there for each of us, he knew his way perfectly when he drove me to the Opéra, gaily talking all the while about Meyer Schapiro's article in *Partisan Review.* Seven years later he walks into a restaurant with his poodle, murmurs, *"Comment dirai-je?"* (How shall I put it?) as he languorously slopes into his chair, the perfect *habitué.* Even the high ceilings in Kappy's living room expose that peculiarly gray, *studious* light in which French men of letters are always photographed. When I first read *Madame Bovary* I saw light as the French essence, present in every room Flaubert pictured for me.

Last night, walking up from dinner to the Pantheon, I saw that light again—not as brilliantly soft blue as the unforgettable night in July '45 when I saw it for the first time over the Pont Alexandre III, but with the same effect here despite the dampness of the evening— the continuously melting light of the Île de France, a light that every particle of the sky soaks in, a light of which your first impression is that it is without limits.

To the Bois de Boulogne in the early aft with Ann and the art historian Robert Rosenblum after a delicious lunch; then to visit with Monsieur et Madame Henri Petsch in their vast *appartement* on the Avenue Mozart. The little rugs and drapes on the walls, the little bookshelves everywhere—in the inner Orient the bourgeoisie can contrive in Paris, little cubbyholes and resting places for comfort, literary and artistic. In the evening to Sacré-Coeur, then by way of Pigalle through Montmartre back to the hotel. The seamy Broadway Paris—stink of piss, too many whores—bars, bars, bars everywhere you look. Going back on the Métro I recited the stations along the route like a chant of welcome to myself.

My thirty-sixth birthday. I write the number but don't believe it. In the last year I have begun to live—and now the days and years rush by so fast that I forget to regret it. The days fill up, they fill up, I am carried along the top of the wave.

Leaving the restaurant on Monsieur le Prince, Ann and I felt so good we sang in the street. A workman in blue overalls leaning drunkenly against the wall growled: "Vous *avez la chance de chanter!*"

Headline in *L'Humanité:* LOUIS ARAGON CONDEMNS U.S. GERM WARFARE IN KOREA. You can see what importance the French attach to a famous writer even if he hasn't had an opinion of his own in twenty years.

Ann is attracted to writers, fits in companionably at a moment's notice, laughingly brings them out in all sorts of funny ways. She got James Baldwin to make up subjects for *Commentary*—by non-Jews. Jimmy: "A Negro Looks at Henry James."

Because of my passion for Henry Adams, I dragged Ann to Chartres. A long line of boys and girls for confirmation passed out of the cathedral; and when they had gone the lights went out, the cathedral went dark again, the stones took over. Gray on gray in great even blocks: the dark cement line between them the only measure of time itself. A cathedral can be entered anywhere, the doors here lead straight in from town. The measure with which people walk—the steps of thought itself.

In the procession leaving the church a young impassioned priest chanted the Ave Maria in full voice all by himself. This will never pass away. At the front the Royal Portal, the figures are a little chipped; the sandy gray dust points, in the same instant perspective, toward the hollows worn in the steps below. But the venerability of the church is its pride; and this, too, will never pass away. So in these middle days full of sun, lurching into summer, there are pilgrims everywhere in this fragile half-restored France, perhaps not going into the church to pray, but to see and to believe that so much is left. How delicate the monuments of Europe are this summer, with what wonder the pilgrims of culture gather around, in lederhosen, in Miami jackets—we are of all countries this summer—to see the monument itself, Chartres.

Chartres, Chartres. I have waited eighteen years for this moment since I first read *Mont-Saint-Michel and Chartres* at college. My first surprise now is of its overwhelming bareness, unassumingness, the union of all forces here, with the great rose window at their head, converging to a common end in the heart. And then I saw the straight "simplicity" of Chartres in all its force, and thought of the stones descending, in their white powdery gray dust to meet, in the immemorial silence and the dark.

I felt like weeping when I saw the boys and girls in Chartres Cathedral—those girls all in white carrying prayer books, those boys with white sashes tied on one arm. I was thinking of Michael and perhaps of all childhood itself, with its infinite dumb expectation.

We bundle into the Italian train carriage loaded down, each of us with a swollen Val-A-Pak and a "portable" Royal typewriter in a heavy metal case. Getting our monumental four pieces into the overhead rack already crammed with the assorted goods of the passengers invariably packed together as we laboriously make our way in! "*Americani!*" they hiss. But once the train starts rolling again, we are tolerated, fellow prisoners.

Pisa: The concierge irritated by our asking for a room together when our passports plainly show we are not married. Nastily made a point of addressing Ann as *Signorina.*

Truly wonderful days with Ann. Right at the tip of the flame: our faces looking at each other as we come.

In the train from Pisa yesterday, a deaf-mute boy traveling with his mother and sister and an older woman. The vibrations of the train repeatedly alarmed him, and without stopping he cried in short wails with his mouth open—*ah-ah-ah-ah!* His face blazed with astonishment and pain. The sound went right through my belly; I hated minding his cries, but I did. *Ah-ah-ah-ah!* It was an absolute protest, from top to bottom. A fat man across the aisle couldn't contain himself even as the woman was taking the boy out at a local station, shouted, "Why don't you leave your cripple home?!" She turned on him. "It's *you* who are abnormal!"

Met Harold Clurman in Florence. He was his usual charmingly studious self as he discussed the cost of superhotel living in Florence. "A thousand bucks a day," he said, grinning. "Come up to the hotel, say hello to Stella!" Stella Adler was in a bed vast and ornate, languid, theatrically beautiful as ever, playfully held out a hand to kiss. Her bra hung over the front of the bed. Reminded me of the forties, when the Group Theater people had gone to Hollywood and Stella in an open car drove me over hill and dale to show me Southern California. She was wearing long suede gloves that went up half her arm, munching a bagel as she drove.

So in a hurry to catch the train to Salzburg, I left my raincoat behind. Telegram from Ann when I arrived at the Schloss: HAVE YOUR COAT. LOVE YOU BOTH.

In John Berryman's mad biography of Stephen Crane. Scooping up a handful of sand on the Asbury beach and tossing it to the sea breeze, "watching it, 'Treat your notions like that,' he said sideways to Arthur Oliver lazily—'Forget what you think about it and tell how you feel about it.'"

And this—"An artist, I think, is nothing but a powerful memory that can move itself at will through certain experiences sideways and every artist must be in some things powerless as a dead snake."

\*　　\*　　\*

There are times in Europe, in the ineradicable strangeness of Europe, when I feel out in space rather than on land. I am swimming to the motion of planets I cannot see. Look: This is me: So let it be beyond praise or blame or disagreement. I am ending my apprenticeship, I am ending my apprenticeship, I am beginning to think. The German who sits next to me at lunch, whom I am prepared to fear and to flee, I can and shall be *me* with him. The Jews I incorporate in myself, I can and do leave as the occasion warrants, as and when some world truth larger than the Jews presents itself. The Christian culture I respect will not bring me a step nearer to Christianity, and I will sit in the courtyard behind their church waiting for them to catch up with me. A truth, a simplicity, a way to God that is beyond praise or blame, just an echo of one's own heart. I am ending my apprenticeship, I am ending my apprenticeship—O joy O joy, so much am I beginning to think for myself. I need not defy anyone or anybody; but can love my own life, wherever I am, even among enemies. And to love the truth even when ridiculed by your countrymen.

Every independent Jew rebels against the Jews—they are the earth from which he is born. Every original Jew relives Jewish history by passing *himself* through it. The trouble with Jewish solidarity—an inexpressible compassion for one's own history. The glory of being in the truth, Jewish or not, is to find a love higher than solidarity. Love may not be "enough," but without it—*niente*.

Salzburg and Salzburg roads, for those who gather here by chance and wait for accidental beings like themselves. Yet the road is perfectly silent, with people sitting like matter thrown off by the sun.

Country roads leading out of Salzburg, and I on a bench with the doctor, singing to the sky in a cracked voice. Now I know why the *ping!* of the radar signal against the moon has stuck with me so long from the time I first encountered it in the newsreel. I sing to break through the silence, and sometimes, you know, I sing to the silence itself.

\* \* \*

Two Jews. I went into a church and sat on a wooden bench and looked up the groins to the ceiling. I floated up there on high like Jesus—not part of the congregation, but a stranger in the church, like Jesus. The only direction I could look was up, to where he lay in the ceiling, high over my head. So he and I were together—in the church but not of it. I waited there a long time, bruising my forehead against the stone ribs in the ceiling, and when I got lonely, talked to him there:

Listen, I am here as a visitor, and so are you. I have so much to ask you. Are you embarrassed to be so much made of here? Are you ever uncomfortable? Is there not *something* another Jew can bring you at last? Funny as it sounds, I feel I am watching out for you in a place like this. So what is the sound of the rain on the roof at night, when you are completely alone in here? What do you feel when the Franciscan brother with the apron dusts you off on your altar, presents you with flowers, bows the knee to you, and crosses himself in the terrified silence between the altar and the street?

Tell me: don't be like Papa God, who has not said a word for millennia. Tell me! Does the scent of all these lilies ever make you sneeze? Will you ever unbend your knees?

UNSERE IST EINE OPTISCHE ZEIT proclaims the great banner in Cologne over the proud exhibition along the Rhine of sparkling bright, ultraprecise German telescopes, microscopes, and camera goods. Ours certainly is a "visual period," especially in a prosperous, resurrected Germany still full of ruins and ruined people exposing every period of its twentieth-century history. Idiot fat caryatids left nakedly standing, from the brown city mansions of Wilhelmine Germany that no longer exist. Block after block after block, loose mounds of brick blowing up the same yellow dust yellow. Rebuilt Cologne is shiny, neon-lighted, looks as hurriedly and cheaply made

as a housing project in Harlem. The pale "American-style" buildings rise above ruins like the pink skin grafted onto the faces of so
many wounded soldiers. The push for *Lebensraum* in flattened
Cologne is ferocious. In Ehrenfeld, hundreds of people still live in
air-raid shelters. A young doctor who visits in the poorest quarter
says, "The automobiles in Cologne live better than many people.
The garages of the new-rich have windows; the people underground have none."

Ann hated to come, she fears Germans so much; but here she is.
And here, too, is Hannah Arendt, now here to accept a literary
prize. Hannah the refugee on Morningside Drive is a great favorite
in Germany, has translated *The Origins of Totalitarianism* to great
acclaim, but is puffed up here, impossible. She condescends to Ann,
calling her "Little One."

Ann's uneasiness in Germany is of course a bond between us, but
she is so disturbed here that I am frightened. My eager pal and
drinking companion on every wild impromptu excursion in France,
Belgium, Holland, Italy, is terrified by being in Germany at all, and
clings to me against the dreary rubble.

No matter how casually Hannah tries to reassure her, we are in
Germany, and we are Jews in Germany. I am endlessly curious about
them—the language, their heavy civility, their terrible seriousness,
the stories my colleagues at the university are always just about to
tell me about the war or the pre-Hitler Left. To Ann they are all
murderers and dominate her dreams. She is a fantastic dreamer (as
perhaps only storytellers can be), wakes up every morning exhausted
by the three-volume story she dreamed during the night. Her sudden utter *homelessness* here makes me realize for the first time how
thin a veneer her wisecracking is, how ready she is to be annihilated. The nights are for powerful dreams, the mornings for despair.

I am fascinated with her but totally unprepared for such an
unceasing flow of temperament: "You have never met anyone at all
like me." Every moment is at the peak of the moment; the flash, the
wild merriment, then the sudden descent, make up a daily drama. At
least in Germany it may not be interrupted. "*Why did you drag me*

*here?"* I get sucked into this drama day after day, amazed by the *ecstasy* she puts into so much emotion.

So we went down the Rhine to Basel this beautiful June day in 1952 and got married. As we entered the town hall for the ceremony, young Swiss recruits in uniform, laughing to beat the band, held up hands to show their wedding rings and shouted: *"Nicht! Nicht!"*

Home again. Nixon is now a senator, but still outraged by "atheistic Communism." Whittaker Chambers on *Time* used to invite colleagues suspected of a radical past to confess to him. And here he is in *Witness*—"No man lightly reverses the faith of a lifetime, held implacably to the point of criminality. He reverses it only with a violence greater than the force of the faith he is repudiating." Faith! Implacably! Criminality! Violence! As Harold Rosenberg says, this guy was never interested in politics.

America, I love you. With all these Dostoyevsky characters running around, I am trying to describe the original myth of America, to *imagine* the promise that has been life for me and millions of immigrants in what I call *The Western Island*. The outpost for so many yet to come, when "in the beginning all the world was America" (John Locke). Reading the history of American settlement, I cannot wait to get us to the final, the destined place, to set the oceans together on each side of, yes, God's own country.

How fervently Europeans in the Renaissance debated the question: "Is it providential, this discovery of America—or merely an accident?" God was so real then, it had to be considered providential, for the white European man, by the very "range of his reason," had access to the secret of creation—knew why the continents had been arrayed as they had been, and so could guess at what lay beyond the seas—to round out beyond the last European cape to Thule. Europe was the center, and Europe's God had appointed the white man to inhabit the temperate zones and to know reason—i.e., to manipulate nature, to bend it to his purpose, and *re-create himself* to it.

The discovery of America had to be providential, for as there was now a new *world* to consider, man the favorite of Heaven alone had the God-given power to deal with it. Which brings us to the atom bomb.

Truman—"We are in a new era of destructive power, capable of creating explosions of a new order of magnitude, dwarfing the clouds of Hiroshima and Nagasaki." As for Russia:

> There has been no challenge like this in the history of our republic. We are called upon to rise to the occasion as no people before us. . . . In this changed, disrupted, chaotic situation, the United States and the Soviet Union emerged . . . on a scale unmatched by any other nation. . . . For our part, we in this Republic . . . are freemen, heirs of the American Revolution, dedicated to the truths of our Declaration of Independence.

U.S. Attorney General James F. McGranery attacks Charlie Chaplin as "an unsavory character . . . making statements that indicate a leering, sneering attitude toward a country whose hospitality has enriched him."

Headline in yesterday's *World-Telegram:* MCCARTHY PLEDGES HE WON'T HOG RED HUNTING.

*   *   *

Wellfleet: Back on the blessed Cape again after thirteen years. I had forgotten the lightness of the air, the cleanness and briskness of the small shrub pine off the dunes, the sand, and sand anywhere I walk off the road. Forgotten the white houses still bright in the afternoon sun, the gold knobs on an ancient door, the plainness of rowboats resting in the grass.

Race Point, Long Point, Highland Light in Truro. So happy to be back, all intermediate visits here rubbed out in the glow of remembering Asya and me in Provincetown thirteen years ago—the dunes just outside town where Eugene O'Neill and later Edmund Wilson lived for a season, coming into town only for supplies—dunes leading to the ocean and the old, long-deserted Peaked Hills Coast Guard Station that constantly drew me back—it so clearly marked the last outpost of the inhabitable world. What is it that haunts me here, drives me to the last possible place?

Neilson professor at Smith. Living in the Neilson apartment at 58 Paradise Road, overlooking Paradise Pond. Paradise enow! Sat down to write about the old scholar-women I seem to see everywhere around here, and who make me wonder what lies behind their external dryness and punctiliousness. The "nice old 'lady'" image they present to the public. Oh dear, old dear, this professional decent drabness—'tis not right, 'tis not nature. That unnaturally stiff lady I saw walking into Paradise Road this morning, the housemate of Mary Ellen Chase, author of a popular book on the Bible—gets through more martinis than I thought possible whenever she invites us in of an afternoon. The housemate walks hard and stiff with such a commanding air. What an attempt to persuade the outside world that the fires *are* well-banked in order to make this appearance without! Took Ann aside as we were leaving and whispered, "*We* know who the real writer is in the family, don't we?"

\*　　\*　　\*

This endless rewriting of American history—of this essentially modern-age story told over and over again from essentially the same "moderate" point of view. The disproportion of scholarly energy to the subject exists, as the mythological invention of America does in *Leaves of Grass* and *Moby-Dick*, to give America *a home in the spirit.* The tremendous industriousness of the first American historians— they were not so much the students of American history as the creators of it. The American writer even in the twentieth century, for all his realism about this society, is still creating some first ideas about the country.

The flight of birds in Homer, in Dante, in Virgil: the prime symbol in classical literature for movement in the world, for unsettlement, for change. The flight of birds: No other symbol has ever meant, can ever mean, so much to the mind for which the world is never simply here and now, and to which the breath of life is a dark line moving away from everything we have in this world.

Just finished washing the dishes, and before I tackle my papers for tomorrow, I sit down to write this. A day, a whole solid day spent fighting with Ann, making up with Ann, going to the movies with Ann, then making love. Such is the doubleness of my life here. Quite apart from the fact that we are going to have a child, praise God, and this will make a woman petulant and strange, especially an artist-woman like my wife, I note for the record—I note it with awe—that the whole bloody day has been spent in the most passionate screaming inner closeness with her. The underlying connection between us, if ever there was one, is gone. I am so sensitive to her every mood that I was still shivering like mad when I walked—and all afternoon.

Yet as I sit writing this, I can still feel in my loins the long delicious withdrawal of sensation, the ebbing of the beautiful fire I knew, we knew, between preparing the sauce and heating up the water for the spaghetti. Not a dull moment. Reminds me of the time we were making love on the couch while the radio was on and it announced the death of Stalin.

Mama yesterday at the hospital in New York. Mama under an oxygen tent, her head wrapped in towels and looking older and more bereft than I have ever seen her. Standing with Ann on the roof walk of the hospital just off the river. A light rain falling, gulls flying, wet brick, the yellow rose I had bought her yesterday in her belt, this rose already swelled and half gone, but the only color in sight on the wet, dark brick roof.

Mama. What a catharsis. Not tragic so much as *awful*. It's like a knife in me to see her gasping for breath. And somehow it was all of a piece to see the rose in my young wife's belt as she looked down on the old woman she cares nothing about.

I prayed to You for her yesterday, and I shall go on praying. The prayer, I know, is not yet to You—it is that prayer will lead me to You.

All over the world, in all religions but perhaps connected with none, there are individuals for whom the spirit is the meaning and the final content of this life, and who will never be content until they have soldered back together the creation and man's awareness of it as the greatest gift. Such individuals, though unknown to each other, are related as they are not to their coreligionists.

I offer this without shame because it defines my solitude—and diminishes it. But I note it because of the loving way in which Ann said about Bellow, her idol: "He had been Orthodox in his youth." (He had laughingly admitted that in the toilet he could not profane a newspaper with Hebrew lettering on it.) Bellow's brilliant speculation now marks the path to our true commitment from the creeds into which we are born.

Who set the space between trees? Who set the space between the first trees and the last? In what mind was this lovely breath of space first designed? And whose mind sees it all still, as a mirror?

This beautiful text from Alfred North Whitehead's *Science and the Modern World* has always moved me so deeply by its subtlety:

Religion is a vision of something which stands beyond, behind and within the passing flux of immediate things; something which is real, and yet waiting to be realised; something which is a remote possibility, and yet the greatest of present facts; something that gives meaning to all that passes, and yet eludes apprehension; something whose possession is the final good and yet is beyond all reach; something which is the ultimate ideal, and the hopeless quest.

I write in order to become that which I write of. I write in order to lay claim to what I would like to become. The hand I write with is already flexed to take possession.

Nature is the world—i.e., only the face of the world. But the face of things is the accessible we confront in all theories of nature.

Which is why we are always questioning the world, despairing of it, trying to get beyond it to that which attaches this world to itself. The task is to *realize* the world without forgetting its mystery.

Saul Bellow, William Maxwell, Brendan Gill here at Smith to talk about *the novel.* Ann was eager to meet with Maxwell, who as fiction editor of *The New Yorker* has taken two of her stories about a New York childhood. Maxwell was wonderful, elaborating on Virginia Woolf's dreamlike projects in fiction. Bellow praised humble realism, from Defoe to Dreiser. Gill was at his most urbane—and under his usual cloak of banter quite nasty at the expense of Bellow, in whom he recognizes a coming star. Bellow does not mix with people who take him lightly, and he went white with shock. But his riposte was mild: "Maybe I can talk about Brendan Gill sometime."

Writing this on the terrace, looking at the last of the ice floes in Paradise Pond. The sun full in my face. I feel absolutely crushed today with the fullness and goodness of the world. Living roots of branches entwined and entangled. I am full, full, full of the world.

Cathrael Kazin born at Cooley Dickinson Hospital, 1:38 in the morning. Dan Aaron sweetly waited with me at the coffee shop until I was let in to see my round little daughter. We are wild with joy. Cathrael is after Ann's beloved uncle Kitriel, "Crown of God," a name Sholom Aleichem derisively gave to the town, Kasrilevske, "Little Crown of God," in which his impoverished characters live. As Tevye the milkman says, "With God's help we starved to death."

Still, "Cathrael" is quite a handful for a newborn. Ann brightly came up with "Katey," after that song the doughboys used to sing in "the Great War"—"K-K-K Katey, beautiful lady! You're the only-only one I adore!"

I wanted to remain at Smith after my wonderful visiting year as Neilson professor, but apparently one sour professor persuaded the English Department to forget it. Whereupon I am invited to Amherst, thanks to Robert Frost, who advised President Cole that I was just the old-fashioned literary type to counteract the semantics and verbal games the English Department presses on its freshmen composition courses. This is all ridiculous, since the English Department dislikes me as much as I dislike the English Department. But we have a wonderful big house on Woodside Avenue, with the most beautiful staircase, a study for each of us. The countryside is delicious, and we have nowhere else to go at the moment.

Amherst is one long street. You just get on, start walking, and trust to luck. There is no easy turnoff, no little side streets and curious alleys. Just one long street. Up and down it goes, and its name is never anything but Pleasant.

On this Pleasant Street, then, life is lived, up and down, past the college and the golf course and the Archer farm. The sidewalk is narrow, and the main street soon empties out into a highway. There is no mystery about anything here. What you see is what you get. An immense, long-suspended quietness trembles behind the blinking face of the lighted pole on our corner. That washed-down, immensely regular, almost convent-prim quality in Amherst people. People who have lived in the same house and have worked at the same college and have looked at the same trees on the same street for a very long time. Up and down this long, sane Amherst street they go. We alone are uneasy here. Love is not enough for two New York writers in Amherst. The country is beautiful, the town mute, the college indifferent.

The leaves are beginning to turn. Many are already past turning, are new colored, gentle-sharp. As I was driving down Woodside Avenue, a homely brown dog wandered into the middle of the street and stared up at me. The street was entirely silent, empty, and as I looked at the dog and he looked at me, I could see that all around him, with his long nose sniffing at me in wonder, the leaves were turning red and green and yellow.

Life is like that these days—a silent empty street, I stopping in the middle of it to be studied by a homely quiet mutt, and the new-colored edge of the world in golden flames of autumn. For how long will I live in this quietness, this newness, this positive strangeness?

God is life; the more of God you realize in the world, the more the world is alive to you. This is all the difference between the believing heart and the nonbelieving. The one sometimes feels absolutely crushed by the amount of life in the world—the constant sense of something weighing on you that asks to be obeyed to the end. The very tension of the joy it brings can be borne as the amount and force of life that you are open to in the end. (To the other, the world is "boring.") But if God is life, a great blaze of life, a surcharge, an incalculable and ever-dominating radiance of life, than it follows that this can never die—not for us!—who, being unacquainted with death as we stand in the sun, cannot conceive of anything to life except its inherent immortality. All this is inextinguishably alive, uncontainable. If you believe in God, you are continually exposed to and can never deny this great and terrible radiance of sheer being—everywhere.

The other night, dining with the head of the English Department at his Frank Lloyd Wright house, I had the strangest sense of retrogression mixed with stylish discomfort. Only this morning did I figure it out. The house is so designed that the main room has only one lamp—tubular—which casts its light upward, so that the open-hearth fireplace is the dominating sight in the room. The room itself constitutes a bleak wooden rectangle. Sitting, or should I say perched, on a cushioned wooden bench, hardly able to see and stupefied by the hickory ash in the fireplace, I felt I was back in some ancient Anglo-Saxon baronial hall, smoky, narrow, and dark—but thank God! all in good taste.

Glorious day. Just back from classes, and the riot of color makes a penumbra inside which I walk. Blaze. How many times have I, when the day is this warm, felt such a blaze within. An absolute sense of freedom, of pure lovingness.

But how difficult, difficult, for two writers who have always taken their freedom for granted, how bitterly difficult for them to live together like this, with a child and manifold duties and responsibilities, quarreling constantly about who does what.

Ann, sweeping the crumbs off the floor after dinner, then throwing the broom down with disdain: "I was not made for marriage."

This is the kind of morning that explains why one lives here. Cold, windy, clear. I got up, very early as usual, to feed the baby, and while diapering her, saw through the bathroom window an absolute drama of lights in the sky. So intense, and many, and much—such a rush of light. It was as if something keen beyond language, utterly nonhuman, was being acted out on the marble edge of its energy.

When I finally got out for my walk, I went automatically down Main Street, to say hello to Emily. Before you come to the

Dickinson house—280 Main Street—there is a yellow house that seems the soul of New England secrecy. Pale yellow picket fence saying, No, no, no, you mustn't even think of coming in! Then the long, arched narrow window of the 1850s, the bleached yellow of the house visibly crumbling into long, fluid lines, until the whole seems to liquefy and disappear into scornful thin-lipped privacy. Finally Number 280. The Dickinson house—high, grand, and proud.

I went in there with Jay Leyda back in the fall of 1951, when he had commenced his minute investigations of daily life in Amherst for *The Years and Hours of Emily Dickinson*, which follows the same relentless coverage he displayed in *A Melville Log*. He is such a zealous investigator, such a nut for detail, that he uncovered Melville's wedding certificate. Melville had actually written in the name of his mother instead of his bride. He led me up and down the backstairs of some empty house in Amherst until he could triumphantly show me Emily's last nightdress hanging in a closet!

Leyda is such a snoop after nineteenth-century lives that he is positively frightening, yet no one seems to know anything about Leyda himself. Even his "Dutch"(?) name is suspect. One rumor is that he was born Irish, then adopted. His manner is elaborate, heavily gracious, but his political opinions are commonplace Stalinist. His wife is Oriental, her background as ambiguous as Leyda's. The dedication page of *A Melville Log* reads: "This book was begun as a birthday present for my teacher, Sergei Eisenstein." Leyda is something of a film buff, but what did Eisenstein the great Soviet film director teach him—and where?

When I stopped for coffee at the College Drug Shop, corner of S. Pleasant and Main, "working-on-my-third-novel" David Jackson, James Merrill's housemate, greeted me with his usual charm. Such a butterfly and so publicly *young*. To be this young and a homosexual in Amherst is to be arch. Merrill is a gifted poet and I admire him for so cheerfully coming back to Amherst with his boyfriend. Jackson asked solicitously after his dear friend "Annie." How they get along. She inspires a fearless affection in homosexuals. And not only in them, God knows. But her husband is sore and hurt and bruised and starved for love—all over.

As I read Erwin Panofsky's charming autobiographical epilogue to the Anchor edition of his essays in art history, I find myself nettled, as usual, by this "humanistic" fetish of our European Jewish intellectuals—no extremes, please, let us be sensible. The Jewish intellectual sees the world through a model, the native culture as his norm. The German Jewish scholars and thinkers brought up on the kind of schoolmaster who, Panofsky reverently notes, not only taught him Greek but Greek *as* history. The case of Hannah Arendt exactly, though being younger, Hannah's reflexes are all from German philosophy, and especially her teacher Martin Heidegger, for whom the pre-Socratics are everything. Hannah would never appreciate E. M. Butler's *The Tyranny of Greece over Germany.*

Russian Jews have taken the messianic type of the Russian intellectual as the nation's liberator, say Chernishevsky and even Tolstoy. Harold Laski for all his socialism never forgot that he was an Oxford man and loved its cultural heroes. With his Russian, his glorious biblical name, his prototypical Jewish face, Isaiah Berlin is as "Levantine" (Anthony Eden's characteristic slur), as exotic as any court Jew in history. But he owes his passion for liberty to England. American Anglophiles like Lionel Trilling and Gertrude Himmelfarb are positively worshipful of Victorians who appeal to their need to appear always correct.

But look who's talking! No one could love America's Protestant thinkers—Emerson, Thoreau, Whitman, Dickinson, Lincoln, et al.—more than I do.

In short, as Kant put it first—"Priests and Jews are civically timid." I would change "timid" to *grateful*. We Jewish intellectuals are always looking for our cultural home.

\* \* \*

She came home jaunty, defiant after an evening out with a loose-limbed schlemiel who teaches here. "You've had your fun in the past, why shouldn't I?"

Quite right! I was not even shocked, things have got so hopeless. But it is not all resignation on my part. My fascination with her sudden enmity never ends—every day is full of drama, so tumultuous, so full of feeling, feeling. What a claim she makes every moment on existence, on everyone in sight, on me. She assures me, and I believe her, that she has an acute sense of personal destiny: "I mean to be up there with the big boys." The other night she woke me up, insisting that I apologize for something I had said or done in her dream.

Having lost Michael before he was two, I don't want to lose Kate before she is even one. And am I in a jealous rage supposed to run out on my job, my students, the Riverside Press *Moby-Dick* I've been editing? I'm stunned by her flaunting everything, but she is seething with anger against everything here, starting with me.

Typically, she has written a story, "Love in the Dunes," all about an episode with someone who resembles Gary Cooper more than her schlemiel. It portrays me as a hopelessly distracted academic fossil.

Alas, the story keeps coming back from one magazine after another, which enrages her even further. I've even carried it back from the P.O. myself. She wants me to admire it, but I really can't go along with her belief that adultery is the main occupation of the faculty at Amherst. She has a sharp, sardonic social talent, is strong on mimicry, but she is so limited in her interests that I could cry. I can't get her to look in on *anyone's* classes here. As for my course in Melville—"*Moby-Dick* is a boy's book." And this when I am editing the book for the Riverside Press edition and am wild with joy at being able—finally!—to get down in my introduction the contesting power as well as the awe with which Melville confronts the universe—

But Ahab is not just a fanatic who leads the whole crew to their destruction; he is a hero of thought who is trying, by terrible force, to reassert man's place in nature. And it is the struggle Ahab incarnates that makes him so magnificent a *voice*, thundering in Shakespearean rhetoric, storming at the gates of the inhuman, silent world. Ahab is trying to give man, in one awful, silent assertion that his will *does* mean something, a feeling of relatedness with his world.

Meanwhile what a comedy we are living—everyone knowing everything. "Love in the dunes" whimpers that he can't understand my disinclination to continue our literary discussions, and his wife has come privately to my office to suggest she is mad enough at her husband to be interested in me. Which she isn't. She just wants revenge.

France: Fulbright professor in American literature. In Paris we called on Dr. Bernard and Selma Weil, Simone Weil's parents, in the Avenue Comte. The kitchen—the only place they could smoke—was crammed with doctoral students allowed to look at Simone's notebooks. Madame Weil showed me Simone's own books, among them the volume of George Herbert's poems in which she had marked "Love," which was to have so great an influence on her—and on me.

Love bade me welcome: yet my soul drew back,
    Guiltie of dust and sinne.
But quick-ey'd Love, observing me grow slack
    From my first entrance in,
Drew near to me, sweetly questioning,
    If I lack'd any thing.

A guest, I answer'd, worthy to be here:
    Love said, you shall be he
I the unkinde, ungratefull? Ah my deare,
    I cannot look on thee.

Love took my hand, and smiling did reply,
    Who made the eyes but I?

Truth Lord, but I have marr'd them: let my shame
    Go where it doth deserve.
And know you not, sayes Love, who bore the blame?
    My deare, then I will serve.
You must sit down, says Love, and taste my meat:
    So I did sit and eat.

Selma Weil was taken with Ann, examined her blond prettiness with intense approval. Waving aside my attempts to question her about Simone, she suddenly burst out to Ann: "How I wish my daughter could have been like you! How I wish she could have had a life normal and happy like yours!"

It is difficult to forget that one is a Jew—even the best people are quick to remind you. After my talk on Scott Fitzgerald at the Centre Universitaire in Nice, the great scholar-critic Denis Saurat burst out at me apropos of nothing—"You know, I don't regard Proust as being truly French. His style is too complicated and dense, *Jewish*."

## FROM MARX TO FREUD AND BACK AGAIN, OR HOW TO BE A JEWISH INTELLECTUAL

> False consciousness is here to stay; it is the happy psychic condition of a mature and still dynamic industrial civilization that has worked back through a religion of transcendence to a religion of immanence based on a supra-primitive fetishism of infinitely variable commodities.
>
> Philip Rieff, *Partisan Review*, Summer 1956

In Stockholm to lecture, I am taken about by the wonderfully charming literary editor of the leading newspaper *Dagens Nyheter,* Olof Lagercrantz, who has written much on Strindberg. We begin our tour at the Jewish Cemetery! Lagercrantz wants to show me the graves of German Jews who obtained refuge in Sweden. Jews are very much on Sweden's mind just now—on the threat of possible invasion in 1940 German troops were allowed to pass through to Norway. And the Swedes made a pile selling Germany their exceptional ball bearings. So I, the American Jewish writer, at a reception in my honor, am led up to the German Jewish poet Nelly Sachs, given refuge in Sweden. She was standing in a corner looking timid and frail. Two Jews introduced to each other in a foreign land because we are both Jews! I felt we were being intently watched by everyone in the room. Instead of merely shaking her hand and murmuring some banalities in English—which she may not speak—I would have liked in homage to quote back to her haunting lines from *O the Chimneys:*

O you chimneys
O you fingers
And Israel's body as smoke through the air!

The Nazis turned this once-romantic, ornamental German poet into a poet of Jewish death. I hear from the literary folk here that Nelly Sachs and Shmuel Yosef Agnon from Israel, an observant Jew who writes in Hebrew, are being considered for the Nobel in literature. What a triumph that will be for us—in Sweden! I envision Agnon wearing a yarmulke when he appears in full evening dress before Gustavus VI to receive his prize. There is something wonderful in this. I am sure that Agnon, who was raised in Austrian Galicia and lived in Germany before moving to Eretz Israel, will read in faultless German the tribute that Jews are supposed to read "when they appear before a king."

Nelly Sachs, the assimilated once-all-German poet from Berlin, and Shmuel Agnon from Buczacz, among the most intense

Hasidim, who in one of his most beautiful stories describes a character so devout that he says, "Hebrew is the connection with the Creation." Nelly Sachs learned that she was a Jew only when she was condemned as one, and piercing as her work is, she was forced to become a poet of death:

O the chimneys!
Freedom for Jeremiah and Job's dust—
Who devised you and laid stone upon stone
The road for refugees of smoke?

O the habitations of death,
Invitingly appointed
For the host who used to be a guest—
O you fingers
Laying the threshold
Like a knife between life and death—

Agnon is a consummate artist, not so much pious as he is fascinated by the traditionalism of Jews living as a religious community, Jews for whom every day was lived in His sight in fulfillment of His edicts. He is all storyteller, neither reverential nor aloof—awestruck rather, positively spellbound by people who believe the Lord is addressing each of them personally, is indeed their shepherd. Their greatest desire is to love, honor, and obey Him—so that after every massacre they reassert this more fervently than ever.

What can you do with a people like that? No storyteller myself, I can only wonder and envy. O God, to believe in God like that!


Robert Frost, who is mostly responsible for my being here, was the first poet in residence at an American college, and likes to return to Amherst, where he is greeted reverently whenever he mounts the steps at Johnson Chapel to give a public reading. He is the Jupiter of the Connecticut Valley, swollen with every possible honor from everywhere, but still so intensely dissatisfied and absorbed in himself that he teasingly attaches himself to this admirer as a possible biographer. He already has an official biographer, Lawrance Thompson, and many an unofficial one, like Elizabeth Shepley Sargent. But he cultivates me (and others) as if no other biographer is enough for him. The other day he invited Ann to tea at a café in Northampton, but alas, warned her that his daughter Lesley, something of a fascist, was about to turn up, "and she is quite terrible about Jews."

In the morning he summoned me to his room at the Lord Jeffrey and triumphantly waved a new poem at me. "It's called 'Kitty Hawk' and I'll bet you can't guess what it's about!" "The Wright Brothers?" "Knew you would say that! It's about chasing a girl down there in 1893!" The "girl," it develops, was his future wife Elinor, who had run away from him when they were high school sweethearts.

What had impressed me in great pieces like *The Hill Wife* was the man-and-woman story, marriage as a Greek tragedy of will against will. There had been a forty-year battle between the Frosts. His son, Carol, committed suicide. My image of Frost has been gained in the small hours of the night, when after dinner at our house, I have to walk him, slightly looped on Cinzano ("never saw any of *that* before") back to the Lord Jeffrey. Often afraid to go to bed, he admits, he then insists on walking me back; whereupon I have to walk him back yet again.

In the dark Amherst night Frost never seems to notice anything, least of all my shivering yawns, in the rambling, fiercely resentful trance into which he falls when he describes his mother taking his father's body from San Francisco to New England, the aborted term at Dartmouth, his "second try at education" that one unfinished time at Harvard. His soul is crowded with ghosts. His life is still unrelieved. Despite all his fame and the baby critics in the universities explicating him for dear life, his life at two in the morning, trudging through the football stadium, the shaky bridge, is still a cry for appreciation, an effort to throw off a curse.

How well I understand that. I have taken a room in Northampton to finish out alone my last year at Amherst.

"I'm not a Jewish nationalist," the woman volunteered as we entered the plane to Israel. "I'm a *progressive*."

Jerusalem the Golden, so divided that we walk the rooftops to get from one Jewish sector to another—but still golden. The enthusiasm—Ben-Gurion proclaims it as a civic duty: "We are living in the age of the Messiah." Alfred North Whitehead thought the Jews were "unpopular" (what a way to put it) because they had no independent state to govern. "The absence of such responsibility has been a characteristic of the Jews for centuries." Well, now they have their own state to govern, and while they are still distinctly "unpopular" with Arabs and others too numerous to mention, there is an understandable thrill in riding the skies from New York to Paris to Rome to Athens to Lod in a plane of the Jewish state bearing the blue-and-white star of David.

Shimon V., the barrel-chested taxi driver who takes us around, boasts that he never gets a "Diaspora Jew" into his cab without working on him to settle in Israel. As he drives us, he shouts in a tone that boasts: "I am at home and I am normal! *We* are at home and now *we* are all normal! I am the most normal taxi driver in Israel and Israel is the only place for normal Jewish people!"

Smiling and at ease in Zion, Dr. Kaplan, head of the new, not-yet-opened museum of antiquities in Jaffa, shows us around the first proud exhibits in what was once a Turkish prison. The squat pillars and high, grilled windows in this great vault must once have been as ominously full of shadows as one of Piranesi's prisons. But now the gleaming whitewashed walls bear neat museum placards identifying the friable clumps of earth and potsherds that can still be traced to ancient Israel.

In short, it's all ours—always was! Archaeology here is Zionism with a shovel. But what meticulous and exhausting effort, what delicacy of touch to keep these shards and brown clusters from crumbling back into the anonymity of earth. Dr. Kaplan translates for us the old Aramaic, Greek, and Latin inscriptions left in the stones, pillars, and roads. Starting from the bottom of recorded time, he read his way up the ladder from biblical times to the present. Everything leads up to the state of Israel, which by its existence has crowned the past and sealed it as its own. So the obstinate Jewish insistence that history does have a design and purpose is confirmed by the fact that "we" are back, reverently staring at stuff dug out of the local soil.

Closing the museum to go home to lunch in his rattly old car, Dr. Kaplan points his ignition key at the cellar below the museum, where old people, on a special reclamation project, are weaving cane seats for chairs.

Jaffa, ancient Joppa, is now just a borough of Tel Aviv. Though there are fewer Arabs around than there must have been, the hovels built into the rock overlooking the Mediterranean are still plainly Arab. The old Arab quarter is a mass of ruins. "We had to blow up the houses because they were in a state of collapse and unsafe," the guide from the municipality gravely tells us, and gravely we look at each other. Being in power eliminates many a doubt and a shudder. Seven hundred thousand Palestinians fled Jewish-held territory. The government's story is that it made every effort to reach peace but was rebuffed. In point of fact Israeli forces expelled many Palestinians; many more left their homes out of fear, and the houses were dynamited. You can see the remains off the Tel Aviv–Jerusalem highway.

Everything is "normal"; *così fan tutti*. We make our way past the

Moroccan whore with a Jewish star around her neck, who is, the guide reluctantly admits, discussing last night's business with her greasy colleagues. The guide blushes but gamely translates to the end, ruefully adding that these "new elements" have brought Israel its first prostitutes.

Of all things to pick up again in Israel—Kafka's *Letters to Milena*. It was to this great love of his earlier life, to the extraordinary Czech patrician who long after Kafka's death was to be a prisoner in Auschwitz and to save many lives, that Kafka confessed something all Jews feel since the Holocaust, whether they can say this or not—

> In the evening I talked to a Palestinian Jew. I believe it's impossible in a letter to make you understand his importance to me—a small, almost tiny, weak, bearded one-eyed man. But the memory of him has cost me half the night.
>   It is not necessary to fly right into the middle of the sun, but just to crawl to some clean spot on earth on which the sun sometimes shines and where one can warm oneself a little.

Kafka lived in a mental dungeon inside a ghetto that was inside the maze of ancient, crazy, doomed Prague. But from the dungeon that was his genius as well as his unhappiness, from the Prague where the Jews of modern times could no longer call up the Golem to help them, he asked just to crawl to a bit of sun and warm himself a little. The Jewish revival since the war owes much, much to the state of Israel—the world owes us this. And this we owe the world, which would be dull indeed without Jews. The real Jewish prophets of *our* time are not just Chaim Weizmann and the socialist statemakers, but the artists and originals—Kafka at their head—who out of endless exile gave the world the gift of their minds.

Still, Kafka dreamed of the sun—and here is the sun. From my window overlooking the sea at Herzliya, where in the golden light the last swimmers are slowly coming in, shrugging the light-beaded drops of water from their bodies, I seem to see not the usual health club but Kafka and Babel, Modigliani, Einstein, and Freud—and all those other Jews of whom Khrushchev complains: "They are all individualists and all intellectuals. They want to talk about everything, they want to discuss everything, they want to debate everything—and they come to totally different conclusions."

Yigael Yadin has some people in to meet us after dinner. Yadin is one of the most vital and most admired people in Israel—commander of the Israeli forces in the 1948 War of Independence, their second chief, a leading archaeologist, and the son of that extraordinary Polish-born scholar Eliezer Lipa Sukenik, who in 1947, in the midst of war, was instrumental in acquiring part of the Dead Sea Scrolls for Israel.

His son, just back from some great conference of Orientalists in the Soviet Union, was scornful of the restrictions the Russians had tried to put in his way as an Israeli, and seemed appropriately aware of his importance. Rather obviously bored with us, but astonishingly made a big pitch for us to settle in Israel. The other guests became quite vehement when I did not seem to take this seriously. Until they became more and more insistent, I hadn't realized that American Jews were in so much danger, and the dear old U.S. of A. itself so much on the rocks. It was impossible to be a Jew and not "come back" to Israel. I disagreed, I even laughed at one point, and the others became so angry, yelling at me, that things dissolved into general laughter only when a man in a house directly opposite us shouted: "Will you for heaven's sake let us sleep!"

\* \* \*

Mailer has me to lunch at the Oak Room in the Plaza. Norman can be studiously correct and most polite when he is not pursuing his favorite demons. But even here at the Plaza he is trying, with a missionary's sweet earnestness, to persuade me that cancer is produced by sexual repression. Cancer or no cancer, there is a fashion show going on in the Oak Room, and the models dip and circle most deliciously as they parade their sexy dresses around our table. Norman, utterly absorbed and intent on persuading me, never looks up for a moment.

A note from "Eliezer Wiesel" thanking me for my review of *Night*, his heartbreaking account of being a boy prisoner in Auschwitz, Birkenau, and Buchenwald and suggesting that we meet. The book, translated from the French, was signed *Elie* Wiesel. A most appealing, gentle man, he lives in a single room at the Master Institute on Riverside Drive—it was once the Roerich Museum— and makes his living as a correspondent at the UN for an Israeli paper favored by the Orthodox.

Meeting Wiesel was an extraordinary experience for me, he is so quietly charming and so strangely humble after his unspeakable afflictions. As we sat together in Riverside Park, he told me that he had written *Night* in Yiddish, then was able to write it over in French, which he had mastered quickly in Paris after his release. He was sixteen when the war ended for him in April 1945. By that time he had been separated from his mother and sisters, whom he never saw again; he had seen his own father, after surviving so many "selections," smashed to death. He had lived in Auschwitz with the constant odor of burning human flesh; he had seen children still alive thrown into the crematoria; he had seen starving men, in the cattle cars transporting them from one camp to another, fighting each other to death over loaves of bread contemptuously thrown them by German civilians.

There are details in his book that can still astonish us at the unflagging cruelty of the Nazis and the sadistic frivolity of those who directed the vast system of human extermination. The infamous SS doctor Mengele, quickly "selecting" those who were to be gassed from the terror-stricken crowds running and stumbling before his eyes, would motion people to death with a conductor's baton! A young boy, after days of being tortured in an attempt to make him reveal where a Dutch prisoner had hidden arms, was put up on the gallows to be hanged. His body was too light, and so he kept strangling in front of the thousands of prisoners who had been summoned to watch the execution and who were marched past the gallows. As they went by, Wiesel heard a man ask, "Where is God now?" And he heard himself thinking: Here He is—He is hanging here on this gallows.

This literal "death of God," as absolute emptiness in the soul, Wiesel experienced in the endless night of Auschwitz. His early religious background interested the French Catholic novelist François Mauriac. When Wiesel interviewed him for his Israeli paper, Mauriac described the ineradicable impression that had been made on Mme. Mauriac as she watched the trainloads of Jewish children being deported from Austerlitz Station in Paris. When Mauriac spoke of how often he thought of those children, Wiesel replied, "I was one of them." Mauriac's singularly beautiful preface to *Night* describes young Wiesel as "a Lazarus risen from the dead," and recalling Nietzsche's declaration that "God is dead," expresses his compassionate understanding of why a boy in Auschwitz should have thought that "God is dead, the God of love, of gentleness, of comfort, the God of Abraham, of Isaac, of Jacob has vanished forevermore, beneath the gaze of this child, in the smoke of a human holocaust exacted by Race, the most voracious of all facts."

What Job-like accusations unite Wiesel to the religion of his fathers! He says that on Rosh Hashanah in Auschwitz, when ten thousand prisoners said with one voice, "Blessed be the name of the Eternal," the young boy defied the Divinity Whom he had come to think of as blind and deaf:

But why should I bless Him? In every fiber I rebelled. Because He had kept six crematories working night and day, on Sundays and feast days? . . .

    That day I had ceased to plead. . . . I was the accuser, God the accused. My eyes were open and I was alone—terribly alone in a world without God and without Man. . . . I stood amid that praying congregation, observing it like a stranger.

 

Ann's father is dead. My mother is dead. I may have been the last person to see the rabbi alive, and I saw my mother die. The rabbi was so weak after being operated on for intestinal cancer that he could hardly speak, was too weak to make the slightest gesture as I happened by chance to be alone at his bedside.

    He looked severe. God, how severe he looked! To my astonishment he suddenly got out of bed, pulling at the IV tubes in his arm, pulling them away, and unsteadily walked to the bathroom, closing the door behind him.

 

As her liver cancer struck, removed her from everything except her disease, my mother wondered why she dreamed all the time. "I can't stop dreaming," she said with a certain pride as she made one last effort to get out of bed, muttering, "I must stop wasting time." As if she had been holding off death until I returned from lecturing on American writers in Russia ("Will they let you visit my old village?") she looked up at me, nodded, and turned her face to the wall. A photograph of Theodore Herzl, all beard and glossy frock coat, had suddenly appeared over her head.

    She never spoke again. We watched over a skeleton, had to stop the nurse from idiotically forcing food down her mouth. The body's collapse was total. She had long since departed in spirit, but her loud

struggling gasp filled the room. The breathing pushed at me fiercely, pushed, and I was caught up in its lonely unconscious bellow.

Saturday night. My father and mother had started married life in
a furnished room on a Saturday night. She had gone to a grocery on
Orchard Street to get food for them, and had returned to find him
weeping. Saturday night, forty-seven silent years of marriage later,
he sat stupefied in another room as I watched her die. Her gasps
rose out of her like fish struggling to reach the surface of a tank;
they drummed so loud in my ears that I could not credit them to
this skeletal face and annihilated body. Louder and louder she
gasped; rhythmic pounding breaths: up, up, up, up. Suddenly it all
stopped. She stopped. There was an easy look on her face. It was
almost a smile.

In an hour they came for her and carried her out in a green sack.


Reading *Herzog*, I am overcome, as usual, by Bellow's merciless
intelligence, the impact and penetration of every sentence. Here is
the sorrowful tale of a man at the end of his tether, cuckolded by his
best friend and totally at odds with himself, a vital new chapter in
the familiar history of the Jewish intellectual. In his radical messianic youth he knew how to save the world; now he can barely save
himself, he is so humiliated at *"their"* perfidy. That this should hap-
pen to *him!* Yet Bellow's writing could not be more removed from
the sorrow, guilt, and turmoil that chain Moses Herzog in his troubles with *his* universe—women. It is Bellow who challenges current
ideologies, who knows that nothing the intellectuals come up with
can help a man whose wife hates him! The essential comedy of this
is rueful and alive, radiant with the contradictions of the intellectual's real life. The reader is delivered by Bellow's vitality even if poor
Moses is not. "Herzog experienced nothing but his own human
feelings, in which he found nothing of use."

Since I am almost too well acquainted with the wife in the story, *and* the lover—and both are easier to know than Bellow himself, complex as his wonder-seeking brain—I am fascinated by Bellow's transformation of himself into Moses Herzog the academic schlemiel. Only Bellow among American Jewish writers gets to the heart of the Jewish experience and its mystery. "Not God is dead, that point was passed long ago. Perhaps it should be stated Death is God." But his inability even to simulate modesty does not make him an idol to everyone. Offer the slightest friendly argument to Bellow about anything he believes and writes, and you get flung out of the window. This made him irresistible to "Valentine Gersbach," another Jewish novelist, another Canadian-born Jew in America. To meet him was to hear bad imitations of Bellow's speculative gift. "There are no concessions in God's circus." He so identified himself with Bellow that he was preposterous, and was so dominated by his image of Bellow that of course he had to take Bellow's place in bed.

Why should the wife in *Herzog* be so cruel to a husband like Moses, no challenge to her? The wife I knew was stupefied and overcome by Bellow's sense of superiority. Her gift was manifestly sexual. You could not look at her without recognizing her capacity for giving pleasure. Otherwise she was the helpless daughter of a pretentious painter from Chicago with a plain Jewish name who in New York assumed a "Russian" name. From time to time daughter Sondra became Alexandra, which was soon Sasha, and innocently pretentious, assumed familiarity with Russian culture. In "real life" she was so occupied with herself that if anyone referred to a recent historic happening, she would sweetly ask, sucking a finger, "Let's see, how old was I then?"

Bellow has his fun, turning the actual childlike wife, whose carelessness and extravagance drove him crazy, into a hilariously affected Catholic convert much occupied with texts of Orthodox Russian spirituality—between adulteries. What a wonderful thing it is to be a novelist, with a wave of your magic wand to turn the grittiness of a totally unequal marriage into the biggest event since the Johnstown flood, the cuckolded husband into a would-be Othello, and the lover's lameness in walking into the rhythms of a Venetian gondolier!

And the actual lover giving adoring lectures on Bellow! At the annual convention of the Modern Language Association, a vast crowd came out to hear him. Was it on *Herzog* or some other Bellow novel? No matter. The lover was so well known, the scandal so obviously cherished, that I saw a pack of nuns in the crowd rushing to hear him.

Teresa Benedicta of the Cross, a Carmelite nun, is in line for sainthood. The cause for her beatification has been presented in Rome by Joseph Cardinal Frings.

In 1891 she was born Edith Stein in Breslau (now Wroclaw, Poland), to an Orthodox Jewish family. At thirteen she "renounced" her faith, declared herself an atheist. But at the University of Göttingen she became fascinated with the phenomenology founded by Edmund Husserl, with its stress on the direct apprehension of an object before reflective thinking sets in. Husserl, born a Jew but a Lutheran convert, was a man of great personal purity and taught the importance of ethical autonomy in all things. She became Husserl's assistant at Freiburg and was much admired by him. Magnetized by the autobiography of Saint Teresa of Avila (descended from *conversos*) she joined the Catholic Church in 1922, lost her teaching job eleven years later when the Nazis came in, the next year joined the Carmelite convent in Cologne.

In 1938 she was transferred to the Carmelite convent at Echt in Holland to protect her from the Nazis. But the condemnation of Nazi anti-Semitism by the Dutch bishops (the German bishops successfully protested Nazi euthanasia, never the murder of the Jews) caused Hitler to order the arrest of all non-Aryan Catholics. Sister Teresa and her sister, Rosa, also a convert, were gassed in Auschwitz.

The Carmelite order in Holland could not hide Edith Stein in her full habit? Law-abiding, handed her right over to the Gestapo? The great Catholic church accepted the Nazi edict that "non-Aryan

Catholics" were to be murdered because they had been born Jews? What was she thinking of in Auschwitz, perhaps still in her habit, side by side with her fellow Jews? Survivors have testified that she was noble, helped others with great compassion. Of course, and the church that could or would not protect her in life will soon declare her a saint.

Gallows humor is big on the West Side. Ann reports a telephone conversation with a friend: "Oh, darling, I'm so blue!" Friend: "*I'm talking from the ledge!*"

Hannah is getting shellacked, but hard, for *Eichmann in Jerusalem*. To believe her violently excited Jewish critics, she is the most terrible enemy of the Jews since . . . since . . . She kindly gave me the manuscript, though we are no longer the friends we used to be. I thought the tone she took to Gideon Hausner, the prosecutor at the Eichmann trial, was deplorable—her usual loftiness toward what she likes to dismiss as "little Jews."

She is understandably severe on the compliant Jewish councils in Poland, which registered the Jews, and the disgusting Jewish "police" in Poland, who helped deliver Jews to the Nazis for deportation. The cupidity of certain council "leaders" in profiting from the ghetto enclosure, in thinking to save themselves and their families from the murderers (they didn't)—beyond anything. But Jews in Poland were a trapped, doomed people. They did not have *any* choice. And that goes for "the banality of evil," with its correlate nonsense that "you must think what you are doing." Eichmann and company certainly knew what they were doing, even if lots of low-ranking murderers were just obeying orders.

Evil is "banal" if you know it only from your reading. Herself a refugee who was briefly interned in France before fleeing to

America, she ignores the fear, the panic, the horror—as well as the essential fact that under Nazi occupation in Russia, there were no Jewish councils, no Jewish police at Babi Yar—the Jews were slaughtered anyway—en masse.

I loved Hannah as a teacher, as I was grateful to Elie Wiesel for being a witness. Their subject—the Holocaust—more and more central to Jews for whom the Holocaust will never go away. And now Hannah has made me suffer because of the tone she has taken to the doomed people, just as Elie's celebrity embarrasses me— always the professional survivor, he now comes on as a *zaddik*, a wise man with many, many books. There has been nothing worth reading since *Night*. As Hannah acts detachment (of course she is as distraught as the rest of us), Elie is now all actor. He described himself to me as "a lecturer in anguish." Hannah gleefully confided to me that *The New Yorker* paid her twenty thousand dollars for its version of "Eichmann in Jerusalem."

We have been coming up to Wellfleet every summer since 1953, the year after our marriage, but the place I love beyond any other in America is now virtually closed to us. The National Seashore, established in 1961, preempted so much land in my favorite spots between Eastham and Provincetown (and a good thing too) that I cannot buy a house though I now have the money. The necessity of a different summer rental every year has added still another vexation to our painful marriage. To remain so "undistinguished" amid the proud properties of our friends Schlesinger and Wilson and Hofstadter, Breuer and O'Connor and Macdonald, Howe and Tate and Levin! So one resentment is piled on another, contributing to the deterioration of a marriage that in our first years naturally flowered in Wellfleet, but that even Wellfleet cannot sustain.

Some day I shall come here alone, even in winter. I so loved the upper reaches of the Cape that after being happy in 1940 in Provincetown with Asya, I came up here at year's end to walk the dunes to the ocean. I used to dream of those summer afternoons when one could go off either to the ocean or the bay or to Gull Pond, Slough Pond, Long Pond.

Somehow it is the *place* I dream—the long stretch of tableland, the high dunes overlooking the Atlantic, dunes half-covered with poverty grass and beach grass. Behind this high sandbank is a path leading through patches of bayberry bushes struggling in the sand, tiny twisted shrub pine deep in the golden sand—tiny plants not set up just to astonish, like Japanese "trees" grown in a pot, but hardy and tough like the Cape itself, twisted by the violent winds that can sweep the beach at the top of summer, and the incessant shifting of the sand.

Wellfleet presents difficulties to a young, ambitious novelist anxious for the plaudits at the cocktail parties on the dunes overlooking the ocean—"Joan's Beach"—and afternoons on the beach itself—"*la plage des intellectuels*," as Dick Hofstadter's wife, Bede, calls it. Ann is a great favorite here, delivering jokes and wisecracks, but is compelled to overdo it because she is not interested in their books and they have never heard of hers. Here she shines in her creamy white pants, martini in hand, engulfed in banter and flirtations, but ends up always "disappointed," mad at me as usual. Alone now, she wanders down at eventide to what Thoreau called the Great Beach.

End of summer. An end, an end, an end. We are through but keep hanging on to each other. I feel like death itself as I watch her at the "violet" hour of the day. The light is fading, and couples in odd corners are getting cozier by the minute. How strange it is to look out from the outermost Cape with nothing in sight but a last fishing vessel. Somewhere out in that thrilling, frightening emptiness is Portugal, even Galicia in northwest Spain. How strange to think that career can be the greatest passion, capable of poisoning a marriage. How little we have made of this last summer. We have used this great half wilderness in a way that cut us off from the everlasting heart of the world beating in our ears as we sat hating each other on the beach.

# PART FOUR

## 1978-1993

Steele Commager, the young classicist, has left Harvard for Columbia and summoned his old New York friends to dinner on Riverside Drive. The always composed and effortlessly dignified Francis Steegmuller was my favorite sight at the party. Francis is the only American I know who wears the *Légion d'honneur* in his buttonhole as if he was born to it. His perfect French was a byword during the war at American HQ in London, *Flaubert and Madame Bovary* is one of the great literary biographies, and only Francis could have turned "The Owl and the Pussycat" into "L'Hibou et le poussiquette." He looked uncharacteristically dreamy and even misty, must have been stricken with nostalgia for old Columbia days. To my astonishment he did something unprecedented and studentlike—he collected the plates and headed back toward the kitchen.

Francis cornered me after dinner and, out of the blue, said very quietly that Ann and I were obviously about to call a halt to our publicly disordered marriage. He asked to buy back the modest little painting of a kitchen scene by his late wife, Bea Stein, that Ann and I had bought ages ago. Thought Francis wanted it as a memorial to his wife.

To my astonishment, it turns out that Francis presented the painting to Bea's *nephew*, a wayward physician with the kind of money that allows him to do just as he pleases. Like going from one profession to another. He left medicine for a Yale doctorate in English and teaches up in Washington State. Nephew, hell! The picture is being returned to me.

How to account for the rest without marveling at my good luck? Judith, just a little nervous but with the most charming voice in the world, telephoned me to say that the good doctor, a friend from their Yale days, had wondered if she could just possibly bring the picture over to me. *As he was transporting the picture, his Mercedes-Benz broke down in front of her office and he was just now too occupied with family and such to perform this mission himself.* Could she? Would she?

Yes, there is a God.

Fell on a heavy patch of ice covering the Sixth Avenue sidewalk, two successive operations at St. Vincent's to restore my broken shoulder. I felt like death until Judith came over.

Stanford University: The Center for Advanced Study in the Behavioral Sciences. Moved into a single room on Oak Creek Drive. Moved in and feel like the unexpected survivor the moment after the battle is over. The field is covered with corpses, and I am spent. But I am here.

Rain—it rains—it rains every day now; and trudging to Bullock's in the rain in this city (which could be on the moon for all we have to say to each other), I feel alive again, not just finished, as when I take my achingly restored shoulder to bed and groan over my bachelorhood, but young—peering through the rain on Fulton Street to the promise of going home, of having a home.

This double state. In my office at the center I work happily on *An*

*American Procession*, happily as I can, typing with one arm. When I go to bed and "face myself," face my mind and past alone, I weep. A spring is released in the dark—and I weep in the emptiness, *for* the emptiness. The brooding silence to which alone I answer between these white white walls.

Okay. *Basta!* "Passive suffering is not a subject for poetry." Or for anything else either. Lights across the way. Deep in northern California's rainy season—plunk, plunk, plunk all day long.

How they straggle in, the members of my procession, my American congregation. How they fall in around my typewriter to show themslves a *family*. I keep seeing Willa Cather on that train doing the long trek homeward to Nebraska, and those lonely reporters from Mark Twain to Ambrose Bierce, Hemingway, and Ring Lardner, hunched down in the dead of night in small-town newspaper offices with the tawny yellow shades drawn against the one street light.

If Judith didn't exist, I could never invent her, ever hope for someone like her. "Smart" all right, like many another Jewish girl from the Bronx—Bronx Science, Mount Holyoke, and Yale Graduate School on scholarships. Gave up Yale to marry. Three children. Life at home a constant battle. Writes and edits for a bloody big bank. But how to describe the plainness and openness of soul, the honesty, the absolute purity in the smallest details of life—the long-cherished pieces from Chaucer through Yeats to Lear always gushing out. And the fun. "Of course I look like a Latin teacher."

Her letters run the blood through me, there is such a fearlessness to her loving.

*Sunday, neglecting work as usual. I just realized, as I thought about our conversation of an hour ago, that with the inoperability of his left arm, Kazin has finally become a right-winger! They do say it happens with advancing age. Well, never mind, my love. I will take you (!) as you are.*

*Call me a lost puppy again, and I will kick your ass.*

*He "accidentally" spilled boiling coffee all over me (luckily I had on my aged-hippy overalls and was not especially burned), and then went off muttering about how I didn't know right from wrong. Not your favorite topic or mine either. I am o.k. I do, however, remind myself in this absurd business of the Edward Lear character—do you know him?*

> *There was an old man who said "How*
> *Shall I flee from this horrible cow?*
> *I will sit on the stile*
> *And continue to smile*
> *Which may soften the heart of that cow."*

*Reminds me of a lady I met in my early Playground Period, when J was small. She had obviously been trained in the social sciences (your favorite discipline by now, no doubt) and chose J as a suitable playmate (the only one in the Bronx, I believe) for her three-year-old son, because, as she told me, he (her son) was strong on self-directed activities but weak on interpersonal dynamics. Which I took to mean that he* enjoyed coloring but had no friends.

\*   \*   \*

*Sweet love I forgot to tell you how truly mortified I was to read the
following in Lehmann-Haupt's review of Anne Sexton's letters.
"Altogether, her style can best be described by her own word
'goopy.' " Does the shoe fit? Shall I wear it? Here I was about to
tell you (horrors!) that I felt pulled to you in Palo Alto like* salt
water taffy. *Goopy, eh?? But then, it is true, I have always
thought of Anne Sexton's poetry as a kind of psychological post-
nasal drip, the symptoms of which are best described on a cough
drop box.*

*Kluck! Litvak! I needed a roomier handbag (now that I carry
around eighteen pairs of eyeglasses, Rilke's* Gesammelte Werke,
*the complete Alfred Kazin correspondence and God only knows
what else). A nice, plain, o.k. pocketbook at Mark Cross turned out
to be $240!! In case you're getting any lunatic ideas, I got one the
next day on Orchard St for $32. I tripped over to Rizzoli & made
myself happy again ordering a bilingual copy of Heine's* Lyric
Poems & Ballads. *Then I sat reading for half an hour in the
charming vest-pocket park between 49th and 48th (I think) the
one in which you walk through a waterfall inside a big plastic tube.
Very aquatic you feel and glub glub.* Then *I paid my obligatory call
on the Gommint king in his showroom at 38th & Seventh. He
eyed my second-hand coat and declared it to be a Givenchy. How do
you know, said I and Myron replied that it had the unmistakable
Givenchy* buttons. *(plain blue buttons with four holes to my untu-
tored eye). How do you like that for* mavenheit?

In a pile of her mother's old German Jewish family photographs,
Judith comes up with an uncle, wounded in the kaiser's army, con-

valescing at a medical rest center. Her uncle Hans lost a leg in battle. A handsome blond young cousin is shown leading an Israeli labor parade in Tel Aviv. He is waving a flag. Our good Roxbury friend Barbara Ungeheuer from the Black Forest, the American correspondent for *Die Zeit*, smiles that the young man looks like the most desirable Aryan selected to keep the Nazi baby farms humming. To make perfect future SS men.

As for the great terrible thing itself—why Germans turned out to be murderers on such a scale—the pit that will never lose its stink—Barbara, who really is a *good* German and born after the war, is silent. "There are unanswerable questions."

Vanessa Redgrave in her new film, *The Palestinians*, dances ecstatically with a Kalashnikov rifle. This most beautiful woman absolutely dream-borne with ecstasy as she dances for the overpowered Palestine crowd. A little stump of an Arab woman bows before her in adoration. The milky white face, the perfect English hair, the white silk shirt and soldier pants. How she dances, the woman you hate to love. But you see what "revolutionary" ideology does for an actress capable of finding a really great part for herself.

That aggressive TV twerp Mike Wallace, interviewing Redgrave on *60 Minutes*, asked her if in *Julia* she wasn't really playing herself. She gravely assented with her eyes on this monkey as if she couldn't believe anyone so dumb and ugly was in her company.

She supports the Workers Revolutionary Party, which gets its inspiration "from the late Leon Trotsky." Considers the Chinese and the Soviets "reactionary."

Redgrave dancing before the Palestinians. It is all a movie. The Palestinians are borrowing their gestures from old silent films. But with Redgrave, the Garbo of our day, as star, in positive ecstasy as she dances with a Kalashnikov rifle, she looks more rapt than if she were being fucked. Which in a sense she is—by the ghost of Leon Trotsky.

\*    \*    \*

I dreamed that I was on my way to Times Square, worried that I had forgotten my glasses, and suddenly found myself in Israel. Everywhere I looked there were planes, with pilots in the cockpits to guard them even on the ground. In a corner of the field tourists were praying.

The books that are gone are gone. The Ann that is gone is gone. I will burrow no more for the lost but rejoice in the found.

Timothy Leary now in California. "Intelligence is the ultimate aphrodisiac." TV commentator—"He's into survival now." After Leary with friend Alpert had been dismissed from the Harvard Psychology Department, Leary hired a once-Yiddish theater on Second Avenue to explain his case to the public. The air was dense with marijuana fumes. I was nodding off in the smoke when, to my everlasting delight, I heard Leary say, "Our predecessor, William James."

In Miami Beach to lecture to a B'nai B'rith audience. O those great white apartment hotels like beached whales (and at a quarter million the apartment, the going price) most successful in blocking the lowly pedestrian's view of the great Atlantic.

O, O, O the white caps and the spavined legs of the elderly Yiddn who hobble about still straining their eyes after the dollar signs that are the only mark of achievement in Miami Beach.

The wretchedly pretentious Eden Roc, where the bedside lamp does not work and the towels are ragged and the vixen behind the counter snarled at the sweet young Spanish-speaking couple who did not know enough to leave her what her brassy hunger demanded.

A packed, madly vibrant audience. First question: "Why does Philip Roth hate the Jews?"

New York snow frozen, snow surrounded, snow drowned. Where do the dead go? What is their secret? I think of Papa in his last years after Mama died, reduced to a pitiful room here in Miami Beach. The Hotel Seagull, which of course he called the Hotel Segal. Old, deaf, endlessly silent, bitter, he was not easy to entertain. To my relief I saw there was a Tchaikovsky program at the town's main auditorium. The Fifth Symphony, the Violin Concerto. The works. At intermission the deputy mayor on stage, and in the most honeyed voice said to the audience, "You are a marvelous audience, a wonderful audience. But please—would you mind not humming along with the music?"

O Father Abraham, beloved Father Abraham, do on earth as you do in heaven. "There was once a rich man, who used to dress in purple and the finest linen, and feasted sumptuously every day. At his gate lay a poor man named Lazarus, who was covered with sores. He would have been glad to satisfy his hunger with the scraps from the rich man's table. Dogs used to come and lick his sores. One day the poor man died and was carried away by the angels to be with Abraham. The rich man also died and was buried. In Hades, where he was in torment, he looked up and there, far away, was Abraham with Lazarus close beside him. 'Abraham, my father,' he called out, 'take pity on me! Send Lazarus to dip the tip of his finger in water, to cool my tongue, for I am in agony in this fire.' But Abraham said, 'My child, remember that the good things fell to you in your lifetime, and the bad to Lazarus. Now he has his consolation here, and it is you who are in agony. But that is not all: there is a great gulf fixed between us; no one can cross it from our side to reach you, and none may pass from your side to us.'"

As Kissinger gloats: "Power is a great aphrodisiac," so my humble-looking but talented and very purposeful classmate Malamud could say that his literary reputation earns him privileges he never expected when he started out. "Are you available?" he asks a dame across the dinner table. Then confides to me, "On the marriage flank I am safe, solid, protected."

I trek through the subway in a daze, not believing what I see as the helpless old fellow with a cane becomes an open invitation to the blaring-radio carriers, the experts in black confrontation. Especially when they are traveling with junky white girls and make a contemptuous show of leaving an empty bottle in the old man's lap as they leave the subway car.

A professional critic, I am fascinated by writing of all sorts, especially the subway writers. Sometimes they even leave a message: HITLER WAS RIGHT.

The new aesthetic at the smartest dinner tables. Norman Mailer in *Harper's:* subway graffiti as a new form of art.

Before dawn. Now teaching at Notre Dame, where it is always before dawn. My dreams are improving. My literary agent called me in some perturbation to announce that Elie Wiesel had taken out a court injunction to prohibit me from writing about the Holocaust.

O my lost Eurydice, I went down into Hades to bring you out, but you are so much at home there!

Sunday, and "two below." Below what? Woke up at 4:30: Was it God or the hour of my death? Papa used to say with the only ironic smile I ever saw on his usually baffled countenance, "Waiting for *Moloch Hamovos*, the Angel of Death! Death the King."

Still, comrades and friends, it may yet not be time. Not with Judith, and *An American Procession* to finish, my children, Michael and Cathrael. No, it is not yet time. Angel—linger behind the door, s'il vous plaît!

Sarah Moore, the civilized-looking, handsome upper-class lady who tried to kill President Ford, escaped for some hours from the tolerant federal prison she has been in. Went over with a Mexican woman prisoner, scaled a very high wall. After capture she is of course interviewed on TV. Sleek looking, hair in a nice bun, friendly and composed, our Sarah talks of her delight in moving about civilization, walking on real sidewalks, happy to see people in a coffee shop.

And what were her plans on getting out? What about her fellow escapee? Momentary tightening of the lips, but the handsome face (one you see at a symphony concert, very refined type, this) comes out with: "Why, I planned to kill her!"

Emily Dickinson. The achievement of such poetry is to roll up space and time—to create another order than the one in experience we have to travel physically. If the mental world is entirely one of relativity, and thus not one in which nature imposes distance and duration on us, then the particular compressiveness of poetry explains why it has this quality of an *exclamation*. The abruptness takes the form of sound, yet what the physical sound expresses is the mental short circuit—the scream of the mind.

An explosion of concentrated material for a moment. And then? The question with lyric poetry of this order is what lasts. The answer is that in Dickinson a drama is created that makes for a wholly new myth and mental order of things. You see life her way and not in the old way, yours:

My life had stood—a Loaded Gun—
In Corners—till a Day
The Owner passed—identified
And carried Me away—

A lyric poem of this order brings a new mental set. And it ends not in a reader's gulp, a moment's sensation, but in a wholly different perspective.

Jean Renoir dead in Los Angeles, eighty-four. The great line I never forget from his 1939 film *Rules of the Game:* "You see, in this world there is one awful thing, and that is that everyone has his reasons."

Papa Pierre Auguste Renoir died in 1919. Jean, in his book *Renoir, My Father* (1962), told of the old painter confined to a wheelchair, still painfully creating works glowing with splendor and sunlight, part of "the tremendous cry of love he uttered at the end of his life."

Almost a year, more than a year (?) since I saw her. So we go, tra-la-la. Is this what twenty-seven years of life with Ann come to? No wonder that all through the night this succession of images and events goes through my submissive head as if there were no rudder, no steadiness, no center. Just the succession of moments, hoping for what is not successive—one after another and another still.

I see that mortality is the daily problem, and that "duration," not to say the now forbidden word, *immortality*, is the only real interest. As dear Mark Van Doren used to say in that wonderful late-afternoon class at Columbia on "The Long Poem" (the day dying to evening as he talked) immortality is the central subject—and not only of literature. I say "The Eternal, blessed be He," because the word *Eternal* is the only rock under my life.

The whirligig of time, etc., etc., whirl all right, dizziness, running. So I walk up the stairs again at 234 Sutter Avenue—not even 234A or 256 Sutter, as the old number became after I left my childhood home. I walk up the stairs, I walk through the hall still smelling of Papa's overalls, I can put it all together again—Mama fixed forever at the old brown scrolled Singer sewing machine next to the one window in the kitchen, the seemingly endless rectangular mirror hung over the table so that Mama's lady customers could survey themselves in the new dresses she had just finished for them.

The dead all gone into the world of light. And do I at sixty-four have a friend against this erosion—anyone except Judith, who has come into my life as such a miracle, so steadfast, that I cannot see even her name without rapture? But thinking of all those losses, of all that silence on every hand, I tremble indeed to think how little I have made of what I thought I cared for most—*You!* The eternal central Other, the You in the life of every Me.

And now Iran, a new war coming, Israel more besieged than ever. The killing. The mullah was asked whether the executions of people deemed torturers and criminals would continue. "Yes, they will continue," he said. And the executions for violating the Koran in other respects of Muslim law, would they continue too? "And those will continue as well," he replied. "We have to purify, we have to renew."

Funny to think that what I said so "handsomely" in the Mennonite Goshen College chapel the other day—the *opposition* to erosion, death, and daily fright embodied in You the Everlasting—should now be the thing most on my mind.

\* \* \*

In Cincinnati eleven people killed in a rush to a rock concert given by the Who. "The concert went on for fear [that] cancellation would make the crowd wholly uncontrollable."

Passover Seder with the Dotys in Notre Dame, plus a lot of Israelis. The Haggadah is such a hand-me-down through the ages, so full of the cracks of time, and the service is such a familiar repetition as it is recited round the table by relatives—all Jews being my relatives—that it is usually hard for me to tell the Jewish religion from the Jews. The strangest thing about any Jewish service now is that our voice, the entreaty itself, is foremost. Yet, as John McDermott said, "The Jews not only invented a God, but a God who spoke to them." So why all this silence now, interrupted only by our praising Him everlastingly and pleading with Him everlastingly? The everlasting Father, "Der Alte" as Einstein called him, the Eternal! Judaism remembers His intervention, His wrath, His creation, etc. But for some time now, silence. Interrupted by our own voice. I don't seem to hear any dialogue. Speak, Father, speak!

O California, how I loved you! I sit here thinking of the walk with my remade shoulder to the Stanford Hospital across from the Oak Creek houses. The fields outside the house *against* which I seemed to walk every morning to therapy with the butter-smooth Polish blond therapist Sue. The fields so much in my purview when I left my room—sky, fields all ranged before me. The effort of walking against the traffic; seemed to take me in the chest. Then, O paradiso! climbing the hill to the Center for Advanced Studies. Will never forget that for sheer momentum my soul was dancing within me. Birds flying, grasses waving, the lovely young girl (how well she knew it) walking early in the morning past Stanford's Greek-letter fraternity houses in a long white dress and carrying flowers. The inexpressible joy of being all myself as I walked up that hill, away from the creepy prof of literary theory, squatting on the windowsill, watching the retired citizens come and go.


O'Hare, waiting for Allegheny 102 to Pittsburgh. The voice of ideology, or the simple unitary answer to *everything*. Vivian Gornick introducing Erving Goffman's *Gender Advertisements* (Harvard):

Beneath the surface of ordinary social behavior, innumerable small murders of the mind and spirit take place daily. Inside most people, behind a socially useful image of the self, there is a sentient being suffocated slowly to death in a Kafkaesque atmosphere, taken as "natural," that denies not only the death but the live being as well.

In short, we are nothing in ourselves but are always being acted on. What a nightmare. What baloney.


I pay Ann's alimony month by month at the City Hall in South Bend. But, wanting more, she has had me hauled up like a criminal before the judge. The cheerful black fellow beside me in the dock hasn't been paying required child support. Can't remember which of his many women he is supposed to pay first.


Elias Canetti in "The Human Province"—"As long as there are any people in the world *who have no power whatsoever,* I cannot lose all hope."

\*    \*    \*

Finishing as visiting professor in Notre Dame. This loathsome Smerdyakov who calls me in the middle of the night always begins with some special insolence, "Hi there, Al," and then proceeds to make some mocking remarks about New Yorkers, etc. The trouble with this nightmare type is that even when I take the phone off the hook and try to get back to sleep, the strange suspicion comes up that he is not *real*, surely an invention I direct myself. So much meanness, arousal of nemesis, seems the product of my own guilt and my own fears.

Lunch with Bellow at the National Arts Club in Chicago. Saul quiet, very cordial, elegant and precise in his speech and manner. Struck by the difference that the many years do *not* make. Sad in a reserved kind of way. Puts things unmistakably, without emphasis. The waiters all bowing to him. O Mr. Bellow! I asked him what getting the Nobel in Stockholm was like. He quoted his son Gregory: "I know Saint Peter's is the largest thing of its kind, but I want to get out of it." I do understand his difficulty in enlarging himself all the way. No doubt the whole quarter of a million—or whatever it was—went to her lawyers.

Judith! Judith! I will see you today!

The intimacies of love make human beings seem more ordinary. Even when the lover is pressing the flesh, he realizes that it is only flesh. If Swift had gone to bed with Stella or Vanessa, he would not have recoiled at the thought, She shits! The Nazi murderers farted, belched, squatted on the can, and trumpeted noisily there like everyone else. Hitler no doubt politely put his hand to his mouth when he burped. Even as he planned genocide at the dinner. *He* was banal, his crimes were not.

I walk up these garbage-laden Upper West Side streets with Judith, and I think how ordinary, how prosaic, dull, brazenly ordinary the Third World is. The still, sad music of humanity. The daily round. Eating, fucking, defecating. Ordinary, all ordinary. The vulnerable perishing body. Ordinary. Nothing out of the ordinary. Except that you haven't *looked.* As Pascal said—"The more intelligence a man has, the more he sees in other people."

New York, or Try to Love Thy Neighbor!

The hills seem to begin at Ninety-sixth, which may be why I always face this corner of Broadway with a certain trepidation. Little lady who looks just like my anarchist aunt Nechama, but tight and pinched, is selling the Spanish edition of the Jehovah's Witnesses magazine.

A Rolls-Royce rolled up Orchard Street yesterday. The Miami Beach plates on this *alrightnik* were just what you'd expect of the heavy advanced-middle-age gent in red slacks wearing a look of total complacency as he parked the Rolls heavily, mountainously, along Eldridge.

New York, or the Big Noisy Terrible Mix. Everyone thrown into the pile, but not yet Earth's holocaust, or the conflagration that took 271 lives at O'Hare and was due, it seems, to "metal fatigue" on the part of a three-inch bolt. This caused an engine and its mounting to fly off the American Airlines jumbo jet.

Oh yes, where was I on the subject of New York? The sick, the elderly—swollen feet in bedroom slippers. Blacks washing cars off Central Park West and to my amazement talking jauntily, familiarly, about something "on which thirty grand were thrown away."

\* \* \*

Faces, faces, how they devour me. It's a movie screen in the street of faces. Seeing Ralph Ellison at the American Academy of Arts and Letters the other day, I was struck by the alternation of pride and furtiveness. So beautifully dressed, Ralph is, and yet always in flight a moment after his face asks your opinion of Ralph Ellison.

As Nichols and May used to say about life on Central Park West, "proximity but no relating." The face problem, the intensity of a certain face suddenly coming at you. Typified in the elevator a minute ago as I was struggling that set of Sholom Aleichem to the P.O. for my sister, Pearlie, in Cambridge. Big, brawny consciously observant gentleman with the most enormously flaring nostrils. Studies me puffing over my package and inquires very tolerantly if my breathing so hard meant the end of my day?

By contrast, my old New York is still here—good Jewish rye and my favorite challah at the Cake Masters on Broadway, where the sweet Chinese girl, or is she Vietnamese, offers me a slice of the rye bread with my purchase of bran muffins for me and salt sticks for Judith. Reminds me of that wonderful old widow neighbor in our tenement who, returning in the morning after a night baking, would leave the most enormous cartwheel of a bialy against the door so that I would find it when I left for school in the morning. Love thy neighbor? In my Brownsville boyhood, nothing easier.

In the summer of 1952 I was Gastprofessor für Amerikanistik at the university, living in that beaten-up suburb of Cologne, my heart beating at my proximity (delayed by seven yrs) to Nazidom. I still couldn't get over the ordinariness of those rain-heavy trees as I walked past them. Like Hitler looking for his underwear. I remember that his so-called will expressed some wish for a "decent," *bürgerlich* life! This from the man who in his "table talk" profoundly announced—"The era of personal happiness is over."

\*   \*   \*

What alone works *all* the time? Spinoza's "God," the laws of nature, "His" laws if you like—and the human mind, "soft but persistent" (Freud). Every once in a while it occurs to this perpetually surprised man that the mind constantly asserts itself—that no matter how secret, silent, ashamed you are—whatever you like!—*it* keeps on working. And recognizes that nothing, ultimately, is so much like reason as the "laws" it seeks. Human nature, alas, is atavism, primitive, stunted, the animal in us always breaking out, seeking not the reason of things but to dominate, to take over, to occupy, and if necessary, to kill.

"Ours, a 'twice-born generation,' finds its wisdom in pessimism, evil, tragedy, and despair." Daniel Bell, *The End of Ideology: On the Exhaustion of Political Ideas in the Fifties*, p. 300.

Des Plaines, Illinois: Sixty-four years old today and who cares? It is all becoming a dreamlike surge to the hereafter. I ask myself, as I did yesterday on the bus returning from that unnecessary lunch in Evanston with the *American Scholar* editor, Joe Epstein (his addiction to Hilton Kramer makes me laugh), What is it all about?—*Where* is it all? All one knows is time passing.

So the only meaning of "God" is duration—the unmoved mover—the lasting—in this shoddy money-crazy existence of too many perishabilities. To hold on.

Edmund Wilson, the perfectionist, always correcting a word, a fact. Still obsessed with the word in his old age—bitterly disillusioned with America and shakily confronting the end. In his Wellfleet kitchen he (with more Hebrew than I could ever master) asked me—*me!*—what the Jewish religion could offer a man in his situation.

It is the animal in us that remembers. Yes. Frank Wedekind in *The Earth Spirit* and *Pandora's Box*: "What you have experienced as an animal, no misfortune can wrest from you. It remains yours for life."

I lost my American Express checks just as I was starting out for the Antarctic, and now the heavy actor Karl Malden with the glint of success in *his* eye holds up a book of AmEx checks and dares me to leave home without them. Mr. Nudnick and Mrs. Nudnick are in despair one minute before the weeds and what-not are climbing up their garage, but are made immediately happy, ecstatic, by the what-not in the commercial. Everything on Tee Vee is contracted into a death-defying cycle of paradise lost, paradise found. All you need to get out of the slough of despond is Kazin's Roto-Rooter, which will unclog your arteries, put hair back on your head, feed your cat as kitty has never been fed before.

Meanwhile the doped-up viewer, half asleep over the box, squinting in disbelief as he is tossed from hell to heaven and returned again by one commercial hitting him over the head after another, realizes that *he too must get going*. Time has been spent but he has not been saved. No sirree, not only not saved but like predigested food passed down the nation's alimentary canal.

June 12, 1979: Anne Frank would have been fifty today. *Times* story from Amsterdam on the Frank family hideout notes that the faded brown walls of the attic room she slept in for twenty-five months are still decorated with magazine photos of her idols—Rudy Vallee, Greta Garbo, Ray Milland, and Ginger Rogers.

West Germans now make up 40 percent of the total visitors: Most of them are young, and many of them, like Heinz Kummerl, a high school student from Hamburg, are clearly stunned by the experience. He sat in the bright sunshine on the steps of the Anne Frank house this afternoon shaking his head and freely conceding that he "simply had no idea."

Otto Frank told Ann and me when we were preparing *The Works of Anne Frank* that the Dutch Nazis who arrested the family smartly saluted Mr. Frank when they saw his old German Army trunk from the First World War marked "Hauptmann [captain] Otto Frank."

Joseph Powers, S.J. At lunch with the Gaffneys in Mishawaka he was comically profane, very much the buddy of ex-priest Ed Gaffney and sophisticated on every topic that came up. His talk on the Eucharist, an hour and a half, showed him absolutely imprisoned within his devotion. He was so hallucinated he impressed me, went round and round the circle of doctrine on the basis of certain key concepts. Best thing he said was about "disremembering" and "remembering." Spoke of the wind (*ruach*) by which the true Christian feels driven—then "the active and performative way in which a Christian behaves."

I was interested but not . . . included. As usual after such sermons I carried away the sense of the Christian *story*, a beautiful story but somehow tautological. I was impressed by Joseph's telling of the "story," not the doctrine floating somewhere within it.

Impressed, that is, by the appeal to the individual human being at his best—if, as Tolstoy said, "God is the name of my desire." My Jesuit: "The word made flesh means—the word made of my own heart." Not to deny oneself as the most beautifully aspiring being! That is beautiful—especially to a Jew tired of just "fighting back." Still, what is it all but a lot of words?

Howard Hughes, the great American money-grabber, the purest product of American *making it, making it,* went crazy because he couldn't take it all with him. He grew a beard all around himself so he could see what he would look like in the grave.

Prisoner, face that wall! Prisoner, what makes you think we take *your* life seriously—or for that matter, any life? You Jews have been so busy defending yourselves for an eternity that you have turned cherishing your existence into an ethical absolute! Well, my friend, my anxious self-protecting friend, my sleepless voraciously self-cherishing friend, *we* have seen so much death and killing, to say nothing of our indifference to the endless poor grubbing in the earth like so many pigs that we spit you out without a moment's thought.

Szymon Dawidowicz, the librarian of the Yiddish Scientific Institute, lost one child in the Warsaw Ghetto, another in Treblinka. Now he is dead. Lucy called me late last night. Tiny, round, gallant Lucy is just my age, grew up the familiar New York Jewish way— Hunter College, once in the Young Communist League with Bella the Abzug, reacted against all that even before she found herself in Vilna in August 1939, to research its famous Jewish past, and was warned by the American consul to get out before the Nazis arrived. Szymon so much older than she—too late for children, but their sweet marriage a triumph over those who meant to kill us all.

Thanks to Szymon and filled up with his past in Poland, Lucy was able to begin and to complete her great book, *The War Against the Jews.* Says she tried writing after her husband's death and now finds herself "inarticulate."

Why does the rain make me think back a thousand years to our only "rich" relatives, Elsie Gilman and her husband (his family owned some of the raw paper from Canadian forests that went into the *New York Times*), grandly *calling* in supper from the local delicatessen when we humbly called on them? My God, what freedom was there to impress poor, forever housebound Charles and Gussie Kazin! What an *air* the Gilmans put into that proud gesture! And how funny, now that we are talking about time (which puts on one funny hat after another before it does the magic act of disappearing from us together), to remember that at our cousin Ralph Levin's in San Mateo, I was talking to Elsie's grandson thinking all the while it was her son.

Judith is the only woman I have loved about whom I have no reserves, no second thoughts. The only one I know whose heart is completely open. Which, given my obsessive memories, is more than I am to her. Everybody so contained, so full of secrets—so full of his and her past life and surreptitious commitments. Which is all very well (I suppose) because while it is wearing, it is most interesting to think how many secrets and "treacheries" we positively live on as we get older.

Anne Sexton read galley proofs of *The Awful Rowing Toward God* on the day she did herself in. W. H. Shurr of Washington State University: "The volume gains in authority, then, as Anne Sexton's intended final work; the book furnishes the pattern, the master-plan, for the whole of her work. Clear also is the fact that the suicide is a consciously intended part of the book."

Judith has left her husband and has found an ap't on the Upper West Side.

*It seems highly unlikely that there will be ice on the NY streets by end April; however, I do wish that you would invest in a pair of shoes with thick rubber soles—preferably ridged soles, so as to minimize the chances of slipping on* anything. *Enough of this foppery in English shoes! Although I said the other day that I love you to pieces, I don't actually insist that you be* in pieces *for me to love (though I can truly say that I would love each one).*

*I had a marvelous time yesterday interviewing people who are setting up a private dining club where corporate biggies can eat lunch far from the riff-raff. $1000 to join, $45 a month dues, plus prices for food that, believe me, Nathan's Famous wouldn't recognize. The rather piggy head setter-upper took me on a tour of the glories-to-be. Mirrored ceilings louvered windows,* luxe. *The most interesting part was the stupendous kitchen, with the latest in automated deep-fat fryers and a James Bond doozy of a garbage disposal.*

*Here is a Polish couplet about a sapphire sky. Today's NY sky is not* sapphire—*the air is green, best to breathe something else. But my mood is green, my heart is green. I'm so happy every time I look at my ticket. "NY/South Bend." Oh God. Oh God. How can I bear to be without you until then?*

Sixty-three people executed "so far" in Iran.

Wasted an hour reading Podhoretz's *Breaking Ranks.* O God, these shallow little publicists who think they have news about themselves for the rest of us because they have gone ideological. A whole book to tell you not why this former Jewish liberal is now on the side of money and power, but what Diana thought of Jason's thoughts about Lionel's thoughts about William Barrett's thoughts.

The man-haters. Adrienne Rich wrote—"A thinking woman sleeps with monsters." But her critic Alicia Ostriker goes her one better: "The culture of the past is a predator; an intellectual woman who absorbs it becomes her own enemy."

Yet these Jews were once horrified by: "When I hear the word *culture* I reach for my revolver" (Göring).

Left Notre Dame August 15, arrived New York Aug 16. A long, hard pull to get here, and now except for my dear Judith, what am I doing in this overcharged, overpopulated, fouled-up city? One John Halpern set fireworks on top of the Manhattan tower of Mr. Roebling's bridge. Had no idea that this might cause extreme hurt to someone or other, but described his action as (*a*) a piece of "sculpture"; (*b*) his protest against the government's economic policy.

Here, ladies and gents, we have a perfect illustration of unlimited "consciousness raising." As Hunter S. Thompson says in "The Great Shark Hunt":

Who needs jazz, or even beer, when you can sit down on a public curbstone, drop a pill in your mouth, and hear fantastic music for hours at a time in your own head? A cup of good acid costs $5, and for that you can hear the Universal Symphony, with God singing solo and the Holy Ghost on drums.

Services at Campbell's Funeral Parlor for Jim Farrell. There was a cross on the stage of this theater where I have seen off so many friends—Harold Solomon, Harvey Breit, Mark Rothko, Sue Kaufman. The scenery in this theater is certainly easily shifted. Over James T. Farrell, a cross! Kurt Vonnegut turned out to be a very peppery admirer of Jim the old radical. "Nice try," he said about the cross. "When Jim arrives at the pearly gates I am sure he will, as always, handle himself well."

Shostakovich in *Testimony*. After his Thirteenth Symphony was banned (it included a setting of Yevtushenko's "Babi Yar"), "Jews became a symbol for me. All of man's defenselessness was concentrated in them."

Pope is in New York. Voices from the crowd: "I am all yours, Pope." "You are our only hope, Pope."

At the last, my mother turned her face to the wall as if in obligation to her religion.

From time to time, refreshed by writers ancient and modern who speak confidently of their belief in God, I think myself a believer. But I have trouble knowing *why* I believe (when I do), for the distance from God to man is so wide that I have never had a revelation. I do not share the confidence of Jews who are sure of the Covenant, of Christians sure that Jesus incarnates the word made flesh. And now here is Karl Rahner, the German Jesuit, for whom theology is an effort to get back to the *original* evocation of the relationship between God and human beings:

> If human beings are hungry for meaning, that is a result of the existence of God. If God does not exist, the hunger is

absurd. The hunger is a longing that cannot be satisfied. A longing for God cannot be taken away. Man is being who does not live absurdly—because he loves, he hopes, and because God, the holy mystery, is infinitely receptive and acceptant of Him.

Panel on Wallace Stevens at the CUNY Grad Center with Harold Bloom as the main attraction. Bloom now looks like my college classmate Zero Mostel, fat and round, round all over, which is funny since Zero was such a street character—rough, plain, and radical—whereas Bloom is as insulated as a yeshiva bocher, thinks all literature comes out of literature and has a mind so utterly refined and removed that his main tenet is that every writer wants to eclipse the writer who was the greatest influence on him. This has a certain application to poetry, that most self-consciously traditional and hierarchic art, but is nonsense if you think that Dickens wrote with Fielding in his mind.

Still, Bloom not only looks like Zero but acts like him even before he speaks, and when he does speak is the most self-conscious dominator of a literary conference I have ever witnessed. His thinking is all flowers, highfalutin interpretation, "gnosis." The line of American romantics *is* the American religion, and links Emerson to—Pater!

Bloom lives in the poets he loves, and clearly thinks himself made up of them. I admire him for this. But when he talks bountifully of Stevens's *Poems for Our Climate*, with many references to Nietzsche and others in the line of his favorite oracles, he cannot (*a*) describe Stevens against the style of other poets, and (*b*) does not by his invocation of his great men show us why the poem is good, what combines and startles and illuminates to make the poem good. What he does is to put the head of Harold Bloom right down on the poem, imprints on it his own mental formation, his signature invocation of Emerson-Whitman-Nietzsche-Pater, and then draw sentence after sentence out of his reading that relates to this imprint of himself on the poem, not the poem itself. I do not understand what this inspiring procession of names in Bloom's special code refers to outside his need to be seen as one of the procession.

The sea watchers on England's South Coast. For them the ocean is a "powerful drug that seems to extend life by exercising the intelligence outside the factors that formed it. Those at the tail end of life are dragged into its pull and immersed in life's origins." Ronald Blythe, *The View in Winter: Reflections on Old Age.*

Reading at Louis D. Brandeis High School, Upper West Side. Young black asked what he had learned from Richard Wright's *Black Boy:*

> The two themes that relate to my life are the desire to escape intolerable conditions and the determination to pursue goals against difficult odds. I live in an area of Harlem that once was good. Crime has now reached the neighborhood like a plague. I'm scared more than anything. But I must be strong. I take knives, sticks, and chains every time I leave the house. I think about why somebody would threaten my life without any cause. I pray every day that the day will come for me to graduate. I would leave this prison madhouse forever.

New York subway in freezing January—each face shaped like an irreversible geological formation. Out of *old* Egyptian earth.

Isaac Bashevis Singer—"Not even in Warsaw did I see faces so wild as here."

\* \* \*

Holocaust, Holocaust, Holocaust. The Jews once held together by their belief in God are now held together, or should I say *scared* together, by the Holocaust. And to cap the sin of the centuries, revived fascists and Nazis "doubt" it ever happened, while *we* do not know nor ever will know "how it could have happened"—how "they" could have "behaved this way." What it all "meant." Unlike the Christian worship of the "sacrificed One," our "sacrifice" is ambiguous.

JERRY RUBIN TO DIRECT DEVELOPMENT AT MUIR: "I hope to actively communicate the opportunities that John Muir presents to the economy, to the entrepreneur and to the investor. Using my knowledge of the media and my communications abilities, I hope to effectively communicate . . ."

Was a member of the sixties group that threw dollar bills from the visitors gallery to the trading floor of the New York Stock Exchange.

Alan M. Greenspan, the "conservative" economist on the *MacNeil Lehrer NewsHour*—he and another Wall Street rightist debating a black Texas congressman, Mickey something-or-other, on the impending Reagan budget cuts of "social services." Greenspan speaks of "the poor." Not people, not people in need, but "the poor." What a grandiosity on the part of this successful Jew, whose particular Darwin is Ayn Rand (another Jew). What a success society we live in! But in the crunch, and the coming worse crunch, America is dividing between those who have "made it," and "the poor." The Left is all windy Utopia just now, the actual complicatedness of our society and their own stake in its complicatedness are beyond them. The yuppie thinkers, like Greenspan and Podhoretz, though they have to sound polite and even "democratic," feel about the failures the way Reagan *looked* in the South Bronx during the campaign: disgusted.

Who says literature is no longer important? Mark Chapman—murderer of John Lennon, constantly carries around a copy of *Catcher in the Rye*—says, "That is my statement," in explanation of the killing.

Judith picked herself up at Ninety-seventh Street and Central Park West after being swiped by a car speeding out of the transverse. The driver stopped for a moment, and without looking to see what he had hit sped on. Judith was knocked on her head, suffered a concussion, for an hour lost sight in one eye. When I rushed over to the emergency room at Roosevelt Hospital she was sitting on a gurney, waiting for the doctor. Says she feels as if she has come back from the dead. There's a shadow over her.

One advantage of getting "old." So many people do not share my past that I am free to invent it.

Pursued all night by the furies: *Must do this, must do that. Do this, do that.* Teach me not to care, teach me to sit still! Teach me to float off at my ease—to "play it," whether "cool" or not. Having tried so long and so hard to reach the main goal, and having gone so far beyond the piss pool off the men's room in the Rockaway Avenue Station, I now ask—all this doing it and not doing it—to what avail? So I dream of that perfect trip with Jude to the fjords, to some small house with its own lake, to the Bach unaccompanied flute sonatas, to being *in* her all day and all night, to that day in Rome amid the line of trees, stopping for a cool, dry wine on my way back from the Vatican museum. More time, Lord! Lord! Grant us enough time. . . . I have never felt so blissfully alive as I do now, when the numbers begin to press.

*You* (because there is no God, only the word at the end of a cry)!

The whole day is made up of obligations, appointments, regularities, like the need to keep my keys in the right-hand pocket of my jacket, my wallet in the *inner* right breast pocket, my glasses in the left, etc. The day is so fixed in advance, the duties are so importunate, that more and more, with the fear that time *may* be running out, I can't wait to get out of bed and to the typewriter even before light has filtered into the Upper West Side.

The strange upshot of all this programming, this busy morning and early afternoon. In the midst of the rain, the turbid flux around my eyes and ears walking past all the porno shit on Forty-second Street, I am moved! Ye gods, to be moved like this—moved just to be alive! Moved because in some totally unexpected, unexpectable way (knock wood), things have worked out! But beyond the daily fulfillment business, moved because one *is* alive, and glad to have this chance, this one last chance still!

Met Judith at the federal courthouse, where she is jurying, had a look at her chic courtroom, admired the Woolworth Building "the cathedral of business" they once called it, then to dinner—past the heaped-up courts, prisons of N.Y.C. power (the old police Headquarters on Centre Street shows its dome as if it were in London)—to Forlini's on Baxter Street. My God, what nuts and nuttesses. In front of us as we ate our heavy meal was a party of young men all with mustaches, all laughing the same way, looking serious the same way, talking money, money, money the same way. All around us fat beefy cops in sweaters, little "Joosh" bail-bond types sucking at big cigars. The aggressiveness just below the surface made my head spin. Because I know nothing of what really goes on.

Almost all the intelligence I see and hear around me is critical—reactions to things, books, etc. Almost all the historians I read are first of all critics of other people's versions of the subject. These "reactions" spring from an intellectual consensus as ghastly as the consensus founded on fear of economic breakdown. Intellectuals whose only horizon is to move oneself a notch above and away from the only company they know.

I don't see much invention, because I think that the common denominator, the ease and superfluity of interchange, is more forceful than ever. All these braying "communications" are the devil, for they come to seem second nature, they get confused with reality.

Literary intelligence (inventiveness, fantasy, the comic sense in all its suppleness and gift for portraiture) must lag behind the reflex of criticism in times like these. The burden of proof is more exigent than ever on people *trying* to escape the web, the "norm" created by all this technology.

We stopped for lunch at the Lorelei in Groton, across the Thames River from the naval base in New London. In the murky dark waters off the restaurant, two swans (such beautiful white fleecy bodies, such prissy ugly faces and show-off necks), anchored unbelievably close to the pier. The tough blue-collar types drinking beer in the vast nightclub spaces of the Lorelei, where at noon the drums were dead, the Sat. nite finery and gewgaws absolutely silent.

My mother, who thought herself the Ugly Duckling. I talked to her a lot—just talked. She became the Survivor. Her lovely sister Schaene was picked up in a Nazi raid on their shtetl and murdered in a ditch. The Ugly Duckling always had a lot to say about handsome attractive ladies *close to her* like Schaene, Sophie, Paula, etc. etc. But in the end she was the Survivor and through her son, still is there, still dominates. He talks to her a lot even now—the old fellow in his sixties or even his seventies(!) still measures other women by her—by her famous moral superiority.

Her hold on me her revenge on other women? She compared herself constantly with other women. After all, a dressmaker. And the big surprise for me is how much my proletarian "saint" was a rival to other women—how far back, back, to the dreary Russian-Polish shtetl, that sexual rivalry went—how much, under all that piety and officiousness from a father who never *looked* at her, the bearded patriarch Isaac Moses Fagelman, lay the woman's hope, her sexual bitterness.

Proletarian Mother and Great Sufferer. The Heroine of the Working Class. Remember how we carried ice together in a great towel from the icehouse on Sutter Avenue. When I described this in my first theme at City College, the instructor, Mr. Burt (fresh from Oxford), frowned: "I don't understand what you're writing about."

In some way the *angst* she planted led to his becoming a writer. In the sleepless nights of his planning—his *whirring*—the brain madly revolving—a certain distinctness in forming so much mind around the object was plainly connected to his concern about *reaching* the object. His recurring dream about not being able to get to a certain place—preparations getting in one another's way for a journey that is constantly being stalemated. All this called for the journey to start again at my desk in the first light of day.

Looking out at the dirty gray front, the ramshackle shops and dreck of Broadway in the 80s (still dreck despite the many years of gentrification)—somehow it all looked like my life with Ann. How many times did our hero walk these blocks, often at night, like a stunned child, after wifey screamed me out of the house? And yet, and yet, how all those years somehow make up a fund of experience, a bank of memory, that is lodged in my brain, so that I cannot help likening myself to Frost, in "Acquainted with the Night." But also of Kate as a Dalton student, doing our "drunk" act with me—wobbling boisterously from one end of the pavement to the other as I walked her to the crosstown bus at Eighty-sixth.

The luck: when I was approached by Carl Van Doren to write the book that became *On Native Grounds.* The luck: meeting Judith by the sheerest accident, living with Judith, loving Judith. The truth is that despite all my kvetching there has been a positively divine gift, yes indeed, of luck and escape, the providential, when I have needed it. The worrier, so much in love with time, worried about time ahead of him, still trying to describe the time behind him, trying to locate the tone of time in all its elusiveness, its silky, adroit elusiveness.

The analyst Leslie Farber dead of a heart attack at Roosevelt Hospital. A sudden death? A great shock to me. What a dear, wise if sad man he was in his last years—and what a change from the peppery, hard-drinking rather mettlesome fellow in naval uniform I met in some Village restaurant during the war years. He was all occupied with dear unfaithful Marjorie in those years—a scrappy unhappy couple they were. She went into a big decline after they finally released each other, got so *finito* she asked him to stop sending money.

Leslie—a sharp fellow, much deepened and saddened by the time I went to him at the Master Institute for help all around. He had a slight stroke, was less interested in my troubles than in seeking a logos by way of Martin Buber! He made me think of my first analyst, Janet Rioch, admitting, "You don't know what goes on upstairs."

In a half dream I see Papa in a crowd, smiling but enclosed by the crowd—unfathomable within the crowd—and being borne away. He was handsome—smiling—in some way he was I—looking at myself as Papa.

Life in the 1980s—a man eating as he watches a massacre on TV.

City University Graduate Center, Room 1511, 4 P.M.: One of those hours, days, moments in which the ecstasy is just being alive. As I say to Judith at such instants, my glass is so full I am afraid to spill a drop. The weather—the gush of spring—eighty degrees—having some money to spend—luxurious feeling approaching the Sabbath—drinking lemony tea in the drab coffee shop across Forty-third Street, tea and poundcake, like Mom's sponge cake, the Shabbas treat. As I sit there in glowing attention I can see the ridiculous red flowers painted on the chandelier getting brighter and brighter.

Shabbas, 7 A.M.: The actor in the White House has had to play many roles *in life* to get where he is now. He is still playing many roles, our Twinkle-Twinkle Mr. Nice Guy. But think of those political "intellectuals," say like Midge Decter, who through this tumultuous period appears first as a gofer at Columbia Records, now as the wife of "Neo-Podhoretz," now as the scourge of homosexuals in *Commentary*, now as director of a super-anticommunist organization called *The* Committee for a Free World. But when you see her on the street, the former editor at *Harper's*, the former this and the former that, is that roguishly smiling Midge, willing to take you on, so to speak, a friendly sort. Still playing some role or other.

In memory alone, thank God, Ann's many faces, above all her many voices. Am I going to keep mourning her when the love—so ragged on my part—is long since gone? The voice used to melt me with its quiveriness. Now, when I hear a door slam, a kitchen drawer being irritably knocked shut, I expect to hear her come on screaming. Just as I still dream of falling out of a window in an effort to keep her from jumping.

The hours fly, the days gather themselves up like so many bundles of newspapers waiting to become the waste material of history. I cannot bear to think of everything flitting by so fast as waste material. *An American Procession* is not only my major effort but my long-sought vindication as a critic—a critic outside the fashionable university opinion.

Stop indulging yourself, Kazin, in anything except work! But don't forget to pray, for God *is* the only continuity and by praying, even by trying to pray, miserable schismatic that you are, you are in the vicinity of His duration, the very hope and sign of the Everlasting.

I pass Holy Name of Jesus Church at Ninety-sixth and Amsterdam every day, but was astonished, entering it for the first time, to see how large it is, how truly *grand* all in good proportion. Just behind all the "greasies," the endless up and down of the street, the concussion that *is* the street. Goes to show, doesn't it—in the midst of this crass city life, there is something distinctly *other*—a promise. Hanging below the lectern: LORD HELP US CHANGE OUR HEARTS HELP US LORD HELP US. COME NEARER—OR LET US COME NEARER.

Devout culture audience at Avery Fisher for Bach's Saint John Passion. To dramatize the Passion of Our Lord! I got tired of the historical miasma in the most anti-Jewish of the Gospels, and could not help snickering to myself over the bent knees (metaphorically) of all the Jews in the orchestra and in the audience. But so it is, forever—we live in a Christian culture, and our lives are entirely secular in practice, Christian in attitude. It is only the silent protest against the majority writing history (and entombing us) that remains "Jewish." Being religiously "Jewish" in this "Christian" society can be so private as to be almost inarticulate.

Fifty years ago this spring! Walking down that wide sidewalk from Columbus to Amsterdam on Ninety-seventh Street I suddenly felt in the puff of warm air that has at last had the decency to surface on the Upper West Side that I was walking those heavily sunlit wide clean streets, Bushwick Avenue, Evergreen Avenue, in that happy high school graduation spring of 1931. Nineteen thirty-one is an improbable date to bring up just now, but I can give back every detail of my teacher Julian Aaronson's kindness to me—playing the Kreisler recording of the Brahms concerto, not laughing over my first story. All that—and Highland Park. All that. What I have most fixed in mind just now, however, is the clean, empty, available Brooklyn sidewalk of 1931.

Leaving my office at the Grad Center I come up against the old lady who has been there forever, shrilling in her thin deadly whine, "Coins! Got coins?"

The pitchman for the massage parlor across Sixth Avenue had the grace to laugh when he accosted me with, "Hey Pop! Check it out! Check it out!"


The god Memory. Listening to a wonderful "BBC cassette" on the radio of my dear old Tchaikovsky showpiece, *Capriccio Italienne,* I seem to hear the roaring, coming, and going of the sound as if I were waking from anesthetic.

And remembering the taste of Passover farfel in a glass of milk of course brings the old kitchen table into focus—the milky enamel kitchen tabletop, with a scar showing the black beneath.


Not to think that all the excitement was in the struggle of youth. Because a life is so short, it is well to remember how consistent it may be.


Sunday morning, 9 A.M. Happy night after happy evening and day with Judith. Lying in bed this morning I thought how fatal "love" was without respect—for some of my previous ladies. The divided man, who sits on the "judgment seat" indeed, full of sharp opinions, but when it came to "love," dissolves into the needy child and the demander in sex-to-the-limit (whatever that means). In any event the split between "judgment" and "feeling" has been near lethal. Looking back at my life with Ann, I must admit to having placed her and myself in a false position. Because her "sharpness"—amusing as it could be—dazzling as her demand on life could be—never impressed me as requiring respect.

"Respect!" I sound like a Mafioso. But the subject is fundamental, not to be avoided in the American pretense that we are all equal to our demands on life.

Afternoon, after the usual acid bath to the nerves in the Sunday *Times* magazine—article "Conservative Brain Trust":

> If American Enterprise Institute has a patron saint, he is Irving Kristol. Mr. Kristol has been busy expanding an enticing blend of ideas that has captured the hearts, minds and checkbooks of American businessmen. The simple truth is that the professional classes of our modern bureaucratized societies are engaged in a class struggle with the business community for status and power. Inevitably, this class struggle is conducted under the banner of "equality." The members of this "new class" occupy key positions in the media, academia and government and are, Mr. Kristol implies, anti-capitalist in their ideology. The corporation, he goes on to say, is "an utterly defenseless institution . . . picked on and so easily bullied." The only defense he can envision is to foster institutions with a pro-business thrust.

You see how little Irving the old Trotskyite has changed from his old Marxism. There is no *thought* on the part of intellectuals—just "class struggle."

\*    \*    \*

Back in New York from my lecture trip in full "wonder shining May." Walked up to Columbia, puttered around bookstores, record shops. Latin-American street actors, street clowns, street villains. People who do not look at the headlines but *look* headlines. For some time, in these cluttered, almost putrefying streets, I have been trying to figure out just what it is that irritates me so much. *Mass.* Everything so derivative, like the disgusting paper and film clichés. I PRAY FOR HIM, headline in the *News* straight from the Holy Father. Reagan and Pat O'Brien embracing at the Notre Dame commencement. Get into the parade, man! What are you doing outside, thinking your own thoughts, figuring out the universe as if it had not already been decided to ignore it?

Times story on Houston, the real United States we now have to deal with. City run by developers, short on all public services, big sports town. Space City USA, home of the Astronauts, site of the Astrodome, citadel of medical wizardry. City held together by its freeways, by what comes into its homes, the airwaves, and by the success of its professional baseball, football, and basketball teams, all of which have been championship contenders in the last year.

Houston's deliberate policy of low taxes and minimal services. Those who run the city say this is the way to unleash growth and development to the benefit of all. The free-market theory of gvt leaves hundreds of thousands of the poor to fend for themselves.

Houston is planned by a "very narrow group, and in many ways a reckless group."

"It's the main show now in the United States."

\*    \*    \*

Waiting for an Amsterdam bus at Seventy-second, I was stupe-fied by the mass mad scene: With traffic being rerouted around the usual midnight excavations, all those buses and trucks (trucks late in the evening, New York *never* sleeps) made such a swirl of noise and confusion at that crossroads that I could not stand look-ing at it as I waited for a bus that never came, and grabbed a taxi. The dark, anonymous man in front, who just drives, whose face you never see, takes your money, lets you out on a street where nobody sees you.

What made the occasion at Temple Emanu-El was the moment when the great Raoul Wallenberg was honored. His sister had come from Sweden to accept an award made to him by the Josephs of Minneapolis. One of the Hungarian Jews saved by Wallenberg was on the "stage"—others stood up in the audience. The not-dead standing up was a thrilling, piercing moment. Not the mourners stood up but those saved from the burning.

The poles in the water. Thinking of the poles holding up the old pier in Coney Island—the rotted poles smelling of piss and studded with shriveled condoms and saltwater taffy. Now all this beautiful peepul of Southampton, all bedecked with golden chains, strolling along the sea, the beautiful sea . . .

My body. My other self. At sixty-six I wonder what surprises it has for me—what surprises it carries deep in itself.

\* \* \*

Visit to Isaac Bashevis Singer for photographs for my book with David Finn, *Our New York*. A big dusty apartment (no curtains overlooking Broadway and Eighty-sixth Street). Singer in his usual thin-lapeled suit and dark tie looking as if he were waiting in line to see his Creator. Delights in his "garbage room"—which drives his German-born wife crazy—lined with endless certificates, diplomas—testimony to his many honors. Framed certificates from some Jewish lawyers' group in Texas next to his Nobel Prize certificate and his election to both the National Institute of Arts and the American Academy of Arts and Sciences.

I found him cagey, depressed, full of sour jokes and unexpected jealousies. "Solzhenitsyn has hundreds of acres in Vermont, is a millionaire, but of course the Jews do not want unlimited acreage, just a bankbook—so they can go off lightly when trouble comes."

The Jews, the Jews, the Jews—the repetition of it even in my own mind sometimes drives me mad—from horrible Begin to our latest martyr, Timerman. Why is it hard for a Jew to forget for one second that he is a Jew? All that history, the constant tug of the past.

In any event the present period of Jewish "success" will some day be remembered as one of the greatest irony. First the Jews get caught in a trap, the Jews "exterminated" en masse. And bango! Atop the mountain of ashes and all this inescapable lament *and* exploitation of the Holocaust comes the state of Israel as the Jews' "safeguard," with the Holocaust as our sanctity. Oh God, this theologizing of "the worst episode in human history" (Churchill).

Driving the long route back from Wellfleet in the rain. I was of course thinking of Emerson and Thoreau in my book. How much Thoreau relies on the word being the equivalent of some actual experience. Whereas Waldo thinks of the word as progenitor—becoming almost equivalent to whatever it creates.

\* \* \*

Southampton, 8:30 P.M.: Immersed in the highway and in thought of the Glorious Fourth while slowly inching my way here (ghastly traffic, almost two hrs to Amityville alone) I suddenly *see* the hulking clouds above and think, How little we take in the strangeness of being in the world at all. What an accident, our interrupting this cosmic bombardment, this ceaseless energy that does not need us for anything!

Emerson says, "Nature is meant to serve." And it did, Waldo, it does. But is it meant to serve just *us?*

Yevgeny Kharitonov, nonconformist Soviet writer, dies at forty as he walks down Pushkin Street, in the center of Moscow, after working all night on a play. He was independent of both official and underground trends in the arts. He was neither a member of the Union of Soviet Writers nor a political dissident:

> He shunned a career and made no efforts to emigrate, he made few efforts to be published and he lived a secluded life, holding a job only to make enough money to enable him to write. . . . An important new element in Soviet art—an independent artist dedicated to pure creativity, a writer not bound or defined by restrictions. He titled the typewritten collection of his works "Under House Arrest," but this referred to his own style of life and work rather than to official repression.

Feigning horror at the oblivion of a writer stripped of official restrictions, Kharitonov described the solution: "To burn only with an internal flame. But to be consumed by it. Then people will believe the poet and will spread his works."

\* \* \*

Monster Begin has killed more than 120 people in Beirut this morning, wounded more than 500. On and on it goes.

BOOK PACKAGERS COME OF AGE: "Hard-cover fiction does not generally lend itself to packaging, but Bernard Geis Associates specialized in it":

> "We put up advances of $50,000 or more, sign up authors, subsidize them, inspire them, edit them, and when the book is completed to our satisfaction, we auction it to co-publishers," said Mr. Geis, who almost 20 years ago published Jacqueline Susann under his own imprint.
> "Our chief function is to court and nurture talent," Mr. Geis said, "and to take a $10,000 writer and make him a quarter-million dollar writer."

You can write about all these partings and deaths—you *can* put something into words. But what the words can never convey is the *wrench*—the unsubduable pain, the shock that remains a shock, is worked into your innermost body until you die.

The reason I do not write fiction is that I am not yet up to human conflict. I still portray people *alone*, whether the characters in my literary history or the people I should like to portray in *Absent Friends*. When I write the story of the lady in Payne Whitney, for example (beginning on protestations of endless love as the guards unlock the barred gate) it will be necessary to show the distrust in both husband and wife—though he has just agreed to smuggle in some gin for her and he is full of cheer (the bastard) as he saunters down Sixty-eighth Street on his way home.

War is logical. The earth is small, its produce is limited. So conflict is instinctive, visceral. And frankly, why not admit how much most of us repel each other?

Early morning, barely six, light gray within the trees, light slowly dripping into the world. The world and my *world.* Wrestling since 4 A.M. or so with Ann's alimony and the monthly payments on the house we have bought in Roxbury. As fearful at sixty-six as I was at six—and at sixteen. Dark thoughts of revenge against the sellers, who indifferently left the house a horror. Wrote imaginary letters of magnificent insult. But the morning time and the nighttime are the seed time of *Absent Friends.* I see myself exuding my dreams, what a mingling—but the mingling is the leitmotif of the book—Babi Yar, New York, the neighbors, my enemies, etc. The hideousness of the literary life apart from literature. Heavy strangers (Ted Roethke), forgotten loves. The shock of just barely remembering someone you once slept with.

The dead piling up around me. The dead getting too many to count. Like the murder statistics in New York just now. Once each "dead" was someone to linger over, as in a detective story. Now they pile up—statistics.

The mixture of remorse and lust, regret and fresh concupiscence. The early morning opening in Joyce and the night closing in Proust. My political despair. The world is icing over. Bottom human nature in control. The rapacity of Reagan, of lawyers, landlords. The show of culture and the destitution below.

Political numbness. Everyone getting dumber. My past means nothing to everyone right after me. The death of the past means I can make it all up! That no one can check on me! Alas, it means that only I am interested in it now. So that it no longer hurts to remember Michael as a boy nudging me in the movie theater when the war scenes of Jews came on. "Okay, Pop, start crying now."

Kafka on the old Jewish quarter in Prague:

In us it still lives—the dark corners, the secret alleys, the shuttered windows, the squalid courtyards, the rowdy pubs, the sinister inns. We walk through the broad streets of the newly built city. But inside we still tremble in the centuries-old streets of our misery. Our hearts know nothing of the slum clearance around us.

The whole bloody day wrapped in dark, persistent rain—sorrow at Sadat's murder. This really tears it, and all the nuts are glad that the peacetime is over. Nuts in Israel as well as Libya.

I had brief visions of getting away for a while from the everlasting anxiety about Israel, but no chance now if Egypt rejoins its Arab Israel-hating brothers.

Woke up this morning thinking of Moshe Dayan (exactly my age), of his withered face, his diffidence in public, his world fame in 1967, the triumphal march to the Wailing Wall—of his passion for archaeology, the Bible, his reading to the audience in which I sat the lament for the fall of Jerusalem by an Arab woman poet, as well as the poetry of Nathan Alterman.

They buried him yesterday on the hilltop at his parents' old moshav in Galilee. The place-names, so dear with the Jewish sense of belonging at last—Nahalal. In his recent book, *Breakthrough*, he described the graveyard as the setting of a dream:

> I am evading pursuit, climbing a hill and trying desperately to reach the top, where I know I shall find a haven. . . . The track leads to the cemetery; but that is not what I am aiming for. My objective is the peak above and just north of it, what the children of Nahalal in my time used to call "the forest." At the top is a cave scooped out of the rock of the peak. I go straight to it and crawl inside. I lie on my right side. And sink into the calmness and tranquillity for which I yearn.

Said he was not a real kibbutznik. A real loner. The famous eye patch hid him very well, as he wanted. There was something about his narrow face that offered nothing to the beholder and yet was soldier-merciless.

Dayan was Israel to me, modern Israel, remote from the Holocaust and pogroms and Europe's eternal everyday hatred of Jews. I liked him being such a bloody Canaanite, so concerned with the land. The TV of the state funeral showed everyone in yarmulkes, and you could hear rabbinical chanting in the background. Not this wolf-man's natural ambience, *what?* That was the rock, the cave, and from it Dayan peering out at us with his one good eye.

Suddenly overcome with grief at the meaningless passing of the hours, days, years—the maddening lurch to the grave. Not yet, O Lord, not yet! Homesick, as always on holiday occasions, for the I-Know-Not-What—Divine Reassurance. I would have liked to cry out in the middle of the unseeing, unfearing crowd how hard it is indeed to love this God who without ever revealing Himself remains—Yea! presence—intimation—shadow and furrow.

To love God is to be grateful for the Creation and the Intelligence that keeps the universe going (while man is forever assaulting it). How odd that the first laws of science are still scriptural—that there *is* a world here rather than nothing.

He never answers but His "world without end" is the only answer we need and can understand. Between us and Him—It—falls the shadow indeed—the ineluctable tangent of our mind. Our mind and His.


The sin in Allied bombing was above all its inadvertence. It was technological fanaticism—a pursuit of destructive ends, but one expressed, sanctioned and disguised by technological means . . . Two distinct but related phenomena—the will to destroy and the means of destruction. . . . The sin was inadvertent in that illusions about modern technology made air war unthinkable before it occurred, and bureaucratic warmaking made responsibility for it diffuse and unclear once war began. It was sin of a modern kind because it seemed to involve no choice. It was the product of a slow accretion of large fears, thoughtless assumptions, and at best discrete decisions.

Michael Sherry


Movies are the very embodiment of our mortality. Flick and it is gone; flicker, move, and movie. The preparations are complex, but the more places you seek out for simulacra, the more the intended *verismo*, the farcical *verismo*, disappears on your hands and calls for still more preparations, expeditions, money. One movie succeeds and replaces another on the production line. Books are now produced like movies. Books now *are* movies. The quick transitions in Robert Stone's *A Flag for Sunrise*, the heightening of the action as the "revolution" approaches—all this adopts the timing of a movie.

Amid the clipped prose with its many hidden quotations, mocking quotations, is what you would get in a really good voiceover movie.

Deep winter, yellow sky last night when I went to bed and yellow sky when I awoke. All the streets and skies and buses and people merge into a gelatinous muddy mess. I am depressed by the inability to walk freely—the sky comes down on me from morning on.

Faces on the supermarket tabloids as you finally make your way to the checkout. The face of Elizabeth Taylor on every cover seems all—the breasts—all-inviting. The face is so sexually open that the instancy of sex, the suddenly bounding nerve, takes you in with the most hurried glance.

Judith is my happiness. Judith is the warm bed, the ready word, the ceaseless interest. The world is not only snowy and cold, day after day this horrid winter; the world is evil and will not get less so. But Judith is the middle of the world, the world within the world. Last night, in an absolute fever of merriment as we were going down on the Columbus Avenue bus to the concert at Alice Tully, I suddenly had a flash: some time in the later thirties on a quiet near-empty Lexington Avenue bus with Asya, enjoying the total quiet with that dear girl in the unexpectedness of a near-empty bus in New York! In the middle of New York's madness, I thought that night, here *we* are safe and quiet! And so it was last night on the bus with Judith.

Incredible luck. Let me for once be clever enough to keep it.

\*   \*   \*

Mailer's protégé Jack Abbott convicted of manslaughter for killing that waiter last summer in an argument about using the men's room. Abbott's lawyer gave him a cake, and Norman Mailer "a specially bound limited edition of an essay he wrote about the media." Nothing excites Mailer's protection and literary zeal so much as a murderer.

The way in which these God seekers *make* God out of language. Karl Rahner (quoted by Thomas Sheehan in the *New York Review*, February 4, 1982): "Wherever a person allows himself to fall into the abyss of the mystery of his own existence with ultimate resolve and ultimate trust, he is accepting God."
Sheehan:

If it is man's nature never to be without a relatedness to matter, and if one maintains that man is immortal as a whole and not just as a spirit, then it follows for Rahner that in death one does not leave the material world but enters more deeply into it and becomes what he calls "all-cosmic," present to and in communication with all material reality, an "open system towards the world," and a real ontological influence on the whole of the universe.

On this hypothesis "certain parapsychological phenomena now puzzling might be more readily and more naturally explained."

Whitehead was right—religion "is what we do with our solitariness." But what is our solitariness but the self not knowing what to make of so much perception locked in—so much sensation without an outlet? Lawrence: "Man has his excess always on his hands."

\* \* \*

New York Hospital: Arrived midnight February 10. A day and an hour that will live in infamy.

Today, Tuesday morning, February 16, 1982, first time the old head is clear enough after the double bypass to put down date and whereabouts. When they wheeled me into the operating room there was such an army waiting for me—so many machines—that I cracked "Los Alamos?" before going under. Woke up immobile, near choking on stuff crammed down my throat. Now bloody intensive care unit—monitoring—endless record-keeping. One medical helot after another staring at EKG screens and keeping records. I am in the world of science fiction, everyone in white—trained, silent, obedient.

Woke up to find Judith had written in my notebook—

*It was*

- *end of visiting hours*
- *too dark to read*
- *time of battery exhaustion for radio*
- *and you were sleeping. So I left. Please call in A.M.*

*XXX*

Wednesday dormant. Silly Wednesday—a Wednesday just like Tuesday and Monday. But I do feel better and sense in the old corpus that I'll make it. Looking back at the argument of the book I see more and more how the "self," Emerson's magic self, was really born of the religion of democracy (in America aka equality) *but* forced to the top, literally, by the innate current of radical Protestantism.

Eliot—man without God is not even "interesting." This is the synthetic literary Catholicism of a poet who obviously has no patience with fiction. After finding man-without-God not "interesting" (shades of DeFoe, Fielding, Dickens, etc.) the next stop is to burn him as a heretic.

My month in the hospital (February 10–March 7) passed like a "dream," a thought, a very bad thought. It passed so quickly that even now I wonder, and perhaps for a long time to come will continue to wonder, what *I* was and where *I* was while my body was the center of attention. Now that I'm home and "recovering," time is like pushing a stubborn ox up a hill. The days seem endless, and I tire so quickly that I am too conscious of time beating away. The old ticker at work in its new connections.

My heart failing was a surprise, a trauma, when I picture what they had to do inside me in that factory of an operating room. (I can't get over the mass of people waiting for me as I was wheeled in.) Now, because of my slowness and hesitancy, I feel the stickiest kind of nausea about so much around me. A mechanical world, as I am newly put together a mechanical man. I crave, more than ever, a departure from this weakness, this routine. I want the Big Surprise.

Anyway, I've been reading *Nostromo*, for the first time. Sooner or later, in every Conrad text, comes the revelation, aka the fascination: It is his compulsiveness. There is an obsessiveness, an obstinacy, a sticking-to-it, an endless preoccupation, and a madly concentrated effort of attention to *details*, important or not. It is not only that his people have long memories, are undeviating fanatics at heart, and have the long view about things insignificant to the rest of us. What makes them stick out, what makes them not of our time, is preoccupation. In Conrad's own grinding determination. Is Conrad the last novelist to *picture* man making the big effort to be larger than his circumstances? The man against the sky. And how well he knows that there is nothing in that sky (nothing in the least) that is a destiny for the likes of him. But he just has to stand out against the sky.

I start with the hospital and end with Conrad. The common note is time—not time everlasting but man making the last big effort to keep it on his side.

Israeli invasion of Lebanon. Yaron Ezrahi, the brilliant Hebrew University political scientist, shocked to see on U.S. television shots of Israeli planes bombing Beirut. These were not shown on Israeli television. Edward Said, in *The Politics of Dispossession*, says twenty thousand died. Robert Fisk, in "Pity the Nation," cites Lebanese sources, based on police, hospital, and Red Cross records, that place the number of deaths at fourteen thousand.

David K. Shipler, front page, *Times* (July 14, 1982), describes in detail the "sleight of hand by which Israel arrived at reduced numbers" of the victims. The *Times Book Review* adds: "The numbers game should not obscure the fact that thousands of innocent civilians died under Israeli bombs and shells. Statistics do not have to be overstated to make the point that it was a horrible war."

Jews on the American scene. The neoconservatives have made it right with the boss their grandfathers used to picket.

I must not forget to record in this book the sight of Lincoln Kirstein on a Madison Avenue corner the other day. Swollen at seventy-five, wearing an original sort of gleaming double-breasted blazer, one hand on a young man's shoulder. L. Kirstein is not only the American Diaghilev, he is the grand factotum of all the arts, the most intelligent, passionate, and indomitable of aesthetes.

\* \* \*

Walking up Madison, I stopped at the Morgan Library to see the exhibition of French illustrated books. God, what luxury, what sumptuousness, what sense of property in a book! Thinking of Gertrude Himmelfarb's sickening essay in *The Victorian Mind*, dismissing sympathy for the poor among the upper classes, I copied this from Blanchard Jerrold's *London Illustrated*, by Gustave Doré— "It is not possible to over-praise the greatness of heart with which the English working classes pass through famine. They alone know how to starve for an idea."

At the International Center of Photography, the Erich Salomon show. Long ago I admired his photographs of international conferences in the twenties—Ramsay Macdonald, Briand, etc., in evening dress with cigars and brandy after dinner. What I had never seen before was the shot of the Reichstag in the Weimar period, with Nazi deputies rambunctious in brown shirts and Sam Browne belts defying the law prohibiting the wearing of uniforms in the Reichstag. You can see them chortling.

Salomon and family, hiding in Holland, were betrayed. He died in Auschwitz.

Menachem Begin in angry meeting with American congressmen returning from West Beirut. Begin responded to Paul McCloskey's question about a "Palestine homeland":

The Prime Minister heatedly gesticulated toward a map on the wall with his cane and recalled the long history of the Jews in those lands. "And you want me to negotiate for a Palestinian state in those mountains and valleys and say this is not my homeland?" He gave a definite "no" in very angry terms to any Palestinian state whatever.

\*   \*   \*

Elinor Arnason, our darling friend in Roxbury, says that her late husband, the art historian H. H. Arnason, was an alcoholic. He briefly attended AA meetings in Washington, Connecticut. One woman, displeased with the social level she encountered in AA, stormed out, saying, "I've never drunk with the likes of you and I'm not going to get sober with the likes of you either!"

Glenn Gould's death hits me very hard. The clearest, subtlest musical mind I've ever heard. He gave back to us a Bach who used to get lost in a volley of notes.

Edward Teller has given Reagan the idea for another super-weapon. The Russian Revolution has kept these neoconservatives in its grip far more than it has the old left:

If the Soviet Union ever launched a mass missile attack against the U.S., tracking instruments would point the lasers at the missiles, the nuclear bomb would explode, the radiation generated by the bomb would activate the lasers, and lethal light beams would flash toward the earth. Instantaneously, these beams would destroy vast numbers of the missiles in flight.

"He flouted the Jewish leadership," Gertrude Himmelfarb says of someone critical of Israel. The president of the Zionist Organization of America—"Recent days have revealed a sense of genuine fear [among] the Jewish people everywhere. . . . Those who criticize Israel need not complain if we sense within this criticism, overtly or covertly . . . elements of anti-Semitism."

Well, here it is 1984 in Roxbury, and there's no television peeking in from Big Brother, no secret police arresting in the night, nothing but ice in the driveway, Benny Goodman and other oldies on the Saturday-night jazz program from Monroe. Our world is ominous, all right, and there is a threat every hour on the hour, the terrible fluency of the news being part of that threat. But we are not Stalinized yet—God bless America! God bless Thomas Jefferson and Abraham Lincoln! God bless the Bill of Rights, the Declaration of Independence, the Shepaug River, and the Vermont Country Store! Hurray for the Portuguese Ele-Fant Bakery just across from the Motor Vehicle Bureau in Danbury, Connecticut!

A night at the opera with the very rich. The magnate Arthur Carter, whose sideline is publishing the *Nation* and the *New York Observer*, had us in his box at the Met, along with the builder Arthur Fisher, an orthopedic surgeon Dr. Leon something. The assembled wives flitted in red—Mrs. Fisher in earrings that Jude is sure cost not less than eighty thou.

So there we were at *La Bohème*, ridiculously overdressed (as always) by Franco Zeffirelli. His sets, while startling, dwarfed poor Mimi, made nonsense of Rodolfo and Marcello, and in the second act produced such a sumptuous street scene that more Parisians surrounded Momus café than can daily be found in the Place de la Concorde.

Between acts we sat down to Dom Perignon, lots of it. The talk itself was desultory—all about your house and my house—though Fisher did mention some impending big deal at Madison and Fifty-sixth. "Parcels" yet! Fisher told me he hadn't been to an opera since he was thirteen, and at the end of Act 2 thought it was all over. In the intermission Carter, having just ordered another bottle of Dom Perignon, delayed our getting to Act 3 because we had to finish the bottle. Or, since he was with Fisher the land and building magnate, was he just less interested in the opera than in discussing some deal?

Anyway, there we were among the rich, observing the poor poor bohemian artists freezing and hungering in a Paris garret.

The Fishers had one of those supersize "stretch limos" waiting at the door to take the rest of the company to supper. We were driven home in his Mercedes by Arthur Carter's chauffeur. The opera performance was not so much undistinguished as drowned in finery. Like the company. Arthur Carter scorns the iniquity of capitalism, at dinner addresses me on the subject of "alienation," and teaches a class once a week at NYU—he gave a million to NYU for a new building. He was so irritable at a private Italian restaurant off Washington Square after meeting his class for the first time that in his limousine afterward he sweetly named for me all the famous Jews in American sports.

January 1, 1987: The New Year opens on a white sky, a feeling of the void. I was lying in bed, thinking of the dinner the other night with the composer George Perle. When I was belaboring Reagan and the right wing, he replied "I hate the Soviet Union." Turns out that his Hebrew name is Gedaliah. I chimed in with my father, Gedaliah, and thinking of the long journey that Hebrew names have made over all the earth for thousands of years, had the fond thought that our names make us a family.

This in my mind, I hear on the radio that the latest, the very latest, news from *Nature* is that scientists have investigated the DNA of women from all over the world, *and have concluded that they are all descended from a single woman who lived approximately two hundred thousand years ago:* "What happened to her contemporaries is not known."

Jews hang together and resent each other as only members of a family can. Both the Old and the New Testament are Jewish in speaking not just of the same family but of "our fathers"—Abraham, Isaac, Jacob. The piercing moment when Joseph in Egypt reveals himself to his own: "I am Joseph your brother." When that great heart John XXIII, born Angelo Giuseppe Roncalli, was elected pope, he actually came to the Jewish survivors of Rome and said *"Sono il suo fratello Giuseppe [I am your brother Joseph]."*

The winter nights in Roxbury are terrible. Already awake by four, all wired up for the book the book the book when it is ridiculous to get up. I feel enclosed by the blackness of rural Connecticut. Only the lights thrown on the ceiling by a passing car assure me that there are people somewhere. Judith comforts herself through bad nights with her tiny radio, but I have only my dolor about *The Almighty Has His Own Purposes,* a book that in my middle seventies I may not live to finish. Since I pay His Awesomeness so many compliments here, I hope He will hold off finishing me until there is a time for me to go mutually agreeable to us both.

Another trouble with being old when you cannot now walk around the Central Park Reservoir without the joggers hurling you against the fence is that we simply do not share the same information. The young checker on my article confesses that he did not know that the Moors had occupied Spain, and that he had never heard of Andrew Johnson, Federico Garcia Lorca, Vladimir Mayakovsky, and Al Smith. I agree with Judith that maybe a checker needs to be such a *tabula rasa.* Then nothing he comes across can be taken for granted, and he can "check everything out" until the cows come home.

\* \* \*

I live in a city full of blacks, in a building full of blacks, but I do not live with blacks. I have never had a real conversation here with any of them. But I do live with black faces. Thinking of the black I saw this morning at the Times Square subway station, surrounded by cops *with dogs,* he looking on in some vague impersonation of a cheerful, even giddy fellow on the cross. I have their faces on my mind, even my soul.

Not to forget the weary suspiciousness with which, toiling and combing upper Broadway, they examine each other. One black outside the Red Apple supermarket to another: "Whaddya staring at me for?" The other: "I don't even know ya! Was just looking!"

Dinner last night with Saul Steinberg. Saul performed as usual. Brilliant, dazzling, every word positively an original perception. Only a "foreigner" can see Americans with such an eye. There is no cozy pause between his flashes, and you feel breathless climbing this mountain after him. I say "mountain" because after all these years in Amerikee Saul is still looking down, in a physical sense, from his eternal perch as a satiric outsider. He bristled when I seemed to be surprised at his claiming to be such a baseball fan. Said he had gone around with the Boston Braves doing sketches for *Life.* I didn't have the heart to tell him that in the U.S. of A. baseball is a matter of local patriotism, real or feigned.

Still, the important thing about Saul is that he has won his unique position in the art world by sheer intelligence, from a curiosity burnished and polished until it positively gleams in your eyes.

On the inevitable subject of *The New Yorker* this week, owner Newhouse having just replaced Bill Shawn with Bob Gottlieb as editor, he gave the most unexpected reading of Shawn's mind. Said Shawn really tackled his job as an artist, putting the magazine together week after week as a sort of novel from every sort of material. Claims Shawn even wanted the magazine to be "unintelligible" at times, putting in Hannah Arendt's bristlingly Teutonic philosophy piece a while back.

*The New Yorker* has had more gifted and unexpected contributors, decade by decade, than any other American magazine I can think of. When they join the team, become writers, artists—and editors—unlike other writers, artists and editors, stars and distinct originals identified entirely with *The New Yorker*—James Thurber, A. J. Liebling, Helen Hokinson, Charles Addams, John Cheever, etc., etc.—they become *New Yorker* personalities as well.

I once met James Thurber at a party, meaning I once listened to James Thurber talking all evening about Harold Ross. I had only to shake the hand of this blind, relentlessly grinning man for him to tell me anecdotes about Ross and the founding of *The New Yorker* that were as familiar as George Washington and the cherry tree. The chief item was the predicament Harold Ross found himself in, one afternoon in Paris, 1918, shortly after the Armistice, when this rambunctious editor of the AEF paper, the *Stars and Stripes*, decided to take a ride on a ferris wheel. No sooner had his little cabin reached the highest point of the trip than the maintenance crew called a strike. And there was Ross, helpless as you can get, and no doubt screaming blue murder. Thurber actually slapped his thigh in irrepressible merriment telling the story.

My old pal Jean Stafford married A. J. Liebling, so I got to meet him after enjoying his work for many years. After strenuous efforts on Jean's part, Liebling finally consented to come to dinner on West End Avenue, though being Jewish himself he had long refused to meet this "sheeny." I never knew a Jew would use this word, but when you get to that pinnacle of sophistication . . . Liebling the journalist of low life, among other places in his repertoire—France especially in wartime was high on his list—had a sound curiosity that led him indefatigably to boxers, jockeys, fixers, finaglers of every sort as colorful material. No doubt this is where he got his professionally tough side.

Inside this fat bald man in a three-piece suit, whose vest seemed about to pop its buttons—it was so tight over his capacious flesh—there was no doubt a too-sensitive self-accusing Liebling still hoping to be let out. On the outside he was the gruff, cosmopolitan journalist with an inside knowledge of the secretly best French restaurants and a bowler that could have come only from Brown's in London.

He had nothing whatever to say to me on arrival or at any time during the evening, stolidly declining to pick up anything Jean dropped in her nervous social chatter to me. She seemed frightened. Liebling came alive only when the meal was served. He pounced at the chicken as if he could not get enough of it. I have never, outside the soup kitchens in New York during the depression, ever seen anyone feed himself with such excitement.

Steinberg's apartment is itself a Steinberg drawing—every drawing tool and slightest piece of paper neatly laid out, every item finished sharp and clear. In his bathroom even his razor brush and shaving cream, carefully lined up at just the right distance from each other, look as if they had been *drawn*. Saul, deliberate and cautious in every word and gesture, says that his father in Rumania (moved there from Odessa) made boxes for a living. Describes his father meticulously cutting boxes.

On one wall Saul's diploma in architecture from the University of Milan. The racial laws had just been passed. His Majesty Vittorio Emmanuele II, the Kingdom of Italy, etc., etc., etc., is pleased to bestow on Saul Steinberg, Jew, the degree of Doctor in Architecture. Saul confronts this object on the wall and asks: "Where is the Kingdom of Italy?" Gone. "Where is his gracious majesty Vittorio Emmanuele II?" Gone. "What is left?" Saul Steinberg, Jew!

How this immensely gifted gracious man charges me up every time I see him.

\* \* \*

An old friend in Chicago was visited by Jean-Marie Cardinal Lustiger, Archbishop of Paris. His eminence was born in Paris Aaron Lustiger, the son of Polish Jews who were rounded up during the occupation. His father survived Auschwitz. His mother did not.

The Jewish-born priest told a reporter the day after his nomination as archbishop:

> I've always considered myself a Jew, even if that's not the
> opinion of some rabbis. . . . I was born Jewish and so I
> remain, even if that's unacceptable for many. . . . For me, the
> vocation of Israel is bringing light to the goyim. That's my
> hope and I believe that Christianity is the means for achiev-
> ing it. I think that in being a disciple of Christ in my way, I
> enter into God's design, a part of a promise made good.

In Chicago his eminence said to his old friend: "You know that the Chief Rabbi in Paris is Sephardic? Well, it's only fair that the Archbishop of Paris be Ashkenazi!"

In the middle of the night, the terrible middle of the night, I writhe sleepless in a bed that is like a raft in a devouring ocean. As I have all my life when I feel myself up against the ropes, I pray to a God who cannot be very real, since he seems to be only a word, a name, a hope, a reach. Yet I pray; it is suffocating to be so bound up in oneself, a tangle of longings, useless memories, and violent recriminations. I pray to get beyond myself, to indicate to this believing unbeliever that there is a territory beyond this bundle tied up so angrily in the night. I pray to be relieved of so much "self," I ask to be extended.

Does any of this mean anything? With all possible doubts and bitterness at the shadowboxing I engage in with "God," I say yes it does out of an impatience to reach higher, to be better. In this monotonously anguishing world one needs another language. One is desperate for grace.

There is a world outside human consciousness, but since without that agency there is in effect no world, the agent cannot easily escape the delusion that mind is the principal. This is where Captain Ahab brought American literature to a boil. Everything is self, self, self. Wittgenstein said that the task of the philosopher is to get the fly out of the fly bottle. But that is not the American way. Starting with Emerson—God is just man transfigured, exists not only in me *as* me—it turned out that the paradox could be forgotten. So "the tremendous farce of human existence," as the infidel Mencken puts it, can be revalidated by keeping man at the center of the picture. God made man in God's own image became—man invented God in man's own image. Only Europeans (Heisenberg) lament that "to the outer limits of space man carries only the image of himself."

The desacralization of the biblical drama in the nineteenth century by agonists like Melville meant that man had become the prisoner of his own perception. This is why Melville despised Emerson's subjectivism. The existing physical reality had been turned into a "mask" for something "deeper" than itself. "If man will strike, strike through the mask! How can the prisoner reach outside except by thrusting through the mask! . . . That inscrutable thing is chiefly what I hate; and be the white whale agent, or be the white whale principal, I will wreak that hate upon him."

The argument for Jesus, not Christ the Lord. That he *was* one of those rare spirits who feel themselves positively commanded by the Holy Spirit, that he was honestly totally filled to the brim with: "My Father, My Father, Our Father, Father, Father." This is Yeshua ben

Joseph the Jew. In some way I have never understood he became identified for other Jews, especially Saul of Tarsus, with *salvation*, the absolute promise and assurance of immortality. This must have been something new in Judaism, and no doubt this promise and assurance were grounded in the increasing sense of Jewish national defeat under the Romans and the expectation that the "world" was coming to an end.

There was certainly a quest for something more than was contained in the Law, but it is impossible to believe that even Yeshua turned into Jesus thought of himself as supplanting the religion he was born into. Still, his disciples, exegetes, and biographers turned him into this everlasting mystery within a religion founded on a mystery: Unless in your heart you believe in me, you will not be saved. Immortality is the theme, the key, the promise—and the threat that it can be withheld. And the meaning of contained in the earthly existence and story of Jesus. Monsignor Ivan Illich, a priest with a Sephardic mother, once said to me with a little smile—"God came closer and closer, so we could at last see Him."

God was now nearer than he had been, and so, it seems, were heaven and hell. This marriage of heaven and hell, promise and threat, becomes the story of his effect on the Jews around him, an effect that widened and widened, taking in most of the Western world and more. This is the most extraordinary intervention in history and remaking of the humanity that can be traced to a single human being. I insist on seeing him as a single being. But the supposedly historical Jesus left scanty remains, became the Son of God, who for so many Christians has replaced the Father. Which always leaves me wondering and even supplicating: What was it in the *example* Jesus left that turned him into a divinity and that has made all the difference in history ever since?

Was it Jesus or the Christians who came to believe that there is no death? Who founded their faith, as Saint Paul admits, on the Resurrection? Without which there is no death. Was it Jesus or Paul who fetched the Gentiles with life everlasting if only you assent to the formula the church presents?

But Jews don't have it so neat. The refrain of their whole history is that there *is* death, that we are always being threatened by it, and that never in the history of the world have so many people been killed en masse and at once as were the Jews in the last years of the Second World War. Yes, the one certainty for Jews is that there is death. It is no longer enough for anyone to suggest that Jesus died for flouting the Jewish Establishment. He died as a Jew. And as Nietzsche said, "He was neither the first nor the last Jew to die on the Cross."

In the same issue today the *Times* carries a story about Israel's ties with South Africa and an obituary of the Rumanian Fascist archbishop Valerian Trifa—his Rumanian Orthodox episcopate is based in Grass Lake, Michigan. The archbishop, finally exposed as directing the murder of Rumanian Jews, was deprived of his U.S. citizenship and deported.

Interviewed in 1984, shortly before he left the country, the archbishop warned that the preoccupation with the Holocaust among Jews would "backfire." "I am a man who happened to get put in a moment of history when some people wanted to make a point. The point was to revive the Holocaust. But all this talk about the Holocaust is going to backfire."

I think of Mark Rothko standing on the steps of his house on East Ninety-fourth, just to get away from the party inside. He was full of grief and talked steadily for an hour about Shakespearean tragedy— the only antidote he found to the many blows—and deaths—in his life. Said he used to be so lonely crossing the Atlantic even after he had achieved fame that he would go up to a stranger at the bar of the *Île de France* and command: "Let's talk."

Can't get over the depression period, was a student at the Yale

School of Fine Arts hitchhiking home to Oregon. The country roads in many parts of the country were usually deserted. A poor old tumbledown truck finally stopped for him. The farmer: "I seen from a long way off, 'That's a Jew!' And I says to myself, 'He may rob me but he won't beat me.' Get in!"

Wall Street Jews are running scared because of current scandals: Boesky. Milken. Levine. Siegel.

Felix Rohatyn testified before a Senate committee about the "cancer called greed" that is threatening the financial industry. Says he is afraid of a vicious backlash.

Abe Rosenthal's *Times* column:

Fear of a particular backlash has led to private meetings among some top Jewish figures in the industry, bankers, chief executive officers, heads of brokerages. The central topic was the fact that so many of the men caught cheating or about to be indicted were Jewish. There was concern that the backlash might carry a decided tinge of anti-Semitism. The anti-Jewish arbitrageur jokes are all around the street.

Room 507, University of Florida Union: My little prison between classes. Students in the morning gathered together before an enormous TV screen. Bowling alleys. Billiard tables. A whole room full of pinball machines. Mirrors everywhere. No matter where I am going, I see myself reflected twice and three times in mirrors reflecting other mirrors. Nothing less calculated to assure myself that the stocky figure in a red sweater is the person I internally imagine myself to be.

That admirable southern novelist and storyteller Peter Taylor at the *News* party. A certain crumpling in his speech after a stroke. Says Randall Jarrell certainly sought his death. Teaching for so many years at Woman's College of the University of North Carolina at Greensboro, he was always falling for some student, but his wife wouldn't let him go.

How different the suffering, perhaps suicidal figure in Taylor's account from the brisk and no-nonsense Randall Jarrell I used to see at Hannah Arendt's moldy old apartment on Morningside Drive facing a park it was fatal to enter. Randall Jarrell on the Upper West Side of New York! It was hard to tell whether Randall was there because he had fallen in love with German or with Hannah Arendt. For him they were identical, though with his usual flair, he announced to all and sundry: "I am too busy translating Faust to learn German."

Hannah the Jew, the refugee, not yet as famous as she would be, turned out to be the intrinsic and everlasting tradition of German seriousness for Randall, Robert Lowell, and other writers of my generation, born during the First World War with Germany and blasted into literature by the Second. Bellow couldn't see her, of course, was turned off by her having the nerve to tell *him* what was great and not great. He retaliated by calling her views "canned Weimar sauerkraut." But Randall couldn't get enough of Hannah the German thinker, just as he couldn't get enough of Mozart, Beethoven, Goethe, Brecht, and any other hallowed German who had become this Texan's daily bread. The most exciting contemporary critic to read, upholding Whitman and Frost against the dreary schoolmarms of the New Criticism, and with nothing in particular to drive him except his insatiable love of the word.

This Florida campus is certainly a change from insurrectionary New York. Wears a benevolent Sunbelt mask, the easy careless look and dress of the young not yet under the pressure of Corporate America or the tenure track. The intellectual innocence is unsullied.

I was asked to take a class reading Arthur Miller's *The Crucible*. One student: "It's just occurred to me. Doesn't this play about witchcraft in seventeenth-century New England have something to do with McCarthyism?"

Forever brooding on *The Almighty Has His Own Purposes*, I walked to the library in a sudden downpour, shivering with cold. Browsing in the religious section, I came on the work of Lev Shestov, who was born Schwartzman in Kiev. Leaving Lenin country, he taught in the Russian Theological College in Paris. He influenced Russian Christians in exile and many English intellectuals, especially D. H. Lawrence, who got to know Shestov through S. S. Koteliansky. Like so many Jewish intellectuals who are religiously independent, dazzled by Western philosophy, Shestov was a Christian up to a point. His most famous text—*Between Athens and Jerusalem*.

Tolstoy knew Shestov's early work, and when informed that Shestov was a Jew, burst out: "No, no! You cannot find a Jew who is irreligious."


Shestov's essential drive is intuitionist. He often sounds just like D. H. Lawrence. All is personal experience, therefore full of abysses from which our culture's belief in logic and the rational continuity of our civilization is completely removed. The ground is nothing but our actual life—the authentic—and to grasp the issues that pertain to this center is to be a philosopher transcending the usual partisan debates (*your* category, *my* category) of philosophy.

Freezing in the Florida rain, I return to the table in the Union cafeteria to hungrily drink two bowls. No one in the place but me and some Arab students horsing around. They all wear sweatshirts reading LONG LIVE PALESTINE.

\* \* \*

Exhibition, *Celebrating the Art from Auschwitz:*

But on a door or a cell, or on a beam, or in a painting com-
missioned by the camp supervisors, are the declarations and
cryptic allusions of people bearing witness to their specific
suffering, to their own impending murder. Who, for example,
was Mirja Braun and why, on July 8, 1944, did she scratch
her name and the date into a brick, adding a Star of David
alongside?

I see from a review in the *Harvard Magazine* that Allen Tate
refused to meet Langston Hughes. Said it was no more possible
than meeting socially with his black cook. I always thought Tate
was the most talented of the Southern "Fugitives," but his con-
suming myth was that he would yet save the Confederacy, and
with people "not of our sort" he was verbally a monster, if an inef-
ficient one. One of those lit'ry snakes, like Jean Stafford. Always
setting up some commotion or other on extraneous grounds. On
the beach at Wellfleet, where we used to meet every summer, I
once urged him to read Bernard Malamud's *The Assistant.* He
replied with a positive sneer that he was not interested in "books
about Jews." I asked him if this interfered with his reading of the
New Testament.

I looked up the Tate episode in the biography of Hughes. While
Tate was willing to meet with L. H. (and another black writer) in
Europe or elsewhere, he could not do so in the South, "unfortu-
nate" as the situation was. And by this time Tate was a Catholic con-
vert—the suspicion was that he and Caroline Gordon had joined the
church to secure their marriage. It didn't. Tate married twice again.
The last marriage was to a former nun. But when Tate was a
Catholic, he was more so than anyone except Evelyn Waugh and
Clare Booth Luce. He once appeared at a reception with an Irish
priest. Robert Frost was there, and being Frost, went over to the

priest. "Father, are you a convert?" The priest was startled and could only say, "No, no!" Frost: "Neither am I! Shake!"

On my way home what do I see but a man standing over a mound of paperbacks, relentlessly splitting them in half and throwing the pieces into a carton. "Why do you do that?" ask I. "You have to split them in order to get them out." "Out?" "For government surplus. They won't buy unless the books are torn up."

Private screening last night of German film on the life and death of Rosa Luxemburg, directed by Margarethe von Trotta. With the beautiful and gifted actress Barbara Sukowa, who even learned Polish for the part. And of course doesn't look in the least bit Jewish, any more than the handsome Polish actor Daniel Olbrychski reminds one of Rosa's companion Leo Jogiches, a Jew from Vilna.

There was not a hint of Rosa's Jewish background and upbringing. To say nothing of Karl Kautsky and other Jews in the great international socialist movement before the 1914 war. The revolution so dear to messianic Jewish revolutionaries and that never happened (maybe there weren't enough non-Jews seeking the Messiah) is at least on the screen *Judenrein*. Von Trotta: "I spent a long time looking for the right actress, someone who would resemble Rosa physically, who was small, Jewish, articulate, unknown to the cinema public and preferably bilingual, but I couldn't find her anywhere."

The "cinema public" may not remember the Jewish revolutionary Rosa Luxemburg (it doesn't remember anything except other movies). But when West Germany put her portrait on a stamp, the public refused to buy it, and postmen even refused to deliver mail that showed her face! In East Germany they used her for propaganda purposes and played down her opposition to Lenin's dictatorial theories. In Warsaw an actress turned down the role because "she couldn't play the part of a Communist." Von Trotta: "The murder of Rosa Luxemburg remains unacknowledged, unpunished, unexpiated. Rosa was the first victim of National Socialism. Her murderers rallied around Hitler."

Which reminds me that the son of one of Austria's leading Socialists, a British officer during the war, told me that when "Aryan" Austrian Socialists were back in Vienna, Jews once prominent in the party were requested not to return.

The film movingly captured Luxemburg's ardor, the lovingness and intellectual brilliance that distinguished her, a crippled Polish "Jewess" who became a leading militant in the German Social Democratic Party and the Socialist International. How vivid she was and remains, how very personal, when you see her supposedly captivating a "Socialist" audience of the time (are any of these perfectly dressed people "workers"?). But you can also see with a sinking of the heart that the flame that burned in Rosa Luxemburg for "socialism" was for others as discardable as the Kaiser would soon be. And the more "Dr. Rosa Luxemburg" talks to workers about the general strike as a way of stopping war, the more you see from their faces that they are a million miles away from her.

Poor Rosa, who like all good Jewish Marxist superrevolutionaries in that land of dreams, the nineteenth century, believed that Jews as Jews belonged to the past. She was not as bad as Karl Marx, who saw the Jews only as an economic factor in the rise of capitalism and had the same social contempt for them that he had for "niggers." Jews, especially if they were not German, were pariahs. Marx was not only the son of a baptized Jew but married to a descendant of the Duke of Argyll. Once, when the Marxes were on their uppers and sent their dutiful maid of all work off to pawn some family spoons, she was accused of stealing them—they bore the Argyll crest. Lev Davidovich Bronstein, better known as Trotsky, rejoiced in the thought that the revolution, if completely successful, would in time eliminate the Jewish sense of themselves as a separate people. Ah yes!

Of course they had a great ecumenical and universalist vision.

The best of us always do. But this always started, as with Saul of Tarsus, by seeking to transcend the Jew in them if they could not deny or eliminate it. The joke is that their "comrades" continued to see them as Jews, often enough as nothing else. When, after Lenin's death, Trotsky went to elite party cells in Moscow to get their support against Stalin, he was dumbfounded to be greeted with anti-Semitic epithets. He helplessly complained to Bukharin, "Is it possible that in *our* party . . . ?"

Poor Rosa indeed! A Polish Jew who helped to form the Polish Socialist Party, who with Lenin and Martov represented the Russian contingent in the Second International, who ended up as central to the formation of the German Communist Party—naturally she thought of herself as transcending "mere" national borders and all national prejudices. When the French Socialist leader Jean Jaurès attacked some position of hers at the last pre-1914 meeting of the International, it was of course Rosa who translated his speech into German.

All that was another world, a world I still like to read about. Were people once this transcendent of "mere" national prejudices? Rosa in her contempt for parochial values, especially Jewish ones, personifies so many lost illusions that she seems unbelievably ancient. But there is a real human being there, which God knows cannot be said about her more dominating fellow ideologues. Marx was an autocrat, Trotsky a murderer, but Rosa is forever endearing. I have left thousands of books behind me in my wanderings, but I still have her wonderfully tender and even lyric 1916–18 letters from prison to Sophie Liebknecht, the wife of Karl Liebknecht. He was murdered when she was, after the failure of the Spartacist revolt they had led in 1919 to form a Communist Germany. Rosa was an extreme left-winger with the most unshakable conviction that she, a pariah if ever there was one, that *she* could rally to a Communist republic—and even help lead one!—a violently embittered postwar country where every good German had only to look at her to think, Jew! Jew!

Wronke, May 2, 1917. Do you remember how, in April of last year, I called you up on the telephone at ten in the morning to come at once to the Botanical Gardens and listen to the nightingale which was giving a regular concert there? We hid ourselves in a thick shrubbery, and sat on the stones beside a trickling streamlet. . . . Just fancy, I heard the same call suddenly here from somewhere close at hand a few days ago in the early morning, and I burned with impatience to find out what the bird was. I could not rest until I had done so. It is not a marsh bird after all.

Just imagine—our little David, with just one stone, the mind of Rosa Luxemburg, was going to topple the mighty German Goliath and through "socialism" transform it into the first truly human society in its bad, bad old history. They slammed the butt of a rifle into her temple before throwing her into the Landwehr Canal.

In Roxbury every inch of ground thick with leaves. Harvest and death at once. As the days get shorter and somehow get away from me faster and faster, time sharply has its way with me. Clock rushes, heart rushes, streets rush under the stampede of all these crowds rushing. River runs, mind races. Can you, oh, can you? Catch up with yourself?

I dream more than I used to. Mama began to dream with fantastic vividness before she died. Never saw her face so lit up, so happy. My dreams are becoming fasteningly scenic, positively operatic, but always, dammit, have the same plot—our hero is lost.

The only relief was a fleeting memory of Dr. Herman Tannenbaum, once the Upper West Side's family doctor to Jewish intellectuals, who talked freely about the terrible state of Norman Podhoretz's hemorrhoids, and even more eccentric than the rest of us, kept a sign in his waiting room: *"Don't feed the dog. She has an allergy."* I don't remember ever seeing the dog.

*    *    *

When I read Pauline Kael's violently energetic, pseudorobust movie criticism, her reactions, so stormily in excess of the commodity she is appraising, remind me why criticism itself is now such a popular commodity. Even a movie sometimes needs to be pondered in silence and time, but what counts for her public is not so much the work as the intensity of her reaction. Reading Pauline, it becomes obvious that no experience in life means so much to her as reliving a movie through and through in order to sound smarter about it than anybody else she is talking to. And the style is one of aggressive conversation on the New York party circuit. The critic as dominator, as know-it-all, as experiencer. As peasant mothers once chewed up food in their own mouths in order to feed the baby, so Pauline chews up the film for the *New Yorker* reader so he will know what to think. With Pauline you also get a sexy superbrash tone, as if she got a charge in the dark to giggle over when turning her collected reviews into books with leering titles—*I Lost It at the Movies; Kiss Kiss, Bang Bang.*

The superior political tone of her voice is striking. On a rare film about the violent war in Central America, of the very rich against the very poor, *Salvador:* "A sensationalistic propulsiveness, and a hero . . . whose hipster hostility was integral to the film's whole jittery, bad-trip tone . . ." On Oliver Stone's strong film about Vietnam horrors, *Platoon:* "The results are overwrought, with too much filtered light, too much poetic license, and too damn much romanticized insanity. . . . Populist sentiments reminiscent of Joad family conversations in *The Grapes of Wrath.* . . . It's like some terrible regression. Stone's gone back to being a literary preppy."

Kael is a Jew who lets nothing, not even the Holocaust, stand in the way of her aesthetic reflexes. In *Shoah* (the Hebrew word for annihilation) the French writer Claude Lanzmann gives us a nine-and-a-half-hour documentary epic made up of people who still have knowledge of the Nazi extermination centers as slave laborers, railroad workers, technicians, bureaucrats, onlookers. There are few enough documentary films of the Holocaust. Of course the damning photographs of Polish Jews lined up on the ravine to be shot were all taken by Germans themselves as souvenirs of their travels far from home.

You would think, wouldn't you, that a Jewish film critic who of course knows all about Hitler's war would find this hair-raising visual document of some historic interest? Kael: "I found *Shoah* logy and exhausting right from the start, and when it had been going on for an hour or longer I was squirming restlessly, my attention slackening." A Czech Jew, Filip Müller, a survivor of the Auschwitz "special detail," tells us that as a boy of twenty in 1942 he was sent, along with "other Jewish prisoners, to work in the incineration chamber of the crematorium in Camp 1 at Auschwitz. His job was to undress the corpses," put them into the ovens and "stir the bodies." Kael approves of Filip Müller: "Müller speaks with urgency in a beautiful, light voice; he's a fluent storyteller who sets his own rhythms and brings out the progression of his experiences."

People in the film telling their stories who do not "set their own rhythms" and do not fluently bring out *the progression of their experiences* fare less well at Kael's hands. Lanzmann speaks French, English, and German, so had to rely on interpreters of Polish, Hebrew, or Yiddish. Kael: "This method of questioning inflates the scale of the film. The theme is, of course, infinitely large, but Lanzmann's method gives the filmmaking itself a deadening weight and solemnity."

The technical difficulties and inevitable slowdowns involved in interviewing so many survivors, witnesses, and (at peace with themselves in Germany), not a few perpetrators—and this in every country in which Hitler's killers came searching for Jews, Jews, Jews— matters not to Kael. She thinks that Lanzmann's purpose in *Shoah* was just to present a work of art! When he said that the film "contains not one unnecessary frame," she thinks he was just aiming for aesthetic form and economy. By "not one unnecessary frame" Lanzmann of course meant that he dared leave out nothing of the terrible time that can still be salvaged and preserved in the everlasting sense of Yizkor, remembrance. Our tears, our anger, our horror, and everlasting outrage may soon all be spent—but we remember. Kael—"When you come out [of *Shoah*], you're likely to feel dazed, and confirmed in all your worst fears."

That's the thing about the Holocaust, it unsettles you for ordinary life, brings up terrors that are simply not fair, not fair!

Bernard Malamud dead. Anne had prepared lunch for him and had gone out. Returned to find him on the floor. We had our bypass operations at the same time—he at Stanford, I in New York—but he had a stroke on the operating table.

Death has come nearer with his passing, for though we could not have been more different and were never easy with each other, we had the same Brooklyn childhood, more or less, were in the same writing class at City College. How well I understood his strong desire not to be called "Bernie." He insisted on "Bern." I remember his scowl when, at a Yaddo meeting, Malcolm Cowley with a condescending smirk loudly addressed him as "Bernie."

He used to walk a lot—for his health. He was very systematic about this, as he was about so many things. He once met up with me when I was waiting for the bus at Eighty-sixth and Broadway. Exhaling fiercely, he told me that he had just done his quota for the day. Remembering himself as a Brooklyn boy, however, he once said to me, "I walked the streets endlessly—looking for my future."

"Future" was the great word in his marvelous novel *The Assistant*—*the* only truly Jewish novel produced by the *Luftmenschen* of my generation.

PROFESSORS OF BLACK STUDIES AT CITY COLLEGE SEE CONSPIRACIES—"The twin plagues of drugs and AIDS were created by white supremacist leaders to keep the numbers of blacks in the world down." It seems the French in Africa were having a problem early in the seventies, "wondering about a vaccine for smallpox they gave in Zaire that was contaminated, and then it produced the results that we are now calling AIDS."

"Did it have to be induced intentionally?"

"Gays were a control population to work on without really getting an adverse reaction."

"AIDS is chemically made in a lab, made in a lab. It is made in a lab."

"The Triumph of the Will" killed off some six million; otherwise it didn't do so well. When I lie awake at night, afraid that I am walking through the valley of the shadow of death, I feel that I am still the entangled Brooklyn boy who all his life has depended on his will. And there I am in the terrors of the night, still trying to . . . outwit death.

When I pray to You to give me some peace, to cease this endless clamor of anxiety, which consists always in asking, "Oh Lord, what am I supposed to do next?" I am really asking for relief from my overstrained will, from the determination to do and even to do over what is expected of me. That is what secularism is—the triumph of the individual will, no matter what the cost to everything crying out in you for another realm of living and being.

There must be an easier world to live in than this! The boundary initially pictured by the will recedes as soon as you reach it, calling for still more resolution to get on to the next. No wonder the sense of failure is such a feature of our inexhaustible drive for success— and adds to the burden.

"In His will is our peace." Eliot is always intoning that, *hoping* for that. That is the truth for natural believers like Emerson, leading him to say, "As for Death, it has nothing to do with me." But how can I believe this, when I am beset by a fear and hatred of death in a society and culture in which death is a kind of failure? In which everything depends on *my* will to eat right, to exercise right, to find the right doctor and perfect medicine that will prolong me on and on? "If only I had done this, if only I had not done that, if only I had not smoked my life away?" In which life is a kind of success contest, the advancing feebleness of the will is already seen as a kind of death.

No contemplation allowed. No mental rest from the race. The pitilessness of the rules under which we live.

And yet it must be possible in some spiritual sense to find an obedience to His will, Nature's will in the fullest sense, that can allay the anguish of my blindly desperate effort to cheat death. That is the crux: to be independent in a new sense of the all-enveloping habit of treating life as nothing more than my personal existence. But how to do this, and where?

And if not now, when?

Astonishing perverse heat in January—sixty-three degrees. Sluggishly made notes on the Hone-Strong diaries of New York upper-class life in the nineteenth century. An age of innocence all right—for those who could remain innocent. Awakened from my near stupefaction by walking with Judith on the park side of Central Park West down to Fifty-ninth Street. The park side, so beautifully built with hexagonal paving stones, is lined with derelicts, one of whom was passively studying his battered naked feet. Another was lying dead to the world on a bench. Someone had poured a lot of dirty park brush on him.

Street after street along the park—the abandoned, the forgotten, the drifters, the hopeless, disgorged as shit. And who wants to look at shit? Year after year in New York it becomes easier not to see the "types" you do not care to see. Across the street are the high apartment houses—bulky, "swell" looking, opulently rising high above the rest of the West Side—the San Remo, the Orwell, the

Beresford, the Majestic, the Dakota—solid, affluent. Doormen in uniform with heavily starched wing collars and just the right look of authority for getting you a taxi in a snowstorm—while in apartments with all those rooms there reside all those contented psychoanalysts, dentists, and anxiously liberal intellectuals. Along this "decent" side of Central Park West, young mamas, papas, or caregivers, rushing their darlings to just the right progressive schools, everyone hustling and bustling their steps on the ladder to success.

Central Park brings back the time some Democratic richies with a vast apartment in the Dakota gave a party to promote Bobby Kennedy's race for the Senate from New York. God knows what I was doing there with the Kennedy faithful, Ken Galbraith, Jackie Onassis herself. I thought I would "drop in" on my way to the lecture I had to give early that evening at the New School. When I finally got to leave, I unbelievably found myself in the same elevator with the Galbraiths and Mrs. Onassis. The Galbraiths had no sooner hit the street than they jumped into the first taxi that came along, explaining that they had to catch a plane to India. I was alone before the Dakota with Mrs. Onassis, who gravely asked me to get her a taxi. When I did so, she astonished me by saying she had no money with her, and would I see her home?

After a vast silence in the cab, she politely regretted the delay she had caused me and hoped she had not kept me from "something important." I admitted that I had a lecture to give at the New School within the hour, and that I would probably just make it. What was the subject of my lecture? I confessed that it was on *Huckleberry Finn*. Much laughter from Mrs. Onassis: "Do people actually give lectures on *Huckleberry Finn?*" "Alas," I said, "I do."

Arthur Miller and I came upon each other in the Roxbury dump on Sunday morning. The setting was more for a Beckett play than for one by Arthur Miller—hills of garbage, of exhausted and now-despised American commodities recurrently ground down, smoothed out, and buried by a tractor, while at the edge of the dump loaded up with discarded tires, machine parts, sewing machines, clocks, radios, you can see Old Bert, the town character, who has been doing this for years, patiently scavenging and cackling at every find.

Miller stands there, tall and raspy, with his usual assured sense of himself, dressed as always in a blue work shirt, work pants, and heavy work shoes. Arthur is a millionaire, has an estate, travels everywhere with the greatest freedom and aplomb, is a steadfast pillar of the American stage and the American scene. So he always comes on straight and strong in that blue work shirt, as a worker should—and opens up every conversation, at least with me, by expressing his bitterness at the *Times*, which has only one drama critic whom Arthur blames for his recent lack of acclaim on Broadway. He has more than one play running strong in London, which unlike Broadway is not afraid of his old-fashioned, brave realism about American society.

We are all intensely personal about life and art and with each other. Arthur's way of being personal is to discourse on the many ruses and snares of power in America. I find him fascinating on this subject and valuable, one of the few radicals out of the thirties who has never lost his suspicion of American society. He certainly knows his social evidence. His plays depend on melodramatic conclusions but are deeply felt, so grounded in family discord and the pain of his father's economic collapse in the depression that the audience easily identifies (as I do) with the pain pouring out on the stage between brothers, between a father and sons. That emotional truth, obviously drawing on once-suppressed rivalry and sorrow in *his* Jewish family, is the secret of Miller's success and rare enough on Broadway.

I shall never forget Lee J. Cobb as Willy Loman in the original production of *Death of a Salesman*. If ever the protagonist of an American tragedy was at the end of his tether, up against the wall, Cobb was the American low man. But it did not need Cobb's bellowing—this was an actor who could not open his mouth without sounding aggrieved fortissimo—to tell me how easily an American devoured by the dream of success feels like a failure long before he ends up as one. Miller had caught the momentum of this—the impossibility of inner peace in a society mesmerized by goals no one except a suicide could reject. And Willy, rigging a fatal accident for the insurance, didn't reject *anything*.

Miller in person talks the *country*, the social weight of people and events. His style in this is wholly ironic—seems to say, "You see? Ever think of this before?" Since I am the same age, another survivor of the terrible thirties and its radical dreams, I enjoy having Miller lecture me. Even in the dump. He brings a certain derision to it, like the blue workingman's shirt he wears to parties. But, oh boy, are social studies *de trop* just now! I almost died laughing when the cop who watches over the dump to make sure that only Roxbury residents can use it suddenly turned on us. "Hey, you guys, will you shut up down there! You're blocking the road!"

Trying to find a place to sit down before my doctor's appointment on East Sixty-eighth. Finally I had an inspiration: Saint James's Church on Madison. At first I thought I was all alone in this chill, genteel edifice. But then I saw homeless blacks trying to get comfortable in one pew or another.

On TV, old newsreel shots of Martin Luther King Jr. rallying blacks in Chicago, trying to enter Cicero against its bigots. Detroit burning. King overheard at one point "I'm tired, I'm tired of . . ." Oh, brother! on this everlasting subject, we're all tired. Even American liberals do not love blacks, enforce toleration for the sake of civic peace. After all, one Civil War was enough!

But the grinding daily sorrow, confusion, bitterness of the black up against white suspicion and fear! Forcing the rest of us against our will into the mystery and history of perpetual victims—Chicago, Haiti, Zaire, South Africa—connected with this race of races. How did so many allow themselves to be enslaved in the first place? The unspoken, inadmissible background, as evident still in the tribal wars in Somalia, even Liberia—they are always selling one another out. And here in America the ensuing terrible morale, so many black males finding it hard to *stay* a father.

Lewis Mumford dead at ninety-four. The last utopian in this technocratic society, whose architecture he was so good at deciphering in the megacity he despaired of.

May 1965, a newly elected member of the American Academy of Arts and Letters, I was sitting on the stage not far behind Mumford, the president that year, when to some amazement on my part (as well as delight), he broke out against Johnson's buildup of the Vietnam War: "I cannot artificially manufacture an atmosphere of joy for this meeting, when under the surface of our ritual a rising tide of public shame and private anger speaks louder than any words, as we contemplate the moral outrage to which our government has committed our country."

There was applause, there were boos; it was all great stuff, highly irregular. I remember the painter Thomas Benton furiously warning Mumford to stop, then storming out of the hall. I heard later that Mumford went home to Amenia with a fever.

That was my Lewis Mumford. In high school, encountering his first book, *The Story of Utopias*, I somehow knew that although utopias were a fantasy and in Russia becoming a twentieth-century nightmare, I felt elated by Mumford's largeness of vision, his passion for a more humane destiny, his obvious links, still, to that belief in the "promise of American life" that had excited Van Wyck Brooks and Randolph Bourne and had been crushed for the next generation by what John Dos Passos to the end of his life called "Mr. Wilson's War."

In 1931, with *The Brown Decades*, Mumford changed my life by documenting what by instinct had long been my favorite period of cultural history in America—from the Civil War to the nettlesome nineties. The book brought home to me the painters Thomas Eakins, Albert Pinkham Ryder, Winslow Homer, and George Fuller; the poet Emily Dickinson; the architects Louis Sullivan, Henry Hobson Richardson, and John Wellborn Root. Best of all, his book instructed me in the building of Brooklyn Bridge, from boyhood an icon in my life.

What thrilled me in *The Brown Decades* was not just Mumford's range as student of literature, painting, architecture, engineering, technics in general, but his feeling for New York—the native city that became his index to so many pleasures and problems in the whole twentieth-century scene that as an increasingly irritated sage he took as his province.

It was never the sage to whom I was drawn but the working critic of a city driven—constantly driven wild—by its excess, the critic of New York as a civilization who had been born in Flushing and had grown up on the Upper West Side. He was the New Yorker tried and true despite everything that another native son, Henry James, called "the terrible town." And Mumford brought an older New York home to me that made an ever-living drama out of the sticks and stones— the title of his book on American architecture—that I had been passing through without actually *seeing*. Walking Brooklyn Bridge almost every day after the war, when I lived on Pineapple Street in Brooklyn Heights, I remembered with joy Mumford saying: "The stone plays against the steel: the granite mass in compression; the spidery steel in tension. In this structure, the architecture of the future, light, aerial, open to sunlight, an architecture of voids rather than of solids."

Thanks to *The Brown Decades*, I came to see New York all over again. Constantly prowling and exploring New York, in search of my future without my knowing what I was looking for, I identified with Mumford's passion for seeking out New York's opportunities. There was the obstinate idealism, merely angry as it finally became, but which in his earlier days was like the incomparable sky of New York, like no other sky as it rose above the spears and pinnacles of Wall Street when you walked down to little old Pearl Street, where Melville had been born.

I knew him briefly, inconsecutively, and never very satisfactorily. He had a public manner, and I could only sigh when in his Sunnyside days he offered a cigarette box, inquiring, "Virginia or Turkish?" The Mumford in his work, not in life, was what I identified with, guessing from the first where the range of his mind would take him—to rebuild the city as a community. Because of his illegitimate birth and fatherless upbringing, he described himself as a child of the city. That was something that for my own reasons I understood very well. Stuyvesant High School, one of the three elite New York public high schools that have cradled so many Nobel Prize–winners. City College, and that in the evenings, but where the great circulating library, built up in tiers like a cathedral—and that it was for us—was positive heaven. Mumford said that he threw himself on the city for his upbringing and education. He was an indefatigable walker, seeker, sketcher of city scenes, who could claim that he had lived everywhere in New York that a writer of limited means could live. He knew the old West Side of backyards surrounded by high wooden fences, where paved paths were too uneven to encourage tricycles, where there was a "gashouse district" from Sixty-fifth Street up, and Broadway was full of vacant lots,

> with visible chickens and market gardens, genuine beer gardens like Unter Den Linden, and even more rural areas. Since for the first quarter of my life I lived between Central Park and Riverside Drive, wide lawns and tree-lined promenades are inseparable in my mind from the design of every great city; for what London, Paris, and Rome boasted New York then possessed.

Sunnyside, the garden city of his steadfast vision, the perfectly planned city he upheld against Jane Jacobs's harum-scarum New York that is just Greenwich Village—this, like so much in Mumford's hopes for New York, fell under the tread of ever-driving greed, corruption, impoverishment, drugs, and indifference. His increasing horror of "megacity" and what he called the "Pentagon of Power" did not have the charm of the Mumford who was at his best in details—*Technics and Civilization, The Brown Decades,* his masterly columns on architecture in *The New Yorker.* His rage was ethical, literary, prophetic, without enough commitment to politics as setting the conditions by which we live. A visionary to the end, he wistfully compared himself to the prophet Jonah, who in his rectitude exasperated even God. Jonah wanted Nineveh punished for not heeding him, and the Lord said to Jonah, perfectly describing New York as it is today: "Should I not pity Nineveh, that great city, in which there are more than a hundred and twenty thousand persons who do not know their right hand from their left."

Suddenly remembered Bellow's confrontation with the Fuller brush man when Saul was living near Bard College. The man was desperate to make a sale, but Saul kept shaking his head, eager to get back to his desk. Exasperated, the Fuller brush man finally said, "Okay, you can at least accept something as a gift, can't you?" Bellow: "I have the gift of life, and it's more than I know what to do with."

Edmund Wilson complained to me in the midst of his Hebrew studies: "I feel as if I have been caught inside three thousand years of Jewish history and can't get out." *He* should talk!

Felix Frankfurter was a favorite of Henry L. Stimson: "A Jew but not a Jewish Jew." The one time I met Frankfurter, he said with an air of congratulation, "Kazin! Oh, yes! I lent your book to the British ambassador!"

*New York Review* threw a big party for Czech president Václav Havel on the stage of the Vivian Beaumont Theater at Lincoln Center. It was all very dramatic—the auditorium dark except for flickering lights at a few seats, while on the lighted, crowded stage distinguished literary personalities—Sontag, Mailer, Bellow, etc.—bobbed in and out of the circle around the charming, sandy-haired, slight, and vulnerable figure of Havel, who was earnestly smoking as he chatted in the friendliest way with these American writers, managed at one point to say that the five years he spent in Stalinist prisons were truly "bad prisons."

Sontag's eyes were glistening after embracing the president—"an old friend," she confessed as she exited the circle around him. "I've been invited to the presidential palace next time I'm in Prague." Fritz Stern, István Deák, Elie and Marian Wiesel, Joan Didion and her husband, John Gregory Dunne, who always looks at me as if he means to bristle about something or other, but then doesn't bristle. Fritz Stern introduced me to Henry Kissinger, who in the most languidly condescending manner said, "Oh, yes, you write literary essays, don't you?" and turned away.

In 1961, when I contributed "The President and Other Intellectuals" to the *American Scholar* issue on the Kennedy administration, Kissinger surprised and even slightly alarmed me by writing me in immoderate praise of my lighthearted scoffing at Kennedy's pretensions as an "author" and intellectual. It turned out that Kissinger was furious at being turned out of the White House circle for not being "entertaining enough."

These literary parties always make me feel, as Van Wyck Brooks used to say about sitting down to write, "that I am on trial for my life and will definitely not be acquitted." Still, there are moments. A murmur of something like dismay went around the stage when someone reported, after a short conversation with Havel, that his favorite contemporary American writer was E. L. Doctorow.

As I was leaving the party, I saw Mailer exuberantly addressing a little group around him, rocking on his feet like a fighter waiting to enter the ring, talking in gulps as he always does. As I passed, I heard him say, "So this guy, wiping the sweat off his balls . . ."

Had a sandwich in the hospital "café." The only empty seat was opposite a glum-looking young fellow in a physician's white coat. He was wearing a yarmulke. Feeling like nothing at all but startled to see a physician so Orthodox—I can never predict how these superbelieving Jews will affect me—I said *"Sholom aleichem!"* the good old Jewish greeting—"Peace to You." He stared at me, muttered or growled something I could not catch, and tore into his grapefruit. He presented as much charm as a politician discovered in a motel room with a doxie. I persisted in conversation; these guys are always so mysterious to me. Asked him if it was in order for an Orthodox Jew to dissect bodies. Testily he informed me that only a Cohane, a Cohen still priestly by descent, was prohibited from contact with a corpse. It was only with the greatest possible irritation that he seemed at all willing to tell me anything about himself. When I asked him if he could work on the Sabbath, he loftily informed me that he had already made arrangements to do his residency somewhere in New Jersey where they would not oblige him to defile the holy day. Never smiled once during this accidental meeting, and why should he? He regarded me as an intruder, a buttinsky—and I, as usual with the super-Orthodox, was equally condescending and superior.

This guy is a closed book to me, just as he has closed himself off from me, a fellow Jew. Yet think of the sacrifices he makes every day in order to be true in his traditional way to "The Eternal, blessed be He and the sanctification of His holy name." Something sacred rising out of the rubbish heap of our present lives, out of all the wretchedness these days in New York tearing me up everywhere I look.

\*   \*   \*

Two weeks ago I had lunch, after doing my physical therapy at the Ansonia, in a café next door that featured croissants "as the French alone can make them." On Monday the excessive weight of modern air-conditioning ducts, pipes, and decorations suspended from a turn-of-the-century plaster ceiling caused the ceiling to collapse. One woman was killed and sixteen injured.

The woman—Miriam Toigo-D'Angeli, a dancer, Brazilian born, Italian father and Soviet mother. Had come to this country for a holiday and was not allowed to go back to Russia, apparently because of her involvement with a prominent Soviet dancer. The Soviet authorities were apparently determined to break up the romance at all costs, even if it meant leaving Ms. Toigo-D'Angeli stranded in New York.

She lived at the top of the stairs in a five-story walk-up at the end of East Eighty-sixth Street. Worked as a tour guide in NYC, showing out-of-towners the Statue of Liberty, the Empire State Building, and "churches in Harlem where the choirs make the rafters ring."

Stopped at Rizzoli's enticing bookstore, on my way to meet Judith at the Alliance Française to see a film. Picked up a book, "Sexual Something or Other," by a woman with an Italian name, Camille Paglia, from the Philadelphia Museum. Links Emily Dickinson to Sade. Now why can't I ever say anything as surprising as that? Academic critics are now living it up in pure fantasy. And the public has never had to read Dickinson or Sade in order to shout, "You tell 'em, Paglia!"

After seeing Judith to Kennedy for her flight to Paris, I settled in for the long boring ride in the Carey bus back to midtown. The driver was one of those little bullies in the transportation business who gets happy when he is shouting. Fare is $9.50! No senior discounts! Have your money ready! He stormed at us when the bus finally took off, telling us where it would stop and where it would not.

Across the aisle two men in superb leather jackets were talking in German. The one on the aisle suddenly turned to me and right out of the blue, in the most be-yoo-tiful English, said, "I hope you admire the works of Isaac Bashevis Singer as much as I do." For years I've joked about my incontestably Jewish face that if I ever land at the North Pole, the first Eskimo running up will ask if I favor Labor in Israel or Likud. I just can't seem to get away from what the nineteenth century called "the Jewish question."

The German was effusive on the subject of Bashevis Singer. Went on and on. Looking straight at me, he even volunteered a few words of Yiddish. He and his buddy were hand surgeons, just back from a medical conference in Denver. Got very friendly. Asked me to recommend a good hotel for the night.

With my fatal gift for associations, I remembered the story I heard in Moscow in 1959, of hand surgeons performing on an operating table right next to another operating table, so that one patient could see what was being done to another. That's Russia for you. And isn't a New York bus drudging in from the airport a show of history, too, what with the driver shouting at us and a most gentlemanly and informed German physician launching into Yiddish to show what friends we all are?

Went lonely to bed and dreamed that Judith was in darkest Europe. In my night, my terrible night, I protested. Sometimes the night comes on like Judgment Day. Then it is indeed that the Lord comes into my sleep and takes a good hard look at me.

Funerals made my mother angry. The living "live and laugh."

*   *   *

East Berlin. Reuters:

We, the first freely elected parliamentarians of East
Germany, admit our responsibility as East Germans for their
history and their future and admit unanimously to the
world—
    Immeasurable suffering was inflicted on the peoples of the
world by Germans during the time of National Socialism.
Nationalism and racial madness led to genocide, particularly
of the Jews in all European countries, of the people of the
Soviet Union, of the Polish people and the Gypsy people.
    Parliament admits joint responsibility on behalf of the peo-
ple for the humiliation, expulsion and murder of Jewish men,
women and children.
    We ask the Jews of the world to forgive us. We ask the
people of Israel to forgive us for the hypocrisy and hostility
of official East German policies toward Israel and for the
persecution and degradation of Jewish citizens also after 1945
in our country.

And oh, yes! the Russians almost officially admit "deep regret
over the tragedy" of having murdered 15,000 Polish prisoners in the
Katyn forest (where the bodies were found in Spring 1943). The
massacre took place in April–May 1940. Some 4,500 bodies were
found. The remaining bodies have never been found.
    From Tass: "The sum of evidence points to the responsibility for
the crime resting on the leadership of the then-N.K.V.D.
Department. . . . The Soviet side expresses deep regret over the
tragedy, and assesses it as one of the worst Stalinist outrages."

Imposing lunch given by the Colonial Dames of America at the
Colony Club in honor of *A Writer's America.* I wouldn't have
believed that the dames were so true to type. All lined up as one

"Mrs." after another. Bosoms, pearls, smiles—the smile of the chair-lady a little tight when, in a discussion of American presidents (our only common interest), I reminded her that Herbert Hoover's father was an Iowa blacksmith. Another lady opinionated generously in my direction that FDR may have been a gentleman (this said very reluctantly), but she couldn't call him "honest." And another actually said, "He *was* a traitor to his class."

Moscow 1990: Everything in the holy Union of Soviet Socialist Republics is in limbo, including the sky. In the thin, watery daylight still hanging on at ten in the evening, a light that shakes you up like vodka, the monotonous bulk of Moscow is overpowering. I have never seen anything like it. Your first impression is that the official huge blocks of Stalinist crash housing are just too gigantic and all the same color. But when you get into the hidden depths of Moscow, away from the hideously wide straight avenues, the blaze of golden domes and the brilliance of blue stars topping the many churches make you gasp at the unexpectedness of everything. No visible connection between the pervasive colorlessness and the wonderful yellows and greens on churches and the occasional old Moscow single houses (one even wooden) in sooty brown relieving the general grayness.

Another world, I keep saying to myself, absolutely another world—and what is going on? On the one hand, here is Communist Russia (perhaps one of these days to be post-Communist Russia), a screamingly packed mass society and clotted bureaucracy, thick with barrackslike housing and creamy white official buildings left over from czarism, flying the red flag emblazoned with hammer and sickle. Then there's the old Christian Russia our hosts from the Union of Soviet Writers insist on showing us—dark sooty monasteries and churches where every wall is lined up and down with precious, opulently colored icons.

God is back! It is not only the tourists who are crowding churches and cathedrals once exhibited as museums. Many a Russian can be seen devotedly crossing himself (more usually herself). At the writer's village, Peredelkino, Yevtushenko smilingly admits that he prayed for the recovery of a sick child. And whaddya know, it worked.

Some of these deeply carved Russian faces with high cheekbones astonishingly recall the faces in medieval paintings. Impassive and above all disapproving of everything they see, these faces speak to me of the long isolation of Russia's once-predominant peasant population.

That long-standing peasant world has left its traces everywhere. The domestic arrangements at our gigantic tourist hotel, the Ukraina, call up life on the farm, as do the square-shaped waitresses whose powerful breasts (set off by their intricately embroidered peasant blouses) seem to promise energetic service. What a joke. Breakfast is all delay and confusion—forks thrown down on a table, but nothing to eat that calls for a fork. No milk. You never know from day to day where breakfast will be served next. When you find someone to ask, she shouts, "I will speak only to the head of your delegation!"

Crowds forever milling around in the vast lobby, waiting for what? My saddest image of Russia is of these people shuffling back and forth, as if they were not yet entirely lost and waiting for Charon the boatman to transport them to a world they have only read about. Meanwhile the incongruity necessary to the simplest arrangement. Only in a Russian hotel do you get elaborate chandeliered ballrooms dominating narrow seedy corridors whose wrinkled threadbare carpets are unraveling badly enough at the edges to trip you. You still have to leave your key, each time you leave your room, to a lady guardian sitting behind a desk facing the elevators. Still, she seems engrossed in her television set and is probably not going through my bags as her fellow Gorgon did when I stayed in this fortress in 1959.

Our hosts at the Writers Union keep telling us that things are changing, changing. The superb Sovietologist Robert Conquest is actually featured on the front page of *Pravda*—or is it *Izvestia?* Down the immensely long, wide endless avenues, engulfed on both sides by the Russian mass. People gathered in queues for copies of the "new" papers—standing in clumps trying to read the copies posted under glass. Still more queues in front of the U.S. Embassy. There the crowd looks more harried, nobody reading books as they wait, like the ones I have seen in front of food stores.

The two longest lines in Moscow—before Lenin's tomb and McDonald's. Pizza Hut coming in—or is it already in?

No neons, or hardly any—no colorful displays. Streets clean (what is there to throw away?), but sudden harsh winds and daily spurts of rain make the dust fly, and I am so allergic to the slightest dot of dust that I cough all the time.

Unbelievable sight of a food shop almost totally empty of food, but with the staff in white uniforms stoically waiting around the desolately yawning bins with that grim Russian patience: "So what is there to expect?"

Saturday night, 7:30 P.M., couldn't get into a café. All seemed closed. But one disco joint had TV screens blaring and a young mob wildly dancing under strobe lights—flash-bang, flash-bang.

At the headquarters of the Soviet Writers Union, the flawless interpreter in his booth has a certain drawl, turning the hot, harsh yammer of the long-winded Russkies into an English more casual than is natural here. The language of the fingers making even more emphases than exist in the extended Russian words. The style not rhetorical, as in Italian streets, but harshly declarative. Why do they have to sound so "strong" and affirmative when they talk? Seventy years of Communism, seventy years of forever proclaiming something or other. The Russian Revolution eliminated real politics but turned every speech act into political impersonation.

Who told me about the Moscow street evangelist who, talking to a listless crowd, spoke scornfully of "Them—with their big buildings"? I suppose he was saying that the true life is of the spirit, and within. But you certainly get an idea of "their" power from the overwhelming mass of the buildings.

The officialness of everything, the formality, the heavy chandeliers, the four-course meals, the meat. As Judith says, they care nothing for the particular comfort or well-being of the individual. The single person lost in the maelstrom, the "tide" of history, the reiteration until you want to scream of the officially declared "We are in a new phase."

At the Sovietskaya Hotel, Christian fundamentalists and Russian nationalists pointedly wearing pins marked GOYIM FOR JESUS.

*Gone With the Wind* a great hit, now a million copies. *Sophie's Choice*, Gertrude Stein, Nabokov, Orwell—all confiscated in the old days. Now grabbed from you.

The wonders of perestroika. How these Russian writers at the roundtable repeat one another! Nevertheless these are individuals who look like us, in situations we cannot imagine, no matter how much we read about them, as if they occupied not only this land mass but another time. The individual details of living here are what are hardest for us Americans to get. The mind-set is beyond us. These people are just now escaping the "Ministry of Truth."

Russians talking: "We cannot go back and we are not going forward. But we are becoming human beings. *Under Communism we burned our hearts away.*"

Louis Auchincloss's experience at the end of the war in France. Saw Russian peasant kids who had been imprisoned en masse by the Germans, put into German uniforms. Had no idea where they were, or what "France" was. All rounded up by the Soviets and sent back to be shot.

I asked if anybody was writing about Trotsky. "Yes, some of it written with racial hatred."

In one month, April, ten thousand Jews left the Soviet Union.

Cars like bugs crawling, in the night still streaked with light, across the bridge. What a joy to see the Moscow River just off our window.

The psychiatrist Dr. David Olds: "They look battered, they batter each other."

At the entrance to the Intourist Hotel in Novgorod, Russian young in jeans trying to sell you their junk, and when you pass on, so Vera Dunham tells me, they inform each other that we're all "Kikes!"

Three hospitals in Moscow just for suicide attempts.

I asked to see Minsk, my father's hometown, and was turned down.

Immediately following the occupation of Minsk, the German city commandant ordered all males between the ages of 15 and 45 to report for registration under the penalty of death. About 40,000 reported and in a field at Drozcy outside Minsk, were segregated in three sections: Jews, Red Army Men, and non-Jewish civilians. On the fifth day the non-Jewish civilians were released. All Jewish members of the intelligentsia were ordered to step forward; the several thousand who did so were marched off to the nearby woods and machine-gunned.

On March 1 the Germans ordered the Judenrat to dig a pit in Ratomskaya Street, an unpaved ravine in the center of the ghetto. On the following morning, after the columns of workers had left the ghetto, Nazi officials arrived and demanded 5000 victims. Informed that the Judenrat had been unable to collect them, the Germans began a hunt for their victims. Dr. Chernis, the woman in charge of the ghetto orphanage, and Fleysher, the supervisor, were ordered to bring their charges in front of the Judenrat building.

Unaware of what awaited the children, they led them, dressed and washed, and carrying the young in their arms, toward the buildings, but when they arrived in Ratomskaya

Street, they were all thrown into the pit and buried alive. When the columns of workers returned at night, several thousand were taken to Koidanovo and murdered there. Others were forced to join the people rounded up inside the ghetto and butchered in the Ratomskaya ravine.

They have photographed an asteroid streaking through space millions of miles from earth and apparently not quite ready to hit us. But the streets of New York in the bitterest weather last week could not rescue the human wrecks sleeping under sheets of cardboard.

Mass for Timothy Stafford Healy S.J. at Ignatius Loyola, Eighty-fourth and Park. The mass itself was so quietly and uneventfully accomplished that I had no sense of the grandeur I used to associate with this in the old Latin days, when the priest with back turned to the congregation seemed to be engaged in some privately holy bigness. And there was that bell! Anyway, we wanted to see a Jesuit funeral for such a notable Jesuit in public life. I remember Healy as a hard-breathing fat man in a ratty old raincoat. As the sermon this morning admitted, "The Rev Healy was no saint," impatient and irascible, a real go-getting administrator who, when I once asked for an appointment, said his schedule was "hairy" at the moment. I remember his ecstasy reading Hopkins that evening at the NYPL celebrating Hopkins and Hardy. I never realized before how over-concentrated Hopkins could sound, and made me think of him as a poet of orgasm without sex.

Enormous crowd, tout New York, his fellow Jesuits in white, but with different scarves, one wearing a bright red skullcap. What a fashion show they do put on, and what assurance, much repeated, that we who believe in Jesus Christ "will never die." What impressed me most was a very pale woman in late middle age with a sort of knitted lace cap, face altogether still and rigid, who while the rest of us were streaming to the exit kept her seat and seemed to be silently saying prayers. I was thinking as I looked at her that there, truly, was someone trying to relieve her life, her soul, by prayer. The link between sorrow and prayer, between the life, the pain, the regret piled up and pent up in us—oh Lord, it was all there in her face.

That, alas, is the kind of "religion" I understand best, and in my own furtive secret way "practice." Jesus: Go into your room and pray in secret to our God who lives in secret.

Wherever there is widespread massive poverty, history is what it has always been. Wherever the ruling ethos of the state is to advance the rich at the expense of the poor, history has not changed.

Livery cab to my ear doctor. Driver wore gloves with sharp white spikes.

Everything in the murder-torn world is like the weather. Judith in tears thinking about all the political horrors we and everyone else seem to be able to do nothing about. But ah! the clean white fellow from Nebraska sitting every day on a rag, corner of Ninety-fifth and Broadway. We cannot get him to agree to a hospital. He is just dying on the corner of Ninety-fifth and Broadway, of AIDS probably, meanwhile tonelessly looking at us and everything else without anger or mistrust. The good Jewish liberals: "What can we do for you?" He would like a hot chocolate. And he could use a Tylenol. Meanwhile smoking a cigarette, just sitting there on the corner of Ninety-fifth and Broadway.

\* \* \*

It is organized religion and funeral bigness that solemnize and magnify death, making a perfectly natural event so awesome for everybody. I like that quotation from the Talmud: "A corpse is without interest." None of this Saint Januarius stuff liquefying on schedule for the faithful in some Naples church.

At 6:45 A.M. this morning the sky was dark but when I finally got myself to get up I was brightened, even if the weather wasn't, by lights across the way. That is my time, the earliest time, when I am still foggy enough after the long bad night to put my soul directly on paper, and when the great goodness of the time for me is that all images are suddenly fresh and surprising. Clear direct contact with a world half formed in my mind and on my retina, but *my* world there for me. As I get nearer and nearer the finish line, and am appalled by how easily bored I am by everything around me so routine and predictable—all of it old, like me—I am drawn with the old excitement to my boyhood, when Papa the painter went off at the crack of dawn to paint bridges and subways, and the still largely unknown wonder of the city loomed so large in my mind that I imagined myself climbing Brooklyn Bridge with Papa and was emperor of all I surveyed in the world harbor of New York.

Henry James lamenting the "general lost freshness." What sickens me in 1993, as it could never have done in the terrible 1933, though Hitler was in power and we were mired in a depression that lifted only with the war, is how limited everyone seems to me—myself not least, how transparent every motive. People have never before seemed to me so narrow and irremediable. The language almost everyone talks around me comes straight out of a TV commercial.

It is as boring to list everything I hate as it is to live with this hatefulness. When you asked my father how he felt, he always replied, "Disappointed." As Pat Moynihan said yesterday of Clinton, what a clatter of broken campaign promises. And the guy hasn't even taken office. Yes, disappointed. Especially with myself, for so much work undone and incomplete, for being so hard on people for coming on, petty and predictable. Where O where did I lose that love for the world that was as real to me as being alive?

Evening come evening comes the darkness I always fear, I droop. Yet for a moment this morning, 6:45 A.M., the world had not yet closed in on itself, there was still light, people were already up to the coming day.

Germans in wheelchairs, handicapped Germans, face attacks by skinheads, some of whom say, "How come they forgot *you* at Dachau?" A couple successfully sued a hotel in Flensburg because their vacation there was marred by the presence of crippled people.

Cold and getting colder. At nine this morning I had a wonderful therapy with dear Maggie Bradley, whose earnestness in tending to my arthritic carcass fills me with such gratitude—not to say surprise—in this unfeeling world that I find myself admitting things about my habits, like praying in the night and admitting that there is no reason to believe in God except that one does.

The *Texas Monthly*, which dotes on reporting Texas as a separate American civilization: An East Texan entrepreneur announced plans for a drive-in funeral parlor where motorists could view the deceased without leaving their cars.

\*   \*   \*

Just back from Gettysburg College after reading my Lincoln chapter. In the bitter cold I finally got to see the battlefield, to see Round Top and to stop at Little Round Top, then the national cemetery where Lincoln spoke. Not another car on the road between the fields, and the vast fields themselves with snow ghostly silent, where for three days, July 1–3, 1863, 93,000 Federal troops and 70,000 Confederates fought it out in such desperation. Everywhere the individual states have put up their own memorials and statues of army leaders. O these replicas, these effigies now dominating the vast fields of snow. What history, what unobtainable memories now. Gettysburg a poor town, mostly dependent on the tourists. The hotel does not serve eggs or orange juice for breakfast, obviously too costly. From where I sat in the restaurant (the wait-resses in Civil War costume), could see cars and trucks regularly swinging round the traffic circle, round and round in an unstopping ballet. There was something so wearisomely routine about their movement that I silently dared at least one car or truck to get out of line for a second, but round and round they went despite me.

A young woman on Ledyard Street opened the trunk of her car to take out a package. A man came up, shot her in the neck, then went off with the package. Bill Cain writes that the Black Studies prof at Wellesley teaches the inmates from a Farrakhan text listing individual Jews as slave traders, offers no other texts to his students, refuses to debate the matter with other faculty, but that the college is trying to "contain" the matter. Black on black on black. My irri-tation with the fashionable distortions of black history, theirs and everyone else's, put me in mind of the story about Julius Rosenwald, the Sears, Roebuck exec who gave vast sums for black education. Once, when he got off the train in Chicago, one porter asked another what sort of tip Rosenwald had left: "You might say he is more generous to the race than to the individual."

Judith says the anecdote makes her relate more firmly to the individual, but the only relief I get these days from the pressure of black misery, black crime, the fearful reinvention of black history, is to think of the terrible, ever terrible history of the race. As always, the novelist is inherently closer to the subject than the historian.

Young black woman in subway concentrating on pamphlet SUB-MISSION TO GOD, HOW TO REGULATE IT, marking it up with red pen.

Towards the end of a hot and happy day at Lollapalooza, hundreds, perhaps thousands, of people started throwing plastic water bottles into the air. The sun was going down and the air filled with bottles, sun glinting as they soared in arcs. . . . Completely safe, the eruption was mildly anarchic, just the right symbol for the whole show: people could go home, having participated in something spontaneous. . . . At the main stage, Frot 242, an industrial dance band, came out and performed dirty, electronic dance music, odd to hear in the sunlight. People went crazy dancing and throwing themselves toward the stage. Fishbone came out and played "Freddy's Dead" over a hyper funk groove; it mixed ska and funk and noise, and the troops streamed to the pit, as bodies cartwheeled in the air over the audience. The pit, dusty and dry, sent up a column of dust.

Near the end of the show the fire dept hosed down the crowd, and the water seemed like some sort of heavenly deliverance.

\* \* \*

America, the land of race. In Los Angeles white supremacists, some no older than twenty, planned to bomb the largest black church and spray the worshippers with machine-gun fire. Prominent rabbis and Jews also to be murdered.

*I grew up without any sense of evil.* It was not in our Jewish communal sense of "decency" and love and social democratic messianism. I missed it, even when it was there, in the books I read. But evil, why evil is just like sunshine; it may seem to hide behind a lot of comforting words at times but just wait, and it will hit you over the head when you are not looking for anything in particular. The trouble with the old Christian belaboring of evil as a constituent was that it fixed on morality, on the Roman Catholic idolization of virginity. Even if you take Calvin's dark warnings about "concupiscence" as not merely sexual but central to the human failure in God's eyes, the initial premise of man as a being almost entirely closed up in himself by his "concupiscence" does nothing but herald God's absolute sovereignty in order to establish the centrality of evil in man's nature. But this evil is limited not just to sexual conduct but to absolute fidelity to the one and only church. Churches are authoritarian by definition, since each church offers itself as the one and only truth and the great dam against the susceptibility to the nihilism so easily felt by man, the temptation to the rhetoric of meaninglessness. Religion as ritual is entirely natural, a persistence of gestures and choreographed responses that arise from elemental responses to our daily universe of arousal, fear, satisfaction. "God" as the "supreme" being, the only unmoved mover, was invented by man as a living metaphor for transcendence and immortality—we all need a Father, a source of our creation, and so must accept the tribunal, the judgment seat He makes of His transcendence—in itself as natural to man in his imaginative sense of time as his expectation of a next day, a next "world" as an alternative to his grinding sense of being locked up in his mortal body.

But evil! Evil is evil against man, it is Cain, it is the murder of our brother. And clearly, from the perspective of the times, the wish to obliterate our "brother" is as strong as the need for sex. Nothing more natural than to obliterate, to tear up the roots of our universal being in the shape of just one other human being.

Black night! Black night!

Long, droning but not uninteresting article by Harold Brodkey in *The New Yorker* on John O'Hara, sort of confiding to you (among other things) about his acquaintance with Carver and his *en famille* knowledge of the strengths and weaknesses of Cheever, Updike, etc. Yet, as always when I read Brodkey, I seem to see him not as an author in command of his material but as a character looking for an author to do him justice.

Jews! David Milch, the creator of the *NYPD Blue* TV show on Channel 7 Tuesday nights, has the same name as the Nazi air chief, Eduard Milch, who was half Jewish or something. When the Nazi racial purists objected to Milch being in the Luftwaffe, his boss Göring replied: "It's up to me to decide who is a Jew and who isn't."

\*   \*   \*

Jesus, the man who took everything on himself. Constantly invoking the Father, like a good Jew, modestly admitting that whatever authority he possesses comes from Blessed be He, our Lord and our God. But Jesus was a genius, and easily exceeded his authority to speak not only *as* a Jew, but as an individual entranced, hypnotized, by the possibility of moral perfection.

But starting out as an unusually gifted and restless "religious person," Jesus clearly comes to see himself as a vessel of the Almighty God. He has been given the word, *The* Word. He performs "miracles," which read like faith curing. He is an exponent, the most astonishing of current prophets. The people in this sacerdotal community flock to him. He has disciples, starting with his own family, like brother James.

But now comes the hard part, the really interesting part. For the "prophet," the self-admitted vessel of the Lord, becomes the victim, the sacrifice. God at the last minute had an angel stay Abraham's hand from sacrificing his son Isaac. But Jesus is not only not spared—not from anything!—God (according to the Christians) means for "my beloved Son" to die in order to lift the burden of guilt and sin we have carried since Adam's fall. This I find an even stranger myth than God testing Abraham's faith by ordering him to sacrifice his most beloved son. We are supposed to believe the torture and crucifixion of Jesus is all a God-ordained design. And in Christianity we are expected (many times *ordered*) to become part of this design, to worship the Cross because the terrible death of the Son was enjoined by the Father—in order to relieve man of the perpetual truth of sin imposed on us because Adam—in transgression of God's strictest order—ate of the apple of the tree of knowledge. God wanted us to remain happy little pagans or puppies in the Garden of Eden! Man has been cursed ever since with the (forbidden) knowledge of evil. Which in truth *is* man's inheritance.

I think of Jesus not as part of the Father's design, but of his willingness to justify the Father by suffering man's evil to himself. He took on the evil as a symbol as well as an affliction. The son insisted that there truly was a Father, that he took on all this suffering in God's name, that the Father was real because the Son was willing to undergo all this humiliation, mutilation, and a despised criminal's death on the Cross in "His" name and Kiddush Hashem, to the sanctification of "His" holy name.

Christianity could make a divine figure of Jesus—"God's Son"—one-third of the Trinity, etc.—only by creating the design of God's own purposefulness in the sacrifice of Jesus. But Christianity includes the Father only to establish the Son, and the Christology is truly named, the Son is the real center of the religion of the "anointed." The emotional content of Christianity is fascinating to this Jew, long wearied of the synagogue's ritual and mechanically repeated praise of the Father. The Son is an active principle to Christians, as Jehovah is only in the Creation and the exigency of the Law. He is the instrument of salvation—believe in me and you shall have eternal life. There need be no death, at least no finality to it.

But what puts the excitement into the good Christian's life is the figure of Jesus, *the man in this life who took everything on himself.* The man who lived all our suffering in this life, and our dread of death. Jesus, the man who really lived all the good and suffered all the evil.

The enduring cruelty of so much social reality in America. Republicans advocate just dropping welfare recipients after two years. There are five million recipients of welfare. Avis Lavelle, an assistant secretary of Health and Human Services, described a visit to a dispirited woman in western Tennessee's Fayette County, who lived in a flimsy shed with little heat and with sewage pipes that emptied into her backyard. "The conditions were so abject there, it made me want to cry," she said. "No heating, just one stove." "Open pipe to the backyard!" said Kathryn Way, a White House aide.

But Republican Representative Nancy Johnson of Connecticut talks like this: "Some women on welfare are more consumed by the feeding of their drug habit than the gut instinct to feed their children."

*  *  *

I don't have the words—the word?—for what I want most to say! Is "God" the final term of my—our—inexpressiveness? Thinking of that woman still sitting in the bitterest silent meditation after the services for Father Healy at the Jesuit church. We were all so busy departing the church, but she looked as if she did not know how to leave, conventionally, with the rest of us. She was rooted, I had the nerve to think, in the church of her own despair. I cannot forget the bitterness she showed (to my stranger's presumption) at all the conventions and trappings enfolding the individual riddle of death.

And now a word from our sponsors. As always, the permanence of slavery among the dark people (Tolstoy's word for the destitute hovering in Moscow).

"Gangster rap, which many of its aficionados see as validating the turbulent and deadly streets of an America denied, is the latest manifestation of hip-hop, which first washed over the country in the mid-70s. Like most of mainstream hip-hop, its market is suburbia." Stanley Crouch—"What is rebellious about a bunch of Negroes going around murdering people, raping people and sitting around a table playing cards and drinking 40-ounce bottles of beer? They are not rebelling against anything. They are a bunch of opportunists who are appealing to an appetite that America has for vulgarity, violence and anarchy inside Afro-America."

I saw on Forty-second Street a man begging, with the following message on his placard. "I am a Navajo Indian and I want to go home to Navajo country."

\*   \*   \*

Philip Gourevich in the *Forward* resists the notion that "American Jewish culture can be understood as a matter of neurosis, cuisine, and television sitcoms":

> Sadly, a large portion—I'd venture that it's close to
> 50%—of the material that comes in to this office for review
> or publication consists of Jewishness as something defined
> from without by persecution or hostility. Sitting in this
> chair on a bad day, you might think that Jews have finally
> succumbed to Sartre's insulting suggestion that if people
> stopped hating us we would cease to exist. . . . Sadder still is
> the fact that many Jews seem to cherish their perception as
> victims. This is a common idiocy of our age, hardly unique
> to Jews: to seek one's value in one's devaluation by others.
> We are hated, so we must be great enough to warrant
> hatred, the thinking goes, we are a cause, and easy
> righteousness is on our side.

Apply this to blacks, who think this as a matter of course, who more and more (so far as I know) think nothing else, and end up hearing that preacher say to them: "Up, you mighty people, Up!"

Hans Morgenthau openly derided on TV during or just after the Vietnam War by McGeorge Bundy. Hans M. once told me he had been ordered by his father to acquire dueling scars. In America he spent a once-unimaginable amount of time with Hasidim.

\*   \*   \*

Dan Pagis's "Scrawled in Pencil in a Sealed Railway Car"

here in this transport
i eve
and abel my son
if you should see my older son
cain son of man
tell him that I

(translated from the Hebrew by Robert Friend)

Stephen Mitchell also translates the original "Cain, son of Adam" as "Cain, son of man." Adam—"man"—human being formed out of the dust of the ground (Adham). Adham, out of the ground.

Auschwitz is decaying (physically) and there is much disagreement how to "save" it so that people will know what it was. One thought is to reconstruct it in part, at least the foundations, but that would be a "forgery." Historians now generally agree that of the approximately 1.6 million victims, 1.3 were Jews and 300,000 were Polish Catholics, Gypsies, and Russian prisoners of war. Already they are trying to collect the names of the estimated 1.6 million victims with the idea of putting them, under glass, on the walls of the "sauna" (where people undressed before being marched into the gas chambers):

> *"But the names of most of the Polish Jews would be almost impossible to retrieve," said Miroslaw Obstarcyk, a historian at the museum, "because the names were left in the ghettoes of occupied Poland after the victims were put on the transports. And the ghettoes and the records of the names no longer exist."*

*       *       *

The fierce cold, day after day. Between the occasional chest pain that comes in when you are least expecting it, and my fear of falling (again) on the ice, and sleeping only on a toehold as it were, since when I am not in the bathroom I lie awake thinking of the next, writing the next, and still the next, it suddenly comes on me in this forest of fears and obligations to think well of "easeful" death. I really have to resist this temptation to "sleep" and "sleep" and "sleep." For death has only one tense, the past, while the day for all its cold is so beautiful, the ice glittering even as it threatens in its unbroken shine. The woods *are* lovely, dark and deep, but how would I know if I bury myself there?

About a thousand foreign Jews each year get to be buried in Israel. One hundred US and Canadian Jews each year. Eretz Hahayim Cemetery on the outskirts of Beit Shemesh. Transportation, coffin, and burial comes to more than six thousand dollars.

"There are people who believe that those who die here go straight to Heaven—a direct line, if you will," said Rabbi Jay Karzen. "And it is said in Cabalistic mysticism that people who are buried here, in holy land, will be the first to come back to life when the Messiah comes. . . . These dead often have children and grandchildren in Israel, so at least they will be visited once in a while."

In the old days the Mount of Olives was the front rank of those rising for the Messiah. But the sprawling mount, east of the old Walled City, has often been a hotbed of grave desecrations and of stone-throwing by young Palestinians. So a more tranquil location these days is the Har Hamenuhot Cemetery in Jerusalem's western precincts.

Jewish apartheid! May Jews and non-Jews lie next to one another! The army's chief rabbi ruled that a Jewish soldier could not be buried in a military cemetery next to a Muslim—Lt. Col. Abdel Majid Hamed, a Bedouin tracker for the Israeli army and who had even taken a Hebrew name, Amos Yarkani. But even Rabin sided with the religious authorities and the poor lieutenant colonel was ousted.

They have been driven crazy by their long, long history. Yet they are not really interested in anything else so much as this history, and they are always repeating it whether they know it or not. And sometimes, if they do know it, they are moved, even happy. It all seems so normal.

When they say "people of the book," they mean their own story. And there are times when the story seems to have eclipsed the event. The story and the fable indeed! It all became a fable, as well as consisting of obvious fables.

Frank Rich complained of *Schindler's List* that the condemned Jews were not "individuated" enough.

Answer from woman in Williamsville, New York:

Jews [were] not uprooted suddenly . . . isolated from their communities for long periods before they were imprisoned. Jews had to wear the star, could not shop wherever and whenever they wanted. The children had to go to special Jewish schools. Jews could not use public transportation, were not allowed to participate in cultural and educational events, were forced to live in certain neighborhoods, were deprived of their livelihoods and hunted like animals.

Finally, when the Germans opened their doors, they were herded into local prison camps, often for months, and families were torn apart. When the trains came to transport the Jews to the concentration camps, they had suppressed their emotions and were totally dehumanized, stripped of all dignity, separated from their children, parents, family and friends. All they had left was a strong desire to outlive this nightmare. . . . There was a raw rage to survive this nightmare, and one's past personality and identity were worthless in this new hellish world. JEWS DID NOT HAVE THE LUXURY OF BRINGING INDIVIDUALITY TO THIS MACABRE WORLD OF TORTURE AND ANNIHILATION. TO SURVIVE JEWS HAD TO BE NAMELESS WITH NO PAST AND NO FUTURE. THEY COULD ONLY LIVE ONE DAY AT A TIME.

Barbara Ungeheuer is back from Germany and tells me that the Frankfurt-Munich express train is named the "Hannah Arendt"!

Orthodox Jews really do believe in a "sky-God." His name may be unutterable, but in their eyes he is ubiquitous, omnipotent, and always *watching*. He is the absolute, and we are as dependent on His commandments as is humanly and inhumanly possible. From believing in an earthly creature instead of this sky-God, the Christians proceeded to internalize Jesus-as-"God," and bit by bit came to believe they were duplicating him and not just sharing his body and his blood in the communion service.

Two happy days reading my son Michael's *The Populist Persuasion: An American History*, which is strong in conception and style, a really first-rate book of American history. And apart from my personal *naches*, I recognize that Michael's knowledge of social struggle in America has put some long needed historical bedrock to my thinking. What a rough, forever raucous country, with so many races, backgrounds, classes incessantly clawing—not just fighting—each other. The history of a country as one populist movement or appeal after another, the "people" as the thematic center. Especially fascinated by Reagan's actual elusiveness even as he acted the role of "everyone's" president.

Terrific replay of Malcolm X's career on PBS. One of the most magnetic personalities in American public life of my time, yes, and inspiring to watch as a *character*, though he was not really going anywhere, could summon up only the same fighting, repetitive words. O God how infinitely tragic the story is, for he was honestly shocked by the doings of that creep the "Honorable Elijah Mohammed," and paid for it. But he was not going anywhere because separatism and black nationalism were already meaningless in the sixties for 11 percent of the American people, while the rest of us remained as distrustful and fearful and fundamentally adversarial as ever. And of course Malcolm's famous eloquence depended on the dormancy of his audience, always looking suffocatingly unanimous and indistinguishable in these old pictures.

Post-modernists now place quotation marks around words like "reality," insisting that the old notion of objective knowledge has become obsolete. Multiculturalists are for new curriculums not on the basis of factual accuracy but on the basis of "self-esteem." Truth and knowledge replaced by opinion, perception, credibility. Spin doctors use pseudo-events and photo-ops to market virtual reality of versions of themselves to the public. For post-modernists the critic counts, not the author.

Gertrude Himmelfarb in her new book, *On Looking into the Abyss: Untimely Thoughts on Literature and Society.* Since all pronouncements, all historical events, are indeterminate, subject to endless interpretation and re-interpretation, this view suggests "a denial of the fixity of the past, of the reality of the past apart from what the historian chooses to make of it, and thus of any objective truth about the past."

Joyce Appleby, Lynn Hunt, and Margaret Jacob in *Telling the Truth about History:*

The more extreme multiculturalists celebrate the virtues of fragmentation. History for them has become an adjunct to "identity politics," which seeks to realign political forces according to votes; ethnic, or social, or sexual identities. Some insist that since all history has a political—often a pro-paganda—function, it is time for each group to rewrite history from its own perspective and thereby reaffirm its own past.

Is the democratic idea of consensus futile? The always wise Tocqueville—everyone is confined "entirely within the solitude of his own heart."

Can blacks tell the truth, are they even in a position to learn the truth, about how their ancestors were sold to the white slave traders by other blacks? Are they ever in a position to learn the truth about their real cultural past, not the bogus history of Africa's onetime cultural supremacy?

Oppression damages people to the point where, as is happening in today's black politics, falsity reigns and truth cannot be found.

*    *    *

America the mix, the grand mix, the mixed-up kid.

Efraim Kishon—

His sole concern is for the fate of the tiny "midget state" to
which he belongs. This . . . was the only lesson a young man
in Middle Europe who had looked all about him in terror and
asked, "What is it they want of me?" could have drawn,
notably when he learned later that *the entire genocidal conspiracy
was known to the political and spiritual leadership of the free world
down to its smallest details as early as 1942. Known to the Pope
who kept it to himself and to Roosevelt and Churchill who obsti-
nately refused to bomb the railroad to Auschwitz. They knew very
well that I and my family were going to be incinerated and raised
not one little finger on my behalf, or on my people's behalf. Given
all this, is it so surprising that your good servant should say today,
unhesitatingly, that as far as he is concerned the world can jump in
a lake.*

From Sarajevo—the Spanish Jews who settled there kept the keys
to the houses they had left in Spain, and the keys were passed on
from generation to generation.

Remembering "Uncle Zayde" Max Kaminkowitz's super-
Orthodox brother with the wispy white beard, so thin and fragile
and contemptuous of us as he stood over our kitchen table saying his
prayers but refusing to eat with us.

*    *    *

Soviet Jewish officials were among the most murderous of Stalin's murderers—L. Z. Mekhlis. And of course Gendrik Yagoda. I remember the famous rabbi Abraham Joshua Heschel (his elaborate family tree hung on the wall of his dining room) trying just a bit forlornly to deny that Yagoda was Jewish. Yagoda, Yehudah!

Kfar Tapuah in Israel, followers of Kahane. Jewish state means expelling the Arabs, "having a Jewish and Zionist education instead of Western education, and putting the media in national Zionist hands. There's a fundamental contradiction between a Jewish state and a democratic one." Bumper sticker: "The laws of Scripture come before the laws of man." Binyamin Kahane (son), "We're going back to 1948, a few against many." Like the Maccabees, who led a Jewish revolt against Syrian-Greek rule in the second century B.C. and also fought Jews who adopted Greek ways. "We're doing the same thing, fighting a cultural war," says American-born David Axelrod; does not have a TV "because the programs spread American culture, which is filled with lust and abomination: sex, murder, theft and idol worship."

Dr. Baruch Goldstein, my son the doctor, my son the murderer. The Kahane group parading his coffin in Jerusalem demand "revenge for his death." One particular fanatic: "A million Arab lives are not worth one Jewish fingernail."

Quite a week, what with the massacre in Hebron, the Russians reverting to their usual reactionary chaos. The Nation of Islam's prize Jew-hater Khalid Abdul Mohammed, whom the Honorable Farrakhan was supposed to be squelching, has come out with an even harsher tirade against the Jews, blaming them for the death of Jesus and saying he prays "that God will kill my enemy and take him off the face of the planet Earth":

"I say you're called Goldstein, Silverstein and Rubenstein because you've been stealing all the gold and silver and rubies all over the world—and it's true, because of your stealing and roguing and lying all over the face of the earth." Elsewhere he referred to Jews as "slumlords" adding, "It's that old no-good J, that old imposter Jew, that old hook-nose, bagel-eating, lox-eating Johnny-come-lately perpetrating a fraud, just crawled out of the caves and hills of Europe, so-called damn Jew."

He blamed Jews for the death of Jesus: "It was the white so-called Jews that set up a kangaroo court to charge Jews with heresy and accepted a thief and a robber named Barabbas over the good black man Jesus, the black revolutionary Messiah."

His February 19 Baltimore speech, recorded on a pair of audio tapes labeled "No Love for the Other Side," sold for ten dollars a set at Nation of Islam gatherings at Howard University and in Chicago yesterday.

Seminar for foreign students on the 1930s: "The Holocaust against the Jews provides a narrative model for the Holocaust against women and blacks." Academic newspeak!

They have found in Ethiopia the skull of the first man. And from the way things are going, it might be just as well for us to be the last.

In Algeria two young women murdered by Muslim fundamentalist gunmen because their heads were uncovered. In Israel Bedouins, who are citizens of the state and have assisted the army as "trackers," more and more bitter about Hebron.

Hashem Mahemeed, an Arab member of the Israeli parliament:

"If there is occupation, there is Goldstein. All settlers are racists. They believe they are the landlords, and have a right to treat the rest of us like . . ."

A car bomb in Israel has murdered, burned, several young girls. Leading rabbis in Israel, including the former chief rabbi of the army, say that the Lord forbids the Jews to give up any part of the land given to them by God, so Jews are permitted to resist the army. Yesterday was Holocaust Remembrance Day. The Pope invited the chief rabbi to the Vatican for a special concert. Vulnerable to every fresh stab of pain at my back, I feel the torrent of murder, malice, race hatred, flooding me like an ocean of shit. And you want me to continue writing about Jews, Jews, Jews! But it is exactly this torrent of raw shocks, of "experience" at its most open and relenting, that tells me it is up to me to write about us as Jews, Jews, Jews.

It is all a story, as the Jews are always a story to themselves and One they worship. They feel that they are unique, that they mark the beginning of history, that they are special in all senses because they are directly under the unrelenting, all-seeing eye of a personal God who is heaven and the creator of earth. Their sufferings are in some sense accepted (not acceptable, for that would violate *their* special covenant with God) because their uniqueness as the favorites of heaven makes the Gentiles jealous and hostile. In any case all this has been written down, in the history found in the Torah and the endless explanations of God's laws that make up the Talmud.

None of this is likely to change, for the fundamentalist strain grows more and more obdurate in Israel, and as we know from the Kahane madness, attracts Yeshiva fanatics in a territorial not religious way because they can no longer stand American religious pluralism. Nobody should count but us. One settler back a year or two:

"We have won the land by our righteousness." Melville in the Holy Land, who saw the miserable remnants of old Jewry as so many insects—"Hapless are the favorites of Heaven."

The secular middle-class Jew is left with the social problem of defending his or her "identity" without confronting the religious claim to specialness that lies eons past, behind what seems only a problem of "prejudice." The individual Jew, especially when confronting the Holocaust, is too busy fighting for life to understand that the Fascist-Nazi determination to "make order" at any price involved eliminating the Jew for conspicuousness alone, the eternal outsider, no matter that racial anti-Semitism no longer speaks in the language of theological anti-Semitism. But the latter supplied the grounds for the former.

Five killed in bus, Hadera, Israel, suicide bomber blowing himself up, wounded. Second such attack in a week. This in the main bus station in this working-class town, in the country's heartland. Most of the survivors had minor wounds, but they told of a scene of blood and terror, of bodies ripped apart and of people too stunned in the first moments even to scream.

From Job to Joseph K—What did I do to get the Fates (or God), so angry with me?

Menachem Mendel Schneerson, the Lubavitcher Rabbi, has died (he was only ninety-two), and the faithful are in such straits that "we are certain that he will now be resurrected," said Rabbi Shmuel Spritzer, a leader of the Lubavitch Youth organization, just before the burial ceremony. "The revelation will come at any moment."

Along Eastern Parkway, Brooklyn, after the funeral: "What alternative is there to believing?" Cf. Babel in *Red Calvary,* quoting a Cossack's attack on him: "This man wants to live without enemies!"

Rabin—"We are paying with blood for ruling over another people. Ruling over another people has corrupted us." He called for the Israeli Defense Force to "become a defense army again and not an occupation army against another people."

The King of the Jews—From Yeshua to the Rebbe. (Alan Nadler on "The King of King's County" in the *New Republic.*) The common way in which he left the world:

> Unlike the other false Messiahs of Jewish history, who tended to die—or to be martyred—in rather spectacular fashion. . . . Not only did he not die before his time, he lived posthumously.
> For more than a decade before his first stroke in 1992, Schneerson had installed the idea of redemption in the center of his religious teachings . . . had . . . encouraged the Lubavitcher Hasidim publicly to proclaim the imminence of the apocalypse. Insisted that their messianic propaganda not be limited to Jews. Lubavitchers called on the world to "prepare for the coming of *Moshiach*" with glitzy full-page advertisers, posters prominently featuring the rebbe's countenance in almost every subway car in New York, highway billboards, bumper stickers and cable television programs.

Never actually claimed he was the Messiah, never denied it.

After he was silenced by his stroke, the messianic claims of the Lubavitchers were not only undiminished, they lost all restraint. Indeed, it was the loss of the rebbe's power to speak that conferred upon his most intoxicated disciples an unlimited license to crown him the long awaited King of the Jews. Dozens of books and pamphlets, in Hebrew and English, were published "proving beyond doubt" that Schneerson was the Messiah. Pseudo-scholarly tracts—including *Good Tidings: Questions and Answers Regarding the Redemption and Messiah,* whose cover featured a kitschy drawing of Schneerson, clad in a prayer shawl and dancing on the mountain tops of Jerusalem.

At the funeral young Lubavitchers singing, dancing, and drinking vodka directly across the street from 770 Eastern Parkway, chanting: "Long *live* our master, teacher, and rebbe, King Messiah, forever and ever."

Woman: "This is the beginning of the *geulah* [redemption], and any minute now the rebbe will rise up and take us all to Israel. . . . Rebbe, wake up! Rebbe, come back!"

Nadler: For Jews there has never been a Messiah who has *not* died.

The flag and the cross are becoming one. Sidney Blumenthal: "In America, as in Europe, the removal of the bipolarity of the Cold War unleashed ethnic and religious tensions that had been mostly submerged for nearly half a century." A Christian rightist: "The old dichotomies of liberal-conservative, internationalist-isolationist, dove-hawk are breaking apart. There are some ideological categories that don't have any history in the politics of the Cold War. The ends of wars . . . bring chaos and recrimination."

\*   \*   \*

William Kristol was vice president Quayle's chief of staff. Blumenthal:

> In January Quayle spoke at a training conference of religious-right activists in Fort Lauderdale, whose theme was "Reclaiming America," and before the event began he stood at attention as the crowd of more than two thousand rose, faced a flag with a cross on it, and, with hands on hearts, recited in unison "I pledge allegiance to the Christian flag, and to the Savior, for whose Kingdom it stands, one Savior, crucified, risen and coming again, *with life and liberty for all who believe.*"

Geza Vermes in the *New York Review* on the history of the Dead Sea Scrolls:

> The Scrolls remain important for our understanding of the New Testament. Essenism, Rabbinic Judaism, and early Christianity all arose in Palestine during a period of profound spiritual ferment. It is no exaggeration to say that none of these movements can properly be understood independently of the others. Their fundamental similarities of language, doctrine and attitude to Scripture clearly seem to derive from the Palestinian religious atmosphere of the period. Some specific resemblances suggest that the early Church may have modeled itself on Essene society . . . a similar form of religious communism was practiced in the early Christian community in Jerusalem. . . .
> 
> By adding to our understanding of the period in which they originated, the study of the Qumran materials will make it possible to see Essenism, Rabbinic Judaism, and early Christianity as parts of a continuously evolving Jewish tradition and of a creative literary process. Compared with the

ultra-conservatism of the Essenes, Rabbinic Judaism appears relatively flexible and open to change, and the religion preached and practiced by Jesus of Nazareth stands out for its religious distinctiveness and immediacy.

The Christian doctrines propagated by John and Paul, for their part, tried to put distance between the teachings of Jesus and those of Christianity; they did so by stressing Christ's eternal divinity and bodily incarnation, the redemption of mankind through his crucifixion and resurrecting, and the trinity of Father, Son, and Holy Ghost (*Jesus the Jew* [1973], *The Religion of Jesus the Jew* [1993]). The teachings of Jesus must be understood in the setting of Jewish religious and cultural history, and of the Christian theology expressed in the New Testament must be distinguished from the life and thought of the teacher, healer, and exorcist whose ethical teachings made him a particularly striking and original figure among the charismatic Jewish men of first-century Galilee.

The superorthodox everywhere are actors playing parts written out for them. And they must obey the written part to the letter. Today's *Times*—"Nearly two hundred thousand Moslems demonstrated in Dacca, Bangladesh, to demand that a fugitive writer, Taslima Nasrin, be hanged and all anti-Islamic activity banned. Ms. Nasrin is accused of calling for revisions to the Koran, but denies the charge and is hiding to avoid arrest."

Art D'Lugoff, interviewed in the *Forward* on the closing of the Village Gate:

"You have to remember that most of American theater was influenced by Russian melodies brought over by Jews, from Irving Berlin to Jerome Kern to Gershwin. The music publishing firms were largely Jewish—and, sure, there were a lot of rip-offs, but blacks were thrown together with Jews during that early period, and there's no question they worked and collaborated together on many projects." The portrayal of exploitative Jewish jazz promoters, the "Moe and Joe Flatbush" seen in Spike Lee's *Mo' Better Blues*, is one particular stereotype that infuriates Mr. D'Lugoff. "The positive influence of the impresarios in this music was enormous. They provided the spaces for the music to flourish. I know for myself Jewish impresarios, people like Barney Josephson, Sol Hurok and Max Gordon, were my idols."

Paul Wechsler, a Tel Aviv University linguist, says in his book *The Ashkenazic Jews* that East European Jews are descended not from Sephardim moving northward and eastward but from converted Slavs, and that many Ashkenazic customs are non-Jewish in origin.

Great lunch with Yaron Ezrahi. Said he got more "secular" when for forty-eight hours after Baruch Goldstein murdered the Hebron Arabs at prayer, not one Jewish cleric had anything to say.

Jews either on top or at the bottom. Jesus on the cross, the most shameful and atrocious of Roman executions, a puzzle and shame to the usual literalists among his own people, tortured and mocked as "king of the Jews," though he never claimed to be a messiah. Immersed in Abba, the Father, whose kingdom was not in the future but now, now, in our hearts through love of our fellow man, he became the "Son of God," a concept meaningless to Jews. And was born and died before Saul of Tarsus invented Christianity. But became God even more than the son of God to centuries and worlds of believers.

Baruch Spinoza, not only excommunicated by his Amsterdam congregation but anathema (officially, he was to be stepped on) to his own people. Refugees from Portugal and Spain who of course were afraid that his "advanced views" would curtail their hazardous existence in Holland. But near the end of his isolated existence as a grinder of lenses, despised as "a dead dog" because he was considered an "enemy of religion," feared by Jews and Christians alike, he was recognized as a prince of thought, a founder of modern philosophy, offered a chair at Heidelberg that he declined because the ruler as protector of God could not possibly protect his belief in freedom of thought at all costs.

Joseph in the pit delivered to become chief court Jew in Egypt! Karl Marx cadging loans from everywhere, pawning his wife's aristocratic family silver, to become the ultimate icon in Russia, giving Lenin and Stalin sanction to direct world revolution! Freud ransomed from the Nazis as a vile Jew ("I would not have charged so much for a single visit"). In exile—"an island of pain in a sea of indifference"—molding the mind of the West as no one else would do it except Einstein.

DeGaulle—They are "dominating." Always at the center of world history and always transforming it, whether they meant to or not. The State of Israel, the Jewish commonwealth resurrected after two thousand years, set the Middle East aflame. Certainly it contributed in large part to the violent religio-political Islamic revolution.

Santayana remembered—"America the greatest of opportunities, the worst of influences"—on this crucial day that may augur the political rule of the Right for a long time to come—way past my lifetime! Born early in the century with the New Freedom, dying at the end of the century in the most reactionary and regressive climate I have ever known.

Robert Pinsky's *Inferno*, the epic invocation that opens Canto 2:

Day was departing, and the darkening air
called all creatures to their evening quiet
While I alone was preparing as though for war
To struggle with my journey and with the spirit
Of pity, which flawless memory will redraw:
O Muses, *O genius of art, O memory whose merit*
*Has inscribed inwardly those things I saw—*
Help me fulfill the perfection of your nature

Israeli soldiers massacred and more than sixty people wounded by suicide bombers (two!) from extreme Muslim group, beyond Hamas. With such heaven-bent suicide bombers, what can the Israelis do?

Yesterday lovely expedition to Christine's Polish eatery at Second and Thirteenth Street. Only Judith could make a bus trip from Ninety-sixth to Fourteenth on Second Avenue pure joy, related to everything and everyone you see. Her passionate interest in "side streets." There are writers who are or want to be avenues. J wants to be a side street. I thought I was weary to death of New York—death in the soul, etc.—but not when I walk or ride with Judith.

From Gaza, suicide bomber's family: "When I saw the flesh and blood of the Jews I was happy." A psychiatrist at Gaza's only community mental health program: "Our own society is somehow com-

mitting suicide. Look at our streets—we are neglectful of everything. . . . There is no mention of the future. In the hopelessness
and helplessness of this world, there is the bright promise of the
next life."

"The bombers have typically been devout single men from poor
backgrounds, in their early 20s, who have experienced a personal
loss or traumatic humiliation at the hands of the Israelis, doctors
add."

"There's a process of brainwashing," Dr. Sarraj said. "You live in a
semi-hypnotic state. You become so overwhelmed with one idea that
you completely isolate yourself from the rest of the world. You have
to conform to the group, and within it you find a new identity."

Notebook left behind by Mr. Radi, a twenty-one-year-old policeman who had prayed regularly, fasted often, and immersed himself
in the Koran, according to his family. "Life is beautiful," he wrote a
month before he died, "but the more beautiful life is to be a martyr.
Paradise is a delicious drink. Our enemies love life but we adore
death, so I am sacrificing my soul and everything I own to God."

Orthodoxy, fundamentalism, as a form of madness, when a cult
and its "commandments" get so internalized that they take over the
whole person.

Some ardently Orthodox rabbis assert that responsibilities for
their deaths (19 young soldiers) lay principally with the PM,
Yitzhak Rabin. Their reasoning: he had held discussions with
his economic adviser one day before, on the Jewish *Sabbath*.
*The terrorist attack was "God's punishment" for his transgression,
said some leaders of a political faction in Parliament known as
Agudat Yisrael.*
    Similarly, several members of the Lubavitcher Hasidic sect
visited the Rene Casson High School in Jerusalem, where
students were still in shock because six recent graduates had

died while on Army duty within the last year. The Hasidim reportedly said they were there to check if the bad luck the school had experienced *may be the result of improperly placed mezuzahs*, small cases of scriptural excerpts attached to doorposts. Angry students went to their principal, Yehezkel Gabbiai, who asked the visitors to leave. "It is unbelievable," he told Israeli reporters, "that in the 20th century someone will really think that one of these flowers, who contributed to the state, died because of a Sabbath desecration or because the mezuzahs weren't good."

Yahweh as demon, exacting revenge because His commandments are not being obeyed to the smallest dot. All of this superstition attached to the figure of the One and Only God reminds me of Simone Weil's observation that when monotheism becomes the content of religion, the loss of faith in the One becomes a loss of faith in religion generally.

The Yad Vashem Holocaust Memorial has rejected a request by a group of Orthodox Jews to remove photographs showing victims of the Holocaust going naked to their deaths. Avner Shalev, the administrative chairman of Yad Vashem, said the institution had a duty to portray history as it happened. He dismissed calls for a boycott issued by Chaim Miller, who heads the Association for Rights of the Haredi Public here.

Dr. Baruch Goldstein, who killed twenty-nine Moslems at prayer in the Hebron cave, is now a cult figure among many Israeli settlers. "He who kills our enemies is sanctifying God's name." Dr. G's face on T-shirts, shown carrying the Torah. A little Arab boy whose father was killed by Dr. G looks on, calls them "crazy," and adds, "I will revenge my father."

Jews so often resemble one another in every particular, but the really great men among them are unlike anyone else—free-minded, independent-minded, "conquistadors," as Freud described himself. Richard Feynman playing his bongo drums when and wherever he liked. At Cornell they are still giggling over Professor Feynman riding around in an open car with a sexy redhead at his side.

William Bennett, the made-over man (I remember him as a sedulous ape to that advanced liberal Professor Charles Frankel), interviewed in the AARP magazine, *Modern Maturity*:

"Are you implying liberals are not patriotic?"
"Liberals say they are patriotic, but the liberal ideology
has trouble sorting things out. It wants to be all things to
all people. The traditional American belief is that America is
exceptional, that this is a special country, that our values are
*not* equal to other countries'. We *are* better, and this is a
better place."

Are we really seeing a change in the American social order? No, just George F. Babbitt having it all over everybody else.

Hate crimes on the rise. Mark Thomas, neo-Nazi leader, publishes *The Watchman*. "It is the trademark of the Jew to make us feel dirty and unworthy." Operates a ministry for racists. The doctrine there, known as Christian identity, says that anyone who disagrees with white supremacy is a traitor who must be destroyed. Fierce-looking man with heavy mustache and aggressive jaw, pictured holding a large Bible. His camp ministry—an atmosphere of paranoia and intimidation.

A Nazi flag hangs in a makeshift chapel inside an old trailer on the grounds. Food is stockpiled in the basement of the main wood-and-stone house in preparation for "a racial holy war." Thomas built a bomb shelter out of a bus he buried on his land. Skinheads welcomed at the compound.

"Their whole religion is based mostly on the first chapter in the Bible." Thomas claims that the Jewish people are descended from Cain who was a descendant of the devil snake and Eve. He claims white people are descendants of Abel, who was a descendant of Adam and Eve. Claims there are two main races, Jews and white people. Everyone else is classified under beasts of the field. They say they need the help of the beasts to overcome the evil Jewish race.

"It's a jungle out there. Move it, shut up, give me the money, have a good day."

The distance between us and God perhaps equals the distance between us and death. After a certain age we are, as it were, reeking of it. But death is the greatest possible mystery. And so is God even when we claim He is within us.

Just back from my annual visit to my tax accountant. Such a beautiful, warm day, but despite my undershirt, jacket, and parka, felt a chill and got some ominous chest pains as I was walking Forty-second Street. Am I scared? Dare I claim to just feeling a piece of nature, its rise and fall in my eighty years? Made me think of how the idea of nature—nature as process and reality—replaced God as His supreme and fickle personal will.

No accident that Emerson called his first book *Nature*, or that Thoreau saw nothing and relied on nothing but nature. Spinoza laughed at the rabbis for saying Yahweh all in his own person determines everything. But all those death-of-God pioneer modern thinkers had just left God for "Nature," and so rather worshipped it instead. Then, then, it too was "immaculate."

Scott Fitzgerald boasted that in the twenties he and Zelda felt they should "never be too tired for anything." Of course Scott Fitz died in his forties and here I am nearing eighty, and feeling too tired for a lot of the usual nonsense. But on! on! no matter what it costs us. With all the down effects of the nitro pill I took yesterday just feeling that chest pain when my warm body hit the slightest chill in the air (not sharp but cloudy, echoing in the chest) I managed to finish my latest piece in good style, delivered same to Silvers at *New York Review* and then wandered down to Chinatown for my meeting with Judith after her jury duty.

I had forgotten what a marvelous flea market Canal Street is. Can never get over the ability of these hucksters of all races to make a living from second- and third-hand junk. The bar and tea room of the Holiday Inn in Chinatown where I sat reading David Remnick in *The New Yorker* on Elaine Pagels was a delight. Fascinated when Judith came in to see this very well-dressed man solitary and silent contemplating his life through slow sips of a martini.

Sidney Lumet in *Making Movies*—The flashes of concentration-camp movies in the memory of the protagonist of *The Pawnbroker* were quickly adapted by the makers of television commercials, who called the technique "subliminal cutting."

\* \* \*

Written on a wall in the West Eighties: "Un poco de luz y no mas sangre [a little light and no more blood]. Cervantes."

Blacks becoming conscious of their background in slavery. Talk of the "Black Holocaust."

We are all recent arrivals here. "Birds of passage."

# PART FIVE

## 1993-1995

Mal. neoplasm prostate
Angina pectoris NEC NOS
Angina decubitis
Hypercholesterolemia
Arthritis

*Dying is much too expensive.*

Lupron Depot 7.5 mg
Eulexin 1, 25
Capoten 12.5
Folic acid 1 mg
Calan SR 240 mg
Prednisone 5 mg
Hytrin 1 mg
Midamor 5 mg
Methotrexate 2.5 mg
Nitro-Dur patch 0.4 mg
Prilosec 20 mg
Baby aspirin
Coumadin 5 mg

J n the midst of death we are in life—and itching to get away for the
weekend. These hot summer days there are so many of us cancer
patients waiting for our daily radiation treatment that no matter

how soon after dawn I get there on Friday mornings so that I can make an early getaway, the crowd in sullen temper is already impatiently massed in the street.

Most days there are not more than seven or eight in the radiologist's waiting room when I show up. We silently take each other in as we wait our turn. There is a lot of silence here, interrupted only by the bossy quick and sharp electronic pulses, *whir, whir, whir!* from the machine presiding in the next room. An almost religiously gentle but startlingly fat doctor overlooks the two young female technicians. He sits in the corner like a Buddha, overlooking the mighty lineup of looseleaf notebooks. Imagine, one whole notebook to each customer! I feel vaguely sorry for him, for he is here from morning to dusk no matter what hour I appear. The head man has a pleasant European accent, is conscious of his good looks and something of a fop. Tassels on his loafers. I can't stand his steady geniality. He shows up only on Tuesdays.

The treatment takes no time at all. Only the waiting seems endless as we study each other. A name is called, the patient enters through the door to the secret room within. A red light goes on. The patient is almost immediately back. In and out. In and out. Reminds me of a barber "college" or army brothel. Nothing about the process takes very long. There is only the slight discomfort in once more depositing yourself without your pants on the cold steel table before the different surfaces of the machine tuck you in and circle around you like some damned planetarium in which you, even cancerous you, are the sun.

Friday mornings, when the wait is longer than usual and the place is so full that people are standing in the back, it is fascinating to see how differently we humble petitioners for life, for still more life, present ourselves. Rarely do you see the desperate cases. For them radiation may be too late. Most of us look as well as people can look at the beginning. For the old this can be a very slow-moving disease. There is one humdinger, a startlingly beautiful Oriental woman in lightly shimmering black who is such a sight in this tiresome room that she sits in her own aura. I can't get over the wonder of this woman in such a place and must stop staring at her. Once in a while there are children. A rare sight—a young black brought in so far gone that people vacate the couch for him. He lies there heaving, one arm dangling to the floor. Although Friday even in the morning is for the very pious dangerously close to the Sabbath, a cluster of heavily bearded Jews surprises me by pushing a wheelchair with a very sick-looking old woman in it. They stand behind her in the waiting room managing in some way to look at no one here, no one at all.

The uninteresting young blond receptionist, not a native to judge by her accent, always has the radio on. She smiles a lot. Observing her in the waiting room day after day, week after week this ghastly summer in which everything has had to wait on my illness, I can see that she does everything by rote, as if taught. She moans softly in disapproval when I fall behind in my payments, then hurls "God bless!" at me when I leave. This is an expression I heard last in wartime Britain, which doesn't suit her. Its greasy good nature grates on me, coming from someone who is always pushing bills at me that get more unbelievable every time I am forced to look at them.

Every day there are new faces. The young girls make me shudder, it seems so unjust. There is a men's group of my generation, all in their seventies, *alte kockers* who sit around recalling old radio shows, solemnly bringing back John Daly, Arlene Francis, Bennett Cerf, Dorothy Kilgallen. It gives me a pang to hear again the best lines of Fred Allen, my favorite satirist from a time when anyone named J. Danforth Quayle would have been straight man to Groucho and not so near the presidency of the United States. "How much would you charge to haunt a house?" Fred Allen liked to ask the nearest pest. Once these men would have met to play pinochle around the pool at Grossinger's. Now they wait, still all good humor with each other, for the machine that is going to postpone our death.

*Timor mortis conturbat me.* When the lifeboat to which I was assigned on that Liberty ship cracked up in the storm, and depth charges from the Canadian escort were being hurled off like mad because a Nazi submarine was rumored to be in the neighborhood, I remember waiting in my life preserver for God knows what, and looking at the ocean so near my face, startled that I was not in the least afraid and more fascinated by the occasion than anything else.

For once, the sense of danger usual in my life was coming from the outside. So here. My cancer is so real to a lot of people that they feel free to probe me front and behind, stick me, prick me, haul me up and down, insert my claustrophobic head into the drum of one CAT scan after another in a process splendidly named Magnetic Resonance Imaging. They are all over me, being in charge as I am not. While my charming Harvard-trained urologist confesses that he loves cases like mine to distraction and seems all charged up, the many technicians ordering me about have so often done this routine that their boredom reduces me to feeling that any preoccupation with myself is in bad form. Except for that enlarged and hardened organ "no bigger than a walnut" that has taken over my life and embarrasses—never pains—me by forever sending me to the bathroom at the most inconvenient times, I am not of the slightest interest to these white coats. I am as unsurprising to them in life as I would be in death.

Yet what an army we are, and behind us what a mass society—all dead. Cancer is the subversive sea licking at the shores of everything supposed to be established and safe. When my mother was reduced to a skeleton and clearly about to enter what as an Orthodox Jew she called "the world of truth," a nurse insisted on stuffing food into her mouth as if she, too, was afraid of death and was determined to keep my mother in the world of appearances. When my friend the historian Richard Hofstadter was dying in Mountain Sinai of leukemia, he kept reaching for the manuscript under his bed of *America at 1750*, the first volume of his projected history of the United States. One of his last remarks: "I've never had any trouble with my will." Anatole Broyard at the last committed himself to a Park Avenue quack, swallowed hundreds of pills a day, chatted brilliantly on the phone from Cambridge, claimed, "I am intoxicated by my illness." It was the cleverest act in Anatole's always clever life. He even got a posthumous book out of it. Knowing Anatole, another nut like me for whom writing is all, I am sure he would have thought the exchange of his life for a memorable death almost fair—if there was going to be a book in it. Of course he would miss the girls. No one I ever knew was so graceful and funny about sex, especially in that memoir of the Village after the war, when books were still as sacred as sex.

The dead refuse to leave me.

Leonard Bernstein's wife, Felicia, groaned "I have smoked my life away." The poet Jean Garrigue must have greeted the news of her lymph node cancer with her accustomed fatalism. When a promised teaching job failed her, she looked up bitterly at the sky and howled: "Existence!" The wry young classical scholar Steele Commager died of throat cancer. Brilliant son of a brilliant father, he was as ironic and disbelieving about everything as his father the historian, as old as the century, was not. Visiting me shortly before he went to the hospital for the last time, Steele, with his usual sense of the absurdity of all things except translating Horace, laughed that he had been forbidden cigarettes and booze, but *commanded* to eat all the ice cream he could get down. My sophisticated and very fastidious friend Mark Schorer from Berkeley, who sniffed at anything remotely considered vulgar, was reduced by a colostomy to carrying his wastes in a bag at his side.

Last night the streets were wet, seemed to reflect the thousand and one brightnesses streaming from the still lighted shop windows and street lamps. There was a friendly fog. The whole thing gave me that strangely familiar feeing of having returned to the end years of the last century—a feeling borrowed from my lifelong fascination with Victorian London, the world of Sherlock Holmes and the Saturday nights of my boyhood, when my father regularly took me down to the Lower East Side for the meetings of the Minsk branch of the Workmen's Circle.

Broadway was so *condensed*, is what I mean, like a stage set, and while furiously lit up, was also deep in shadows.

I have never lost this association between shadowy dark streets and suddenly finding myself in another century. When I first came to Rome and stayed on in winter, I would walk in the shadows covering the narrow alleylike streets between shut-in palaces and churches as if in a trance of memory. I had been here before! And if I came out into Trastevere on a busy night, the glittering arc lights over the stands selling everything under the sun plunged me back into the Brownsville open market on Belmont Avenue, alongside which I grew up.

Joe Liebling used to say of the streets painted by Maurice Utrillo that they made you want to weep. For me the old Jewish streets of the Lower East Side, where I have never lived, tell me something of Charlie and Gussie Kazin before I knew them. I am still looking for them on this dark Saturday night. They were married on a Saturday night, which is about as much as I will ever know of their wedding. The year is 1913, something like that, not far from the nineteenth century. They are very much alone, which is the chief reason they ever married in the first place. So far as I can figure out—there were no birth certificates for the likes of them in czarist Russia, and they were as unsure of their actual birthdays as they were about everything else in the dark past. Mama was twenty-four, papa twenty-six. She was a seamstress from a heavily Orthodox family, so large that she seems to have felt lost by contrast with the good-looking favorite—whose name was Schaene.

Gussie must have considered herself unmarriageable in that narrow hole of a shtetl. No one ever told my mother that she looked just like Emma Goldman, whose round bespectacled face and thick body never kept the men off. Gussie fled at the first opportunity with the brother she loved, who decided to try his luck in a place called New Haven. Schaene and her husband were murdered when the Nazis reached their town.

What I would give to bring to life the first encounter of the two whose lifelong silence with each other left me with such a sense of their solitude—and of mine. The young fellow from Minsk is an orphan, will never get over the day his father Abraham died in New York in his twenties, leaving his mother to bear a posthumous son and to flee with the two boys back to Minsk. Where she marries again, puts my father into an orphan asylum. He will learn to fend for himself, will prove adventurous enough in America to go West as a painter on the Union Pacific Railroad before turning East to find a Jewish girl to marry. He will always seem to me the lonesomest man in the world, more like a son than a father. I learned to love him, my kid sister never could.

The newly married couple had just a furnished room—his? hers?—to return to after the ceremony. She stopped on the way to pick up some food for them. He must have gone on ahead, for when she reached the room she found him weeping. She told me this in later years. She told it with a certain contempt, I thought. "Like when you was a little boy," she added.

Jerzy Kosinski has committed suicide, sensationally of course, putting his face into a plastic bag while sitting in the bathtub. From the moment I first saw him in the seventies, working the crowd as the newly elected president of New York PEN, smiling exuberantly, laughing his way around the room as he described himself as "the latest Polish joke," I was impressed by the talent he put into becoming a celebrity—as an actor from afar to play a role in this country. I soon found that I could not believe a word he said, he was such a public entertainer.

No doubt this had much to do with his being a survivor, though in his first years here he was not crazy about identifying himself as a Jew. And for all the atrocities visited by Polish peasants on the little boy in *The Painted Bird*, the book that so violently introduced Kosinski, it is not clear why he is always on the run and easily singled out as a victim. I remember Elie Wiesel, another celebrity created by the Holocaust, going up to Kosinski at a party, demanding to know if he was a Jew!

I followed Kosinski's ascent from afar, fascinated by his intimacy with big players—Oscar de la Renta, Henry Grunwald, Abe Rosenthal, Warren Beatty, Marshall Field's heir. He had once married the widow of a millionaire, now lived with the daughter of a German baron. He played Zinoviev, the famous Russian Bolshevik, in Warren Beatty's film *Reds*. I was surprised one day to get a card from him announcing that he was a fellow at Yale and inviting me to attend the dedication of a Holocaust memorial—in New Haven.

I was even more surprised to read a piece on the op-ed page of the *Times* in which he described himself visiting hospitals at night to read to patients. He would carry the slip cover of one of his books in his raincoat, and when asked for identification would show it as the only credentials needed. Enough, it seems, for him to be welcomed into the hospital. Where he would sit himself down at some stranger's bed and like a ministering angel proceed to read, proceeding, sure that whatever the hour, the patient needed to hear from the works of Jerzy Kosinski.

This self-portrait of Kosinski as a kind of Walt Whitman in the Civil War hospitals was such a piece of intrusive arrogance that I was staggered by Kosinski's clout with the op-ed editor at the *New York Times*. I pictured myself in the New York Hospital after my heart operation. Nauseated, no longer sure which world I am in, I am unable to read anything, to understand anything but my helplessness. My dinner tray lies intact, the food looking more repulsive by the hour as I pray for someone finally to come and take the mess away.

In comes Jerzy Kosinski in his raincoat. Like Prince Myshkin in Dostoevsky's *The Idiot*, he is looking for some poor soul to befriend. Smiling at me warmly, he removes from the famous raincoat a few pages he has xeroxed from his latest book, and in his most vigorous Polish accent proceeds to read, read, read, although I am swimming in nausea. Myshkin-Kosinski concludes his reading with a fraternal kiss on my feverish brow. With a sigh at so much suffering he moves on to another bed.

We had one real meeting. Out of the blue one day he invited me to his apartment on West Fifty-seventh Street. I found myself on a sofa so ridiculously too deep that I felt my host had me at his mercy. As if the shelves thick with photographs of famous people were not enough, Kosinski name-dropped at such a pace that I felt myself sinking deeper and deeper into the sofa—especially when he recounted how a famous French Nobel biologist "practically died in my arms." I had clearly been invited so that I would champion his cause, to write about his work in a purely literary spirit. He had just been accused in the *Village Voice* of not always writing the books he published. But instead of discussing his work he built up such a picture of the elevated circles in which he moved that I felt a great desire to depart but couldn't seem to extricate myself from the sofa.

His final anecdote made my head spin. Kosinski told me that when Pope John Paul II was still Cardinal Wojtlya, he was privileged to show His Eminence around New York. At the corner of Fifty-seventh and Sixth there was a newsstand with the usual super abundance of girlie magazines. His Eminence was shocked at the display and wanted to know why it was allowed. "What kind of people sell this stuff?" he demanded of Kosinski. "Well, Your Eminence," replied Kosinski, smiling faintly as he recalled his answer, "they're usually Jews."

In the plane to Dallas I read a remarkable interview with Harold Bloom that amounts to a dialogue with himself. What a driving myth-maker about every writer he takes up—and what a prodigy. His roommate at Cornell told me that he had all of *Measure for Measure* by heart. His redoubtable Cornell professor M. H. Abrams still talks of him with awe. Says that while still at Ithaca he had only to take up Chinese before he passed his teacher.

The most startling product, for his age, of the old Bronx, Yale Professor of the Humanities Bloom looks just like my rough old City College classmate Zero Mostel, once Samuel Joseph Mostel, who certainly earned his nickname not only by his spectacularly low marks in school but by driving teachers crazy. Zero never stopped acting. He was sinuous as a monkey for all his girth, as loudly dominating in life as he was taking over the stage in Ionesco's *Rhinoceros.* When he robustly played Tevye in *Fiddler on the Roof,* he took over the whole town, the people, and what was left of the czar after Zero got him in his teeth. You forgot that the original Tevye was a pious little milkman with too many daughters whose only daring in this life was to sigh, "With God's help we starved to death."

Zero was so histrionic on all occasions that you had to laugh even when he was clearly taking up too much space on this earth.

The French novelist Christiane Rochefort and I had just been seated at a Chinese restaurant on West Seventy-second Street when I saw Zero at the other end of the room and vaguely waved. I had seen him many times on the stage, but he had not seen me since college. To my horror, he remembered me all too well. Seizing on a book I had written about a Brooklyn childhood—Zero had one too—and which he apparently disliked with all his well-known contempt for anything not in his rambunctious style, he told me off in stark colors right over the heads of everyone else in the restaurant.

Mademoiselle Rochefort's English was not up to Zero's, and she was totally bewildered, even frightened, at the onslaught. Zero finally subsided, smiled as if he expected applause, and turned back to his dinner.

The round prematurely shapeless Bloom is all literature, positively lives it. He gives the appearance in public of a slightly exhausted Falstaff—one of the many Shakespeare characters he knows right down to the ground. He has so many baby critics in his train that he seems to enjoy his fame a bit wearily. But reading his interview, I become merry. Bloom has so assimilated all the great English and American texts that he has them talking to each other. Not a man to be frightened by the scare word *canon,* his canon has Freud reading Shakespeare and Shakespeare seriously taking account of Freud. I like his contempt for all the little commissars now in the English department insructing us to look down on so many classics, but I can't agree that they are moved by "resentment." They don't look up enough to any real achievement to be resentful of it. What old Yale types so resented in Bloom that they got him out of the English Department and deposited him in a chair of the humanities was the Bronx, the Jew, the impudence that he brought to his gifts.

Talk of resentment! The wife of a Yale English professor said to me one Sunday morning as I considered renting her house for the summer, "My husband is not here. My husband is in church, on his knees, praying for the death of Harold Bloom."

Question: "What is the difference between The International Ladies Garment Workers Union and the American Psychiatric Association?"
Answer: "One generation."

Writing this in the hospital waiting for my old-fashioned arthritis shot, a solution made up of gold. The gold syringed into me week after week, left buttock one week, right buttock the next, is not the kind some doctors enjoy up front. The head surgeon of the cancer hospital across the street makes eight hundred thousand dollars a year. Information leaked by Elly B., to whom it was leaked by a dominating figure in the cancer business.

Which leads me to think of my own doctor, who has gently taken care of me for years, has twice saved my life, and whom I love, not least because his grandfather was famous in the old Jewish trade movement for standing up to anyone (he was once in jail for this) in behalf of what used to be called the "downtrodden." And they were.

But oh Lord, how we have all "risen"! A millionaire patient's photograph next to his desk. The big bash New Year's Eve. What waste. The champagne flowing, flowing. The flowers alone must have cost a sum, and there was such a spread of food on the big round table dominating the room that you felt you had to compliment the hostess every time you passed. The young girl waiter in tuxedo was so agreeable that I half expected her to curtsy.

All this to meet with bald plump reps of the East Hampton crowd in evening clothes. The doctors at the party bore the same white glassy look of superiority that comes from standing in your white coat over some trembling wretch in his underwear. A psychiatrist sympathetic to Alfred Adler, who believed that personalities were often formed from the need to compensate for some physical deficiency, laughingly regaled me with names of the withered arm group whom he calls the "Captain Ahab brigade"—the dominating types who more than made up for their affliction—Kaiser Wilhelm, a pugnacious governor, a famous philosopher, etc., etc. He reminded me that Stalin belongs to this group, and ended: "Boy, did he compensate!"

As people said their goodbyes, one doc embraced the host and said in Yiddish, "Here's to an even better time next year!"

Every other year or so some old student of mine, now doing extremely well, insists on taking me to lunch in order to laugh off the B- or C I gave him at Amherst or Berkeley. Ridiculously ornate lunch this time on Fifty-eighth Street, from the investment banker Michael S., the sauciest of the lot. The food on my plate was obviously chosen for the picture it made, as radiant as the French countryside in May. Otherwise it was inedible.

The way to the men's room is a padded elevator.

I asked Michael about the surgeon who makes a million p.a. He politely informd me that a client, a gynecologist, makes two million. When a patient asks for satin sheets during her stay in the hospital, he decides that she is open to any bill. This, he adds quickly, enables him to charge other people less.

\* \* \*

326

Baby born in a stairwell in a Coney Island housing project thrown into a compactor ten stories below. The mother is nineteen years old. Second time in six months a baby was thrown down a chute into a trash compactor.

Young woman, twenty-one years old. "What we're saying is, if they throw a kid down the incinerator, that kid should be punished." A twenty-five-year-old man who refused to give his name. "But you never know what's going through her mind. She may be going through some depressing problem, like she had AIDS or something."

At Pasternak's grave in Peredelkino, the lovely Moscow suburb where so many writers live, we drink to him, typically Russian routine of toasting the dead, presumably wishing them well. Yevgeny Yevtushenko tells the story of the two young poets who under pressure to denounce Pasternak for *Doctor Zhivago*, actually asked Pasternak for permission to do so. After taking this in, Pasternak ironically gave permission. What disturbed him, Yevtushenko says, was the fact that they two were skipping and jumping for joy as they went off. Their consciences were clean.

Yevtushenko: "I am happy to tell you that both these bathstids came to bad ends."

I was uneasy in my mind when I went off to Gerald Freund's joint birthday party for Saul Bellow and me—we were born the same week in June 1915—but it turned out to be even more of a jolt than I had expected. I "shoulda stood in bed."

I have known Bellow for more than half a century, have admired and celebrated his fiction, and feel I understand the springs of his talent—which have to do with his innate sense of the primitive sources of life. He is like a character in a Greek tragedy—his many apprehensions, his famous moodiness, his acute and unrelievable sense of a world that may actually be dying before our eyes—these are not "personal" and neurotic, whatever the self-fulfilling fatalism he brings to his relationships, but an intuition (with the cycles of Jewish disaster always in his mind) that we are all up against forces we can hardly name, much less master.

No other American novelist in our day has so directly addressed the universe at large with Kierkegaard's "fear and trembling." We are so secular now that like Job's comforters we think religion consists just in supplying the word "God" to the riddle of human pain. But Job asked the right questions about our fate, and Bellow does too.

The trouble is that Bellow is also a university intellectual, loves teaching, and since he helped to edit the text of the Great Books used at the Robert Hutchins's University of Chicago Program has moved in the company of its conservative Big Thinkers. He has been much influenced by the traditionalists Allan Bloom and Edward Shils, has even had Shils vet his novels in manuscript. The university at Chicago thrives on absolutes, no doubt because the city has been described by Bellow as the last word in civic piggishness. I know a professor of law there who advocates repealing *all* social legislation written in the twentieth century. Bellow says that in Chicago "my modernity was all used up. I became a college professor in order to cure my ignorance."

At our birthday party Bellow gave me a turn. I knew that like many Jewish intellectuals from the immigrant working class and forced to their knees before the altar of Marxism during the depression, he had been moving right. The Jewish working class was now just an occasion for nostalgia. As Jules Feiffer said when asked why so many of his friends were getting divorced, "They can now afford it."

Bellow at college had helped to edit a Trotskyist student paper. After uselessly losing his heart to Adlai Stevenson in 1952 and 1956, he moved steadily right. (Stevenson, well known for his private dislike of Jews, was once seen coming off a plane with a novel by Bellow. When asked what he thought of it, he replied: "I wouldn't know. I don't read Yiddish.") My heart sank with each fresh report of Bellow's contempt for the lower orders not only in Papua ("who is the Tolstoy of the Zulus, the Proust of the Papuans? I'd be glad to read him.") but in America. The ex-Trotskyists now so hot for the right had never believed in American democracy. But I was not prepared when I entered our birthday party for Bellow's vehemence about liberals. When I said that I had been troubled by the conservative line on the *New York Times* editorial page one week, Bellow flashed out: "How can you call a paper conservative that publishes Anthony Lewis?"

After exuding a lot of irritation the rest of the evening, Bellow took himself off without saying goodbye.

Gingrich our next president? The total demagogue. On becoming Speaker yesterday acclaimed FDR as the greatest twentieth-century president—and the liberal Democrats for "ending segregation." America, the land where anyone can say anything—the advertising fever and the self-promotion habit are in the blood. The mob of newly elected Republican congressmen acclaim him as if they were trained seals. And Billy Kristol's advice on this "great day": Keep beating up on Clinton, make him your "punching bag."

In the Atlanta airport I saw a young woman just standing there, holding up a placard BAN LIBERALS. When I ventured to ask her just how she would enforce this, she shrugged. "Well, maybe I should have said, 'Ban Liberalism.'" When I foolishly pressed on and asked how *this* was to be done, she scowled and said, "Where you from?"

Facing me as I write is the cracked much-mended photograph of a clean-shaven young Russian Jew who died on the Lower East Side just about a century ago. A poor garment worker, he wears a frock coat and a white evening tie in which to have his picture taken.

I have needed to have this photograph near me ever since I found it—the only one of him that has survived the century—at the bottom of a pile of family photographs. He died perhaps twenty years before I was born and I have only the barest outline of his existence. I have never known anything about his life in Minsk before he became part of the tidal movement of Russian Jews to America. No one was ever able to tell me with any confidence just how old my grandfather was when he died, why he died at such an age—how his widow could have had his body thrown into one of those now unlocatable mass graves in which poor immigrants were buried in their first ravaging decade here. All I was ever able to pick up from his first-born son, my father, who seemed to me even as a boy to be a perpetual orphan, was that the young man in the photograph, my forever absurdly young grandfather, was "somewhere in his twenties," that he *may* have been a union organizer, and that I had been given my Hebrew name in the usual tradition of naming the newborn after the nearest dead ancestor. So there was a chain linking me to the undiscoverable past! My nearest dead ancestor, the only one with whom I have any connection, was called Abraham. The name was everything to me, but the name was pretty much all I had of him. There was all this silence about him. It was not like the besetting grimness with which my father and mother ever divulged anything about their first lives in the old country. There was no family saga, no great background to attach themselves to. Mine were intensely humble people—totally without *yichas*, family pride and prestige. The thing that as I grew up drove me crazy was their sense of their insignificance in the "promised land"—"Charlie" Kazin always condescended to by successful relatives, helpless feeling, shy, waiting to be accepted for a painting job by the steward of the Brotherhood of Painters and Decorators, to be smiled upon by his own folk in the Socialist Party of America, the Workmen's Circle, the Minsk branch (No. 99) of the Workmen's Circle.

Groups, institutions, public buildings, the Eastern Parkway branch of the Brooklyn Public Library just to sit in—to these my father could attach himself to. But he seemed to have no familiar and easy name for his own father. He never mentioned the dead man unless I pressed him for his memories. He could hardly bring himself to mention the death, the shock of that moment back on the Lower East Side—he was four or five—without looking as if he had been struck in the face.

There were just a few strangled words for what happened after the death. The young man's widow was "with child." When she was delivered of a second son, he was of course named Abraham after his dead father. My grandmother apparently knew no English, and must have been so terrified of the strange land that she never registered her son's birth in New York.

I have never been sure of my grandmother's name. There had been, glimpsed for a second and then totally lost, one other photograph of my grandfather—and of her. In the patriarchal tradition he alone is seated, the supposed center of the family, its mainstay and support. She stands, one hand on his shoulder. My father as a little boy is happily curled up at their feet. My grandmother is sharp-faced, looks determined. No one is smiling.

My father lived in silence even when he included me in his walks and expeditions around New York to parks, museums, David Mannes's midwinter concerts at the Metropolitan Museum of Art, the Philharmonic's summer concerts at Lewisohn Stadium. Once the show, the concert, the expedition was over, he had nothing to say.

Each of these occasions was epochal for me, a discovery of the great city of New York, to be remembered in every detail, like the mighty Egyptian figures in the Metropolitan Museum who in the old days presided over the great central hall, or (after a Lewisohn Stadium concert)—the amazing sight in the Bickford's cafeteria, Broadway and 137th Street, of people no better dressed than we actually cutting into a boat-shaped slice of watermelon with fork and knife instead of thrusting their faces right into it.

When my father volunteered to say anything to me at all, it was to go over again those first adventures in America which I knew by heart and loved because these, like books, gave me the connection I craved with America itself. He had managed to get himself to America in 1907. With his solemn pride in being even a little part of America (a pride I hungrily grabbed at) he liked to remind me that 1907 was the peak year of immigration. "1907! There was more than a million of us at Ellis Island that year!" He had been sent up to Albany by a Jewish immigration society to work at a potash factory near the Hudson. He had worked in the Chicago stockyards shaking cattle skins free of salt, had been a stitcher in the Hart, Schaffner and Marx factory.

Intoxicated with his freedom to go anywhere in his new country, he went further west painting box cars on the Union Pacific railroad. He was offered a homestead in Colorado. "In 1912," he wrote in a pathetic reminiscence, jealous when both his children began to publish, "I decided to go east as I did not hear from my mother for six years." He needed to get married, and of course there were no Jewish girls in Colorado.

None of his talk ever contained the slightest reference to me, any hope for me. He was as alone with himself as he was with his dead father Abraham. After my mother died and I would regularly phone him: "Papa, how do you feel?" he would respond exactly the same way, "As well as can be expected."

It was this silence, so much self-containment, that drove me to make a myth of my grandfather, to turn him into the only hero in my family, to regard his absence as something I could fill up, not in imagination, but with my helpless love, my longing.


I have no imagination, I just react. Here I sit at the end of another century, old like the century itself, still beginning my day as I have ever since I was a boy—writing up things in my notebook as if my peace depended on it.

It is all very strange, as strange as I have always felt to myself. I am a grandfather twice over, near enough the finish line to be more and more haunted by the past. But as Faulkner said, the past is not even past. I was ten years old, a repeated failure in the Friday morning arithmetic tests at P.S. 125 on Rockaway Avenue, when I wondered if I should not end it all. The school would call my mother in, not knowing that she had no English. The shame of my nothingness in school, of my family's ineptitude in possibly having to account for it, to deal with it, was more than I could bear. There was a skull-and-crossbones in the corner pharmacy advertising iodine: POISON, FOR EXTERNAL USE ONLY. I bought the smallest amount of it for a nickel, carried it in my pocket for days deciding what to do. I could not let us down.

There were just two steps from the street to the front door of 256A Sutter Avenue, steps off which we used to bounce a Spalding rubber ball to be caught on the fly. The outer door was glass, enclosed in an iron frame, and there were iron bars across the glass to protect it. Inside the short hall, before you took two steps to the long hall, were the buzzers for each family in the tenement. It seemed to me that the same names had, like ours, been there forever. People were too poor to move much, but in the depression there were evictions. Bad weather never stopped city marshals from turning a family out, dumping the furniture into the street while it rained. People dropped coins into a can to help the family move. My mother was enraged by evictions and once led a pack of women to put the furniture back.

At the end of the long hall were the mailboxes. I hated the very look of them, dead flat on the wall. Any time I opened our box to find a typed, official-looking business-size envelope, I dreaded having to open it and explain it to my parents. It always brought bad news.

There were three apartments on this ground floor, just before you got to the stairs. The center one was for the Polish janitor, who with his bitter wife and butter-colored daughter were the only non-Jews in the building. My mother was from Poland and was afraid of Poles. A blond girl from a Polish family, another violinist, sat next to me in the Franklin K. Lane High School orchestra, and we often walked away from school on Evergreen Avenue carrying our violin cases to the cemetery in Highland Park, the most secluded place in which to pet. Little did I know that she would become one of the city's first policewomen.

I made the mistake one day of showing Anne where I lived just as my mother was washing the windows that faced on Sutter Avenue. The girl's blond hair shone on our street, and struck at my mother watching us at the window as a physical threat. She was overcome with fear, was hysterical when I got home. "Are you planning to marry this *Pelishe*?" she demanded.

Three apartments on one side of a floor faced three on the opposite side. We occupied the right corner on the second floor. It was the thirteenth apartment in the building, so was numbered 12A. Superstition was rife. My mother from Dugzitz, a *shtetl* no one but "Dugzitzer" ever heard of and which I have never been able to find on any map of Poland, regularly instructed me, when I opened our front door to leave for school, to put out my left foot first. This, I learned from all the associations with "sinister," the left side, was misinformed. It was the left you were to distrust. My mother was remarkably active, a tireless home dressmaker whose sewing machine kept us alive when the building trades collapsed in the depression and there were no painting jobs for my father. But she had no knowledge of the trans-Jewish world I could walk into any day.

On the landing between the first and second floors was the opening from which the clotheslines extended to a twin tenement across the yard. I loved to watch my mother haul in the lines when it was her turn to put out our clothes to dry, to hear the pulleys rattling as she worked the lines back and forth. The yard was never quiet. There was always someone in it, singing to the back windows in an appeal for coins—*Italiener* yelling up operatic arias, Jews crooning nostalgic songs like *Beltz My Old Home*, meant to wring tears of recollection about the Old World from which, without exception, all parents seemed to have come. We thoughtfully wrapped the pennies in newspaper before flinging them to the singers in the yard.

The center apartment across from us impressed me whenever I stopped in to see a boy named Eugene. There was a beaded curtain between the rooms and the copy of some famous English painting that showed a stag at eve drinking from a lake. Catty corner lived the only family whose son was known to be a "bad one." He was a failed boxer who, after getting repeatedly knocked out in bouts at Canarsie, had taken to pilfering and was seen skipping from one roof to another just ahead of the police. I was always hearing about people in the neighborhood being taken down to the Liberty Avenue police station, once actually saw Lepke Buchalter of "Murder, Incorporated," who eventually "got the chair," threatening a storekeeper. We ourselves were innocent in everything. My father's pants were once lifted from a chair near an open window. My parents never stopped giggling over this.

There was no doorbell to apartment 12A, just a metal slab that whistled when you turned it to the right. The long unlighted hall from the front door to the icebox at the end of the hall, just before you turned left into the kitchen, smelled bracingly of the paint on my father's overalls and was lined with empty seltzer bottles in the slats of a wooden box waiting to be picked up the next time the seltzer man came around. My mother and I regularly refilled the icebox from a yard two blocks away, one square chunk at a time, carrying it between us in a large towel.

The kitchen was the largest room in our apartment and the center of everything. The toilet occupied one corner of it, right next to the sink. My mother had her brown Singer sewing machine at the window. Our kitchen was her little dress shop. There she met her customers, the neighborhood women who often sat around the kitchen without much on, waiting to be fitted.

It was a long time before we got steam heat. For most of my childhood a big black country stove in the kitchen provided the only heat in the apartment. When I was small, my mother in deep winter made up a bed for me on kitchen chairs next to the stove.

One horrible morning the stove gave out completely. My mother finally managed to get hold of the landlord, an immense, powerfully bearded Jew named Wishnevski. He clearly disdained us, walked in as if he owned us as well as the kitchen, muttering that he got no profit from us, we were dirt, of no account, a terrible bother. Looking the stove over with contempt, he suddenly, with just his arm, threw it over. My mother screamed. I made a mental vow to kill him when I got just a bit older.

This was my introduction to the real world of Brownsville beyond my family. How far removed we were even from the rest of Brooklyn, where "New York" was another world. We had been dumped by real-estate speculators into the farthest recesses of far-out Brooklyn, near unknown unapproachable Queens on one side, and on the other what was still the wasteland of Canarsie, Jamaica Bay, the great Atlantic itself. Once this was all farmland, then the subway came out and reached its terminus in "New Lots."

All I knew was that my immediate world was Jewish, that everyone and everything was Jewish, Jewish all day long. Little did I know that Brownsville–East New York would become all black, a most desperately poor and despised neighborhood always in the crime news. The tenement in which I spent my first twenty years would be demolished to make room for a housing project named after Langston Hughes. Mike Tyson, the former heavyweight champ who went to prison for rape, came from Brownsville.

So at various times did Aaron Copland, the painter Max Weber, and Daniel Jacob Kaminski, who became Danny Kaye. The great Nobel Prize physicist I. I. Rabi, who liked to say, "If I had stayed in Poland, I would have been a tailor." Joseph Hirshhorn, who somewhat later named his art museum in Washington after himself, thanks to the uranium he spotted in Canada. The astonishingly erudite art historian Meyer Schapiro, after whom Columbia named a building. Julius Garfinkel, who became John Garfield and first starred in the Group Theater's production of Clifford Odets's *Awake and Sing*. My sister, Pearl, had a schoolgirl crush on Julie. When I asked him for an autograph I could triumphantly bring back to her, he asked, "What should I write?" "How about 'Sincerely, John Garfield'?" His face fell. "How do you spell 'sincerely'?"

I woke up one day in Brooklyn Jewish Hospital to find that over my bed, and over every bed next to me in the ward, was a plaque marked with the name of the Jewish donor. It was like waking up in a family cemetery.

It was another world then, before Hitler. We were not Zionists. The oppressed of other races were not forgotten, though we knew no other race but our own.

My father revered the Yiddish labor paper, the *Forward*. This impressed me more than anything else about him. When he exultantly read from the *Forward* to me, with its news of the international working class, he was not alone. He was full of pride in what he was reading aloud, positively worshipping every item. In his excitement he read at breakneck speed, as if afraid that someone would stop him, read so fast that I would laughingly beg him to slow down. The *Forward*'s masthead carried the opening line in every Socialist Bible: "Workers of the world unite! You have nothing to lose but your chains!" Sometime in the twenties a black man was lynched in Pennsylvania. The flaming headline across the face of the *Forward*—POGROM IN PENNSYLVANIA!

When I sat on my parents' bed in the front room, which looked beyond the ailanthus trees to a distant horizon pierced by distant church spires, I could see that there was much I needed to learn. My kid sister, Pearlie, and I lived for the new books we freshly borrowed every other day from the Stone Avenue Library, which had more space for shelves than the Glenmore Avenue Library. But at the moment I was also transformed, because of the women who were always there, by the life that throbbed in our kitchen.

An enormous horizontal mirror rising over the kitchen table drew everyone to it. The women in their slips waiting to be fitted or to try on a new dress were always looking themselves over as if I were not sitting at the table over my homework. A loud, busty girl named Yetta, standing before the mirror, laughed merrily when her mother reproached her for pulling at her dress to show more of her breasts. "This is what the boys like, Ma! This is what the boys like!"

The kitchen was always full of women. They were the most vivid thing in my life. My father was outside all this, read his paper in the "dining room," where we never dined. Then, bit by bit, thanks to the adult books I could now read without a teacher's help, thanks to my father's silent inclusion of me as we walked New York, as we went up against the awesome city by ourselves—just the two of us!—I saw a public world very different from my mother's kitchen.

There were still open-air trolleys in the twenties that went all the way down Brooklyn straight to Coney Island. These became my ecstasy. People sat happily crowded together on benches that spanned the width of the car. The conductor easily made his way up and down a platform along the side to collect the fares passed down to him. You knew you were getting closer to "Khuny Hilund," as my mother called it, when grass appeared between the tracks. Soon there would be a whiff of cool salty air right off the ocean. Another world, another time, paradise! Everyone knew it, because one unforgettable summer afternoon, amidst the excited clanging of the trolley bell as we got into Coney Island and I prayed that such a sun, such a day, would never vanish, people started singing.

I read and read and read. Everyone read a lot, even the tough guys on the block who always beat me in a fight. My sister and I had fraudulently obtained extra library cards so that we could be sure of having enough to read. As I made my way home from the library, I made sure to impress the boys standing in front of Epstein's candy store with the advanced titles I had picked up.

I was fourteen or fifteen when a boy named Willie, with whom I was always fighting and arguing, took me aside one day and said in the most aggressive way, "I'm reading a poet I bet *you* never heard of." "Yeah, who?" "His name is Ezra Pound."

It was a feisty neighborhood. A boy you hardly knew would suddenly decide he couldn't stand the look of you and punch you around. My cousin Nat on Herzl Street—always pronounced "Hoizl"—was like that. We were born enemies. In winter the snow was never cleared, piled up in yellowing pissed-on hills and icy barriers through which we cut tunnels. Nat liked to trap me, keep me in a tunnel. His bitterness against me was like bad breath and lasted for life. I could never understand it. He just hated my guts. His father was my mother's brother, but his father, another hater, was not in the least like my mother.

The world was like that, full of people who couldn't stand each other. As young Germans like to say about the Holocaust, the world is full of unanswerable questions. I was just beginning to try some out. As the years mounted I was happiest when alone, reading and beginning to note in my school notebook what I thought of the books I was always reading. I was getting used to being with people and yet not being with them. I was my father all over again. Somehow I knew there would be trouble ahead, that I would pay for this cherished solitude.

While the revolt of the Warsaw Ghetto in 1943 was crushed and the ghetto shut down, the survivors were pulled out of their houses and deported to Auschwitz and Treblinka. Some escaped only by throwing themselves to death in the street below. Poles on the other side of the ghetto wall stood around laughing and cheering.

This is my most searing image not so much of the terrible war— there were even ghastlier scenes—as of the division that runs through life, marks each us as nothing else does, and explains why life never really changes. In the end everything becomes a question of personal experience that you cannot share whatever your love for the other and your magnanimous ideas about anything and everything. The sheer physical difference, the uncrossed line, between actors and bystanders, stage and audience, doers and onlookers, women and men, the work of art and its profuse commentators, the judged and the judge, the hanged and the hangman, the afflicted and their comforters, the young and the old, the fiercely alive and the merely watchful, between the glowing act of love and everything said about it!

Simone Weil said that the only real question to be asked of another is "What are you going through?" And another even more fiercely independent Jew: "The Kingdom of God cometh not with observation." No, it doth not. I know this as a critic of other people's books, as a tiresome moralist even to myself of other people's habits and choices, as a spectator, merely, wandering New York all my life in constant amazement at the number of people walking briskly alone talking to themselves, glowering as they sit fiercely alone on park benches, fiercely adopting attitudes as they talk to make a point, then just as surely drooping away from this make-believe height as soon as the others are gone.

Science, seeking confirmation, proof, objective testing and proof, cannot avail itself of this cardinal human loneliness, but literature can. And this with language that is always failing and stumbling, breaking the writer's heart with its mere approximateness to the thing in his mind. Besides, language is always asserting its primitive authority, is a halting servant but can be a terrible master. Science progresses all the time, literature never. How should it "improve" over the centuries when its very subject is the enigma, the inaccessibility of the human condition? The beast in the jungle only *seems* to threaten us, being outside in its "jungle." The final act, when it comes, will be to show us where the failure of our expectation lay. The fall of man is only too real when it comes to ourselves.

But that is a marvelous fable, isn't it, coming from a writer virgin, who acted in life only by writing, writing, who had left his own country behind while hardly finding one in England's upper classes, who became part of England only by changing his citizenship when England went to war in 1914? Yet Henry James manages now to make his reader feel like an accomplice. He proved that whatever his withdrawals as a man, his valor as a writer was enough—and overreaching. The mere spectator transcended himself by plowing to the depths, in a hundred European hotels, the exceptionality of his own condition. He never read *Moby-Dick*, but he would have understood Ahab saying, "How can the prisoner reach outside, except by thrusting through the wall?" James himself, in old age: "The starting point of my life has been loneliness."